1975

FOURTE

IRAQ UNDER GENERAL NURI:
My Recollections of Nuri al-Said, 1954–1958

Nuri al-Said at the age of twenty-five, when hospitalized by the British in the American Mission Hospital in Basra in 1914, as a Turkish prisoner of war. This photo was given to Mrs. Wilhelmina Zeigler, who was then nursing superintendent of the hospital. (Photo courtesy of Mrs. Zeigler.)

IRAQ UNDER GENERAL NURI

My Recollections of
Nuri al-said, 1954-1958

BY WALDEMAR J. GALLMAN

THE JOHNS HOPKINS PRESS, BALTIMORE

To Marge, John, and Philip

PREFACE

My work on Nuri was written after my retirement from the Foreign Service. It is based largely on my personal notes and recollections covering the four years I was ambassador to Iraq, 1954–58, and on talks with Iraqi and American friends of mine who knew Nuri and understood the situation in Iraq. It is in no sense an official publication. The views and observations appearing in it are my personal ones.

For some valuable information appearing in my study on Nuri and for helpful suggestions on its content and form I am especially indebted to Dr. Majid Khadduri, distinguished authority on the Middle East, formerly on the faculty of the Higher Teachers College and the Law College of Baghdad and later professor at The Johns Hopkins School of Advanced International Studies, and Director of Research at the Middle East Institute, Washington, D.C.; to Mr. Hermann Eilts, a Foreign Service officer who served with me in Iraq and who subsequently was assigned as Middle East specialist to the American Embassy, London; and to John Gatch, a Foreign Service officer who had also been a member of my staff in Iraq and who was later attached to the Office of Near Eastern and South Asian Affairs of the State Department. Their help and encouragement made this work possible.

WALDEMAR J. GALLMAN

Washington, D.C.
1963

CONTENTS

Preface *vii*
Introduction *xi*

    I *Iraq, 1954* *1*

   II *Nuri's Background* *9*

  III *Meeting Nuri* *15*

  IV *Prelude to the Baghdad Pact* *21*

   V *The Baghdad Pact* *66*

  VI *Nuri's Domestic Policy* *88*

 VII *Nuri as Arab Nationalist* *133*

VIII *Nuri on Israel* *167*

  IX *The British in Iraq* *172*

   X *The Americans in Iraq* *182*

  XI *The 1958 Coup and Its Aftermath* *200*

 XII *The Nuri I Knew* *219*

Epilogue *231*

Suggested Background Reading *232*
Index *233*

INTRODUCTION

This is the story of Nuri al-Said as I came to know him through almost daily contact over a period of four years. My association with him began in the autumn of 1954, shortly after he became prime minister of Iraq for the thirteenth time. It continued until a few days before his violent death at the time of the Qasim military coup in the summer of 1958. The last four years of his life were crowded ones for him and crucial ones for Iraq and her neighbors.

Nuri himself, unfortunately, kept few records of his activities even when in office, and that was for most of his life. During the last years he was repeatedly urged by his intimates to write his memoirs. He half promised to do so but was too engrossed in the problems of the day to make a start. He left texts of his public speeches and statements, some scattered letters, and his short work, *Arab Independence and Unity,* better known as "The Fertile Crescent Plan." Because of this dearth of material giving insight into his character, personality and views, I felt impelled to record my impressions of him as I observed him working during his last years on the problems critically affecting Iraq and her neighbors. My story covers only a brief portion of his life. Even so, I hope it will contribute toward a fairer understanding of him as a patriot, Arab nationalist, and statesman.*

Modern Iraq embraces most of the land lying between the Tigris and Euphrates rivers which was once known as Mesopotamia. From the early part of the sixteenth century until the end of World War I, Mesopotamia formed part of the Ottoman Empire. Situated on the fringes of the empire, with the local authorities left by Constantinople for the most part to their own devices, the province suffered from neglect and indifferent administration. Following the defeat of the Turkish forces in the Middle East by British and Arabian troops in 1918, the modern state of Iraq emerged. Its sovereignty, however, was at first considerably circumscribed. The United Kingdom, under the 1922 Treaty of Alliance, held a mandate over the country. It was not until 1930 that this treaty was superseded by one providing for Iraq's entry into the League of Nations and the termination of the mandate. Even then some limits were put on Iraq's sovereignty and independence. Under the new treaty Britain retained air bases in the country and the right of transit across Iraqi territory for British forces. In 1955 these remaining bonds to her independence were removed by a Special Agreement which also cleared the way for Britain's entry into the Baghdad Pact. In breaking the Turkish hold on the Middle East, bringing about the formation of modern Iraq, and securing for her a place in the family of nations as a fully independent state, Nuri played a significant role.

Nuri's contributions to Iraq's welfare, however, went beyond these solid political achievements. He made a significant contribution in the economic field also. When the exploitation of the country's oil deposits began producing large revenues, he helped to establish a Development Board which directed the expenditure of these revenues on projects which secured

* There is a biography of Nuri available, Lord Birdwood's *Nuri as-Said; A Study in Arab Leadership*, published by Cassell and Co., Ltd., London, 1959.

and developed the country's economy. Chief among these was the building of dams for flood control and the construction of irrigation systems designed to improve land under cultivation and to reclaim land that had reverted to desert. Toward the end of Nuri's life the Ottoman Empire's neglected province was beginning to take on the aspects of biblical Mesopotamia.

When in 1954, I was appointed ambassador to Iraq our Secretary of State informed me that he considered Iraq to be a country of key importance in the Middle East. He hoped that Iraq would eventually join with Turkey, Pakistan, and Iran in regional defense arrangements for the area. He felt Iraq's participation in such arrangements was crucial because of the effect it would have on other Arab states. Iraqi leaders were known to be inclined to participate, but their relations with other Arab states and with their own people posed a problem. On August 4, 1954, Nuri returned to power, and on October 30, 1954, I arrived in Baghdad.

IRAQ, 1954

Disastrous floods and an unsettled political situation marked the spring of 1954 in Iraq. The effects of both carried over into summer when Nuri returned to office, and both influenced the course of his government. The floods, among the worst in Iraq's history, caused damage estimated at thirty-million *dinar* or about $84,000,000, and came within inches of inundating Baghdad. The political situation was so unstable that between the end of April and early August Iraq had three prime ministers. The effects of the floods led Nuri to give priority to flood control in the country's Development Program. The uneasy political situation led him to impose, with characteristic firmness, a series of security measures. April, with the country thus shaken economically and politically, found Western-educated Fadhil Jamali in office as prime minister.

One of the most pressing problems facing Jamali's government was relief for the sufferers from the floods. In this difficult situation Jamali became the target of strong criticism in Parliament and of equally strong attacks by the press for the way he was handling flood relief. When he took office Jamali had hoped that he had Nuri's backing. However, when these attacks were made on him, mainly by nationalist and leftist elements, Nuri's followers in Parliament, members of the Constitutional Union party, would not come to his defense. Their silence led Jamali to offer his resignation. The Palace accepted and, as it had done for a quarter of a century whenever the situation seemed to call for determined action, turned to Nuri. He agreed to try to form a government, but wanted Jamali in it. I was informed by friends of mine who were close to the Baghdad political scene at the time that Nuri wanted the support of Jamali's amorphous group of liberally inclined followers to offset the opposition of his chief rival, Salih Jabr, and his Umma (Populist or People's) party, and that of scattered leftist elements. There also may have been some pressure on Nuri from the Palace to make room for Jamali, for Jamali was close to the Crown Prince, Abdul-Ilah, who occasionally entrusted Jamali with missions of personal interest.

On religious grounds, too, Nuri wanted Jamali in his government. Prime ministers in Iraq made it a practice to give representation in their cabinets to both Moslem sects, Sunnis and Shias. Jamali, a respected Shia with experience in public affairs, met Nuri's needs in this respect.[1] But Jamali was in no mood to be accommodating just after being left in the lurch by Nuri's men in Parliament, and so, with a show of independence, he declined Nuri's offer.

Jamali's refusal must have come as a surprise to Nuri. He had helped Jamali frequently in his public career. Actually, on previous occasions and occasions to follow, Jamali did show his appreciation of Nuri's help and a readiness to meet his wishes. (This cannot be said for all whom Nuri launched on a public career. Far too many of these, when once established, conveniently forgot what they owed him and went their independent ways.)

---

[1] In the Moslem world the Sunnis outnumber the Shias. This is the case in Iraq, too, where there are more Sunnis, trained and experienced in government, than Shias. This makes it difficult for a prime minister to balance his cabinet. Actually, among the Arab population in Iraq, the Shias outnumber the Sunnis. It is the Kurds, living in the North, who tip the numerical balance in favor of the Sunnis.

But Nuri's real attitude toward Jamali, and estimate of him, I think, was revealed in remarks he made to me shortly after he had named him head of the Iraqi delegation to the Bandung Conference of April, 1955. Nuri began with an explanation of what motivated the devil worship of the Yezidis, a small religious sect living in the Mosul area of northern Iraq. The Yezidis, Nuri explained, recognize the supreme goodness of God. God's will, however, is constantly threatened by the devil. God, being the personification of virtue, does not have to be propitiated. But the devil, always on the alert to do mischief, needs to be. Hence the devil worship of the Yezidis. Jamali, Nuri confided with a mischievous wisdom, was his personal "little devil" whom, he had found, it was judicious to propitiate from time to time with various appointments.

After Jamali had declined his offer, Nuri made no further effort to form a government. Some observers thought Nuri felt the Crown Prince was not really serious in asking him to form a government at that time. In any event he decided to bide his time, apparently convinced that without him at the helm conditions would become even more chaotic and before long he would get another Palace summons. To dissociate himself from the political scene, he went to London ostensibly for a physical check-up and visit with his two grandsons.

The Palace now turned to Arshad al-Umari, an independent then living in Istanbul. In a long public career, including a term as prime minister from June 1, 1946, to November 14, 1946, months when Iraq was grappling with the aftermath of the war, he gained a reputation, not unlike Nuri's, as a man of action. He agreed to become prime minister but only on an interim basis, just long enough for new elections to be held. He took office on April 29, 1954, and elections were called for June 9, with the promise that they would be free.

The immediate effect of announcing free elections was to encourage many independents to announce their candidacy. The Istiqlal or National party, representing strong national but anti-Western groups, and the Umma party, representing moderate pro-Western groups, entered the campaign. A National Front, composed of National Democrats, the Istiqlal party and diverse left wing independents was organized. All told there were 466 candidates for the 135 seats in the Chamber of Deputies.

Eyewitnesses gave me a description of the campaign preceding the June 9 elections. The prevailing atmosphere was neither calm nor disciplined. It was one of the liveliest campaigns in Iraq's history, with political rallies in all parts of the country. Some of these turned into anti-government demonstrations of such violence that the police had to intervene to safeguard lives and property. Banners offering a wide choice of salvation were freely displayed. Sound trucks blaring forth the virtues of would-be saviors cruised the city streets. Garden walls of private homes were painted with slogans which, in support of National Front candidates, denounced the West and advocated neutralism. By election day, the air was so charged that police had to be stationed at various polling places. When the votes were counted it was found to the consternation of the Palace and conservative elements generally that the newly formed National Front had won fourteen seats. Arshad al-Umari seemed to have lost his touch.

At first glance fourteen seats in a body of 135 seem very few to be disturbed about. Actually this small group had the means for considerable troublemaking and the conservative element did have grounds for feeling uneasy. As a closely knit and well-disciplined unit, it could obstruct the work of Parliament and, with such a forum at its disposal, it could appeal as well to leftist groups and disgruntled individuals in the country at large. This was an opportunity the small, determined minority had sought for a long time.

The new Parliament held its brief inaugural session late in June and then adjourned until the fall session. The free elections had been held and now it only remained for Arshad al-Umari to resign. He did so on July 23 and the Palace once again had to search for a prime minister.

Palace soundings soon revealed that none of the likely candidates was enthusiastic about becoming prime minister with the political atmosphere so charged. The role the National Front might now play caused particular uneasiness. Faced with this situation, as Nuri had shrewdly calculated, the Palace once again turned to him. He was still in London, and Crown Prince Abdul-Ilah himself undertook to approach him. Relations between the two had never been congenial. Nuri's strong-mindedness and Abdul-Ilah's insistence on having a say on all decisions of any importance, did not make for an easy relationship. What happened now strained their relations still more. Abdul-Ilah tried several times to reach Nuri by telephone but got no answer. The intercession of the Iraqi ambassador in London, Amir Zayd, King Faisal's [2] granduncle, was then sought. He did not get an answer from Nuri, but he did get his consent to meet with Abdul-Ilah in Paris and discuss the offer. When they met Nuri agreed to become prime minister only on certain conditions. The Palace was to approve the dissolution of the recently elected Parliament and the holding of still another election. Political parties were to be dissolved, and Nuri was to have a free hand to revoke press licenses. It was only after these conditions were accepted that he returned to Baghdad to become prime minister.

He moved with characteristic vigor. On August 4 he addressed a letter to the King requesting the dissolution of Parliament and new elections. He wanted, he explained, a popular mandate for his program. He had all political parties dissolved and personally announced the dissolution of his own Constitutional Union party, pointing out that all who felt capable of representing their country could now compete on an equal

---

[2] Faisal II. Iraq's monarchy began on August 23, 1921, when Hashimite Prince Faisal became Faisal I. He ruled until September 8, 1933, when he was succeeded by his son, Ghazi. Ghazi ruled till his death on April 4, 1939. Ghazi's son was then a minor and Abdul-Ilah was proclaimed Regent on April 5, 1939. The Regency lasted till May 2, 1953, when the young King came of age and was crowned Faisal II. The monarchy ended with the King's death July 14, 1958, in Qasim's coup.

basis. He revoked press licenses. In a subsequent public statement, obviously aimed at Communist and National Front groups, he cautioned the public to be on guard against those who, while serving "foreign interests," speak in terms of democracy, liberty and peace. The meaning of this mild warning was made clear on September 1, twelve days before the elections. On that day the government published amendments to the Penal Code which extended its authority to deal with Communists and other leftists. Peace Partisan and Democratic Youth activities were placed in the same category as Communist activities and outlawed. The Council of Ministers was empowered to deprive any Iraqi convicted of Communist or associated activities of his nationality and deport him. Further, the Council of Ministers was authorized to suspend temporarily or permanently any association, professional or labor, if its activities were deemed detrimental to public order.

These provisions, together with Nuri's firmly established reputation as a strong man who would not hesitate to use repressive measures if he thought them necessary, effectively discouraged the opposition and prepared the way for Nuri's overwhelming victory in the elections.

The elections took place on September 12. The campaign preceding them was in marked contrast to the June campaign, and on the surface everything was calm. Public rallies had to be licensed, and most of the applications were rejected. Very few slogans were painted on walls. In the final days of the June campaign there was considerable undisguised pressure by local officials on unwanted candidates to withdraw. In September, little of this could be detected, since all the pressure was behind the scenes. On election day no extra police were called out, and balloting was carried out quietly.

On election morning 116 candidates stood unopposed. Balloting had to be held in only ten constituencies in the Baghdad, Basra, and Sulaimaniya areas, where twenty-five candidates contested the remaining nineteen seats. The vast majority of those elected were former members of Nuri's dissolved Constitutional

Union party. Added to this bloc were a number of pro-Nuri independents. Eight candidates who had belonged to the Umma party, two from the Istiqlal and one from the United Popular Front, all running as "independents," were elected. The opposition could therefore muster hardly a dozen deputies.[3] Because this was the Parliament that was to remain in office for almost three years, years marked by extraordinary activity in the fields of foreign affairs and economic development, a further breakdown of its composition is advisable.

Racially the membership consisted of 116 Arabs and nineteen Kurds. From a sectarian angle there were seventy-three Sunnis, fifty-six Shias, and six Christians. Eighty-eight of the deputies had sat in the preceding or fourteenth Parliament. All but sixteen in the new Parliament had previous parliamentary experience. Known landowners, as distinguished from tribal leaders, numbered forty-nine. There were forty-two tribal leaders and eighteen businessmen. The professional class was represented by twenty-three lawyers, five of whom had previously been judges, and by three physicians. Nuri not only had a formidable majority, but also a fairly representative group. He was in a position to do much for Iraq at home and abroad. I will give an appraisal of how effectively he used this opportunity in subsequent chapters.

On my arrival in Baghdad in October the opposition had been cowed, Nuri had a Parliament to his liking, and his program had begun to unfold. In the domestic field one of his immediate objectives was to complete the flood control measures of the Development Program. In the foreign field he was determined to put Iraq in a stronger position to meet possible aggression. In both these areas I was fortunate in having the means for ready and constant contact with him. The Agree-

---

[3] The dissolution of the preceding Parliament did not effect the Senate, where some opposition to Nuri persisted. Under the Monarchy the Iraqi Constitution empowered the King to appoint a Senate. Tenure was for eight years with reappointment permissible. The Senate was not to exceed one-fourth of the total number of elected deputies.

ment for Technical Co-operation and the Military Assistance Understanding between our two countries served this purpose well.[4] The atmosphere was charged but stimulating. Activity was in the air.

[4] The text of the Technical Aid Agreement has been published as Department of State publication No. 4592 and the text of the Military Assistance Agreement as No. 5739. Both are available at the U.S. Government Printing Office, Washington 25, D.C.

NURI'S BACKGROUND

A colleague of mine who had served in Baghdad some years before my time gave this thumbnail sketch of Nuri: "He was a Kurd by birth, a Turk by education, and an Iraqi by profession."

This arresting summarization is much too succinct to be fully accurate. I repeat it here because it calls attention to Nuri's colorful background, his varied experience and his complex character.

How much Kurdish blood Nuri had I do not know, but Iraqi friends of his say he had some. He certainly had characteristics which were typically Kurdish, such as physical and moral toughness and courage. He was born in 1889, but not in Kurdistan. Baghdad was his birthplace and that seems appropriate as he spent most of his life in the service of Iraq. His family, it was believed, traced its ancestry and residence in Baghdad back three hundred years, to the time when the head of the family was no less a personage than a mullah, Lowlow by name. Lowlow, a Sunni, one day suffered an extreme indignity. Invading Persian soldiers, members of the rival Shiite sect, stabled their horses in his mosque. Lowlow took immediate action. He set off, alone, for Constantinople to report to the Sultan himself. He returned with an army and drove the foreign desecrators away, but not before they had murdered his wife and children. Once more the Sultan came to his aid. He sent Lowlow a new wife, a young Turkish inmate from the royal harem and decreed a monthly allowance in perpetuity to the Lowlow family. Despite this early close tie with Constantinople, the family was accepted and respected in Baghdad as Arab.

Nuri was very young when he began his formal education. He was eight when he finished the first stage, under a mullah's care and guidance at the local "infants school." Concentration there was on memory training which might explain the phenomenal memory he displayed later in life. His father, Said Taha, an esteemed civil servant in the employ of the Turkish government, felt that it was not too early to decide whether his son should prepare for civilian or military life. The higher civilian positions in the government were reserved by Constantinople for the Turks. An army career on the other hand was open to all peoples of the empire, up to the highest levels. This must have influenced Said Taha in choosing a military career for his son. The choice turned out to be a happy one. Directly from "infants school" Nuri entered the primary military school in Baghdad where from the start, it is said, he felt completely at home. In 1903, when not quite fifteen, he left home for the Military College in Constantinople. He had done well in Baghdad, though he was about two years younger than most of his classmates at the college. Shortly after his arrival there, his father died. His mother, in Baghdad, was preoccupied with the care of his four young sisters and he was left to manage his own affairs. He stood up well under these responsibilities and the strenuous demands of cadet life. In September of 1906 he was graduated and commissioned at the age of eighteen. He returned to Iraq where he was assigned to a mounted infantry unit engaged not in glamorous military activity but in the distasteful civilian duty of collecting taxes on livestock from nomadic tribes. He had four years of this. How many taxes he collected is not recorded, but in pursuit of them he got to know the Iraqi countryside and the way of life of the sheiks and their tribes. It was during this period that he married into the prominent Iraqi family of al-Askari.

In 1910 Nuri was called back to Constantinople for further military study. He had been chosen for the Staff College course. In 1912, during the Balkan War, his active military service began. He took part in the campaign against the Bulgarians. However, during these years Nuri was not absorbed exclusively with military matters. In the course of them he developed a taste for politics as well.

The "Young Turk" reform movement had started during Nuri's early formative years as a cadet in Constantinople, and it gained momentum in the years leading up to the outbreak of World War I. The movement had its repercussions among the Arab peoples of the empire who saw it as a possible means of gaining greater cultural and political freedom. Sometime during 1913–14 Nuri joined a reform group called al-Ahad, or the "Covenant," among which were some Arab military officers. In the first years of his association with this "cell," Nuri thought of it only as an instrument to gain autonomy for the Arabs within the empire on a federated basis. It did not take him long, though, to see that the Young Turks, should they come to power, would make few if any concessions to the Arabs. To this disillusionment was added the conviction that if war broke out and Turkey threw in her lot with Germany, as seemed likely, the empire itself would not survive. So, as early as 1914 Nuri came to feel conscience-free to work for complete Arab independence. He had already by then, in mind and heart, broken with his past. By the spring of 1914 his Turkish masters surmised what he was up to and prepared to arrest him. Nuri moved quickly. Undetected he left Constantinople by ship. He found his way to Cairo and from

there to Basra where he immediately made contact with an
Iraqi group of revolutionaries under the leadership of Sayyid
Talib, head of an influential Sunni family. Not long after his
arrival in Basra he became ill. He was placed in the American
mission hospital. When, after the outbreak of the war, the
British occupied Basra they moved him to a convalescent home
in India, near Bombay, where he was kept for over a year as
a Turkish prisoner of war, but a privileged one. He enjoyed,
it seems, just about every privilege except the freedom to move
very far from his bungalow "prison" home; and the only thing
he was made to suffer was boredom. Toward the end of 1915,
to his great relief, he was moved from India to Egypt. There,
in Cairo, he enthusiastically joined a group of Arabs and
British who were planning the Arab revolt. T. E. Lawrence
was a member of this group, and on June 5, 1916, Arab independence was proclaimed in the name of Sherif Husayn and
Lord of Mecca. In July, in response to a summons from King
Husayn, Nuri left Cairo for Jidda. From there he set out to
join the revolt. The desert campaign, in which Nuri established his reputation as a military leader, lasted a year and
a half. After the collapse of the Central Powers, and with it
the Turkish rule over the Arabs, Nuri continued in the public
eye. During 1918–19, as chief of staff to Prince Faisal, Husayn's
son, he was in London and Paris, closely following the discussions on the future of the Arabs. After these talks he remained
with Faisal for several months, mostly in Syria. In the autumn
of 1920, at the request of his brother-in-law Jafar Pasha, who
had been named minister of defense for Iraq, Nuri returned
to Baghdad to become Jafar's chief of staff. It was on his arrival
in Baghdad that Gertrude Bell saw Nuri for the first time and
recorded those widely quoted first impressions of hers: "The
moment I saw him I realized that we had before us a strong
and supple force which we must either use or engage in difficult combat." In the years that followed, her appraisal proved
accurate and her advice sound.

August 23, 1921, was a happy day in Nuri's life, for on that

day he saw the fulfillment of his fond hope in the crowning of
Faisal as king of Iraq. Now he felt free to devote his full
energies to placing his young country on a sure foundation.
For a time in 1921–22, he was given leave from the army to
help organize a police force. Thereafter, for the better part of
nine years, he concentrated on building the army, providing
facilities for training officers, and organizing the Ministry of
Defense. During some of these years he was minister of defense.
Then on March 23, 1930, he became prime minister of Iraq
for the first time. Thirteen more Iraqi prime-ministerships
were to follow before he became the first prime minister of the
Arab Union in May, 1958, two months before his death.

During the long period of Nuri's public life, Iraq experienced many troubled and uneasy times, and some very violent
ones. In between being prime minister, Nuri held some other
portfolios in addition to serving in Parliament. He was minister
of defense frequently and foreign minister several times. But
it was invariably during periods of particular stress that one
found him in office as prime minister, called there urgently
by King, or Regent, or Crown Prince.

The list of Nuri's achievements as a public figure is long
and impressive, but this is not the place to recount and weigh
these accomplishments in detail. I call attention to them here
only to make it clear that by the time I came to know him
he had experienced much and had done much for his country
and his people, and was firmly established as a powerful figure
in the Arab world. A few milestones in his career should, however, be mentioned to emphasize the breadth of his skills and
interests. To him must go the credit for founding the Staff
College in 1921. He was prime minister in 1931 when the Capital Development Works Scheme was announced, the forerunner
of the Development Program administered later by the Development Board. He played a role in the negotiations that
led to the termination of the British mandate and to Iraq's
entry into the League of Nations. He, more than any other
Iraqi, was responsible for the termination of the 1930 Anglo-

Iraqi treaty and for placing treaty relations between the two countries, through the Special Agreement of April 4, 1955, on a more favorable, realistic basis. He pleaded well and often at council meetings of the Arab League for a healthy, constructive Arab nationalism. And he made his voice heard on behalf of a free world, as opposed to one dominated from Moscow, years before he helped make the Northern Tier alignment a reality through the Baghdad Pact.[1]

[1] For information on Nuri's background I have drawn on talks I had with him and with his friends, and on some of the books listed in "Suggested Background Reading," at the back of this book.

MEETING NURI

A few days after my arrival in Baghdad, Nuri left for the North where he was to spend two weeks observing the troops on their annual maneuvers. I did not meet him until he returned. However, when I made my first call at the Foreign Office to arrange the details of my reception and presentation of credentials, I felt his presence. I found the foreign minister, Musa Shabandar, in telephone conversation with him, and the subject of the conversation was our arms aid. The "coincidence" of this conversation taking place during my call on the Minister revealed the characteristic directness of Nuri's methods and his preoccupation with a subject that was to recur in almost every talk I had with him in the next four years.

It developed during my talk with Minister Shabandar that Nuri, although the arms agreement had been reached only six months before during the closing days of the Jamali government, was already becoming impatient about the rate of deliveries and was critical of the type of equipment Iraq was getting. If the agreement was to be helpful to him it was vital, he insisted, especially at the beginning, that deliveries be made promptly and that something more impressive than trucks be supplied. He needed immediate delivery of some impressive equipment to strengthen his position with the Iraqi public. To date, little besides automotive equipment had arrived and that was slow in coming. Nuri wanted to know whether something could not be done right away to improve the situation.

While I was still in Washington preparing for my assignment to Baghdad, our Military Assistance Advisory Group (MAAG) had urged Washington to speed up deliveries in order to arrest mounting criticism among Iraqi military chiefs. I was invited to attend the conference in the Pentagon at which this recommendation was considered. The standard procedure for processing requests for military aid was explained. This operation took time and did not allow for short-cuts. Within those limits, I was told, requests from Iraq would be given every possible consideration. Immediately following that conference, we were joined at luncheon in the Pentagon by Shabandar, who was then ambassador of Iraq in Washington. During the luncheon I gave him a picture of the morning's deliberations, emphasizing the assurances given me.

While listening to him in the Foreign Office reciting Nuri's complaints, I remembered that day in the Pentagon and reminded Shabandar of it and the assurances growing out of it. He listened attentively but promptly indicated that he did not find these assurances sufficient. In spite of them, with ingrained Arab suspicion he asked: "Could it be that Israeli protests are causing the delays?"

I assumed that was not the case and told him there were no grounds for his misgivings. That ended my first call on the Minister for Foreign Affairs.

Having presented my credentials on November 3 as scheduled, I waited for the Chef de Protocol to arrange my first call on Nuri. He, however, did not wait upon ceremony. Immediately after his return from the North he asked to see me at once, and alone. He placed particular stress on just the two of us talking together. I was to meet with him at his home.

Early in our association I learned that Nuri preferred to

transact business at his home, where he was freer from interruptions. Moreover, in the last years of his life he was very much a lone worker. He confided in few and sought advice from only a few intimates. He was secretive and did not want to be observed too closely. He never used documents in his discussions nor seemed to keep a record of his talks. He had no staff, only a few factotums around him. He needed access neither to archives nor to a secretariat to accomplish what he wanted; he relied heavily on his extraordinary memory.

I found dealing with Nuri at his home very satisfactory. He was seldom prime minister only. Most of the time, he acted also as minister of defense and foreign minister. Once he left his home in the morning and crossed the Tigris into the heart of Baghdad he was forced to shuttle between various ministries and it became difficult to arrange appointments. Therefore I always tried to see him the first thing in the morning at his home.

There he was invariably waiting on the threshold to greet his visitors. He was punctual himself and expected punctuality from his callers. He was impatient, too. When he fixed the time for a meeting, he was ready for it some minutes in advance, alert, taut and exuding energy. He was waiting for me like that at the door of his house the first time I called on him.

He was rather small of stature, but was slightly heavier than the pictures I had seen of him which had been taken while he was still leading an active military life. His face was arresting. It was friendly, smiling, lined by hard and troubled living, set with dark, constantly alert intelligent eyes. He was an animated conversationalist. His speech was usually accompanied by the constant clicking of his amber beads, the prayer beads of the devout Moslem which are used so generally by Arabs as conversation beads. While he talked and busily flicked the beads, he still remembered to offer from time to time a little tin box of assorted colored pastiles that was always lying on his desk. In stark contrast to the ornamental beads and multicolored lozenges, there was also always near at hand and usually in sight—a reminder of constant, continuing danger to his life— a revolver in a leather case.

Another physical attribute which bears mentioning is Nuri's deafness. When I first met him it was not noticeable as he did not appear to have difficulty in following what was being said. During the latter years of our association, however, he wore a hearing aid at times. Just at that time an American company brought out one of the smallest but most effective hearing aids ever produced. Nuri's friends at the Embassy decided to give him one, and I was to make the presentation. At first I had some reservations about the project. After all, Nuri might resent the gift, interpreting the gesture as a gentle hint that he had perhaps been missing some of the fine points I had been trying to convey to him. But I did not hesitate long. After all, Nuri was very understanding and would, I convinced myself, receive the gift in the spirit in which it was being offered. And so he did. Far from showing resentment, he was touched by the thoughtfulness of his friends and with all the enthusiasm of a child getting a new toy, immediately began in my presence to experiment with this neat little gadget.

It was never easy to determine the extent of his deafness, and he even seemed to use it at times to his advantage. He had his days. There were times when he heard everything distinctly; there were others when he heard in part only. And there were those times when there was no meeting of the minds at all.

On that first call Nuri lost no time on preliminaries. He greeted me with a warm but brief welcome to Iraq and escorted me briskly to his study. Immediately he came to grips with what was on his mind. After observing the troops for two weeks on their exercises, he felt that some tanks for training purposes were urgently needed. A minimum of six would do. A few more would be helpful. The important thing was that they be supplied at once.

Having made known his immediate need, which seemed

modest enough, he proceeded to give his estimate of Iraq's capacity to help herself. This turned out to be a more serious matter. What Iraq was then spending from her own resources on arms, he said, was the limit she could afford. If the United States and the United Kingdom felt more should be spent, then the money would have to come either from the United States or the United Kingdom or both. Iraq could muster additional funds only by diverting some now going into such vital fields as public health and education. This he would never sanction. If the Iraqi Army were called upon to fight with what it then had, it would give a good accounting of itself but the chances were that its armament would prove to be inadequate. If Iraq was to play the role she should in the defense of the area, Iraqi forces should be fully equipped with modern weapons. He estimated the cost at fifty million pounds sterling. Whether these long range requirements were met by us or the British made no difference to him. In any event, he felt that for the most effective defense of the Middle East it was important that the Iraqi Army be equipped with the same type of weapons as the Turkish and Pakistani armies. (While Nuri made only this passing reference to Turkish and Pakistani arms, he obviously knew something about the details of U.S. aid going to Turkey and Pakistan.)

The very next day at Nuri's request I called on him with Colonel van Ormer, head of our MAAG mission. Nuri was brisk in plying the Colonel with questions. He wanted to know what recommendations on Iraqi needs he had been sending to Washington; what types of equipment would be included in the first consignments; how the system of "offshore procurement" worked (under which we bought from the British and gave to Iraq); and what Pakistan was getting in the way of arms aid. He seemed satisfied with the answers he got and then wanted to discuss the problem of the defense of the whole area. He maintained that what was essential for securing the Middle East from Soviet aggression was an assured, steady, and uniform flow of modern armament, along with dependable maintenance and replacement, to the area from the Caucasus to the Persian Gulf. His formula, though compressed, covered everything, including uniformity of treatment: he wanted to make sure that Iraq would be on an equal footing with Turkey and Pakistan.

After the business at hand had been disposed of, Nuri was ready to relax and engage in light conversation. He asked the Colonel what he had been doing before coming to Baghdad. When he learned that he had been in Greece, also with a military aid mission, he questioned him about his experience there and asked for an appraisal of the Greek Army. The Colonel praised the Greek soldier. Nuri listened politely but with a trace of amusement. When the Colonel had finished, Nuri, with that twinkle that so distinguished him when he was in one of his lighter moods, commented: "That's very interesting. Times have certainly changed. Back in my days in the Balkan War we always feared the Bulgarians, but never the Greeks."

IV

PRELUDE TO THE BAGHDAD PACT

The defense of the Middle East against outside aggression had preoccupied Washington for some years before my assignment to Iraq. Secretary of State Dulles had personally given the problem much thought. With other leaders of the free world he had explored at first the possibility of establishing a Middle East Command with a Middle East Defense Organization (MEDO). Among Arab states Egypt was to play a key role in such an organization. In May, 1953, Secretary Dulles and Harold Stassen, then Director of Mutual Security, made a sounding expedition that covered eleven countries, an area extending from the European Mediterranean region to the borders of China and Asia. When they started their journey it had already become apparent that neither Egypt nor any other Arab state was greatly interested in the MEDO concept. Nevertheless, the two made stops in Egypt, Jordan, Syria, Iraq, Saudi Arabia, Libya, Israel, Greece, Turkey, Pakistan and India.[1] On June 1, 1953, shortly after his return, Dulles re-

[1] Iran was also to be visited but when it was found how preoccupied Iranian authorities had become with the oil dispute with the British, the idea was dropped.

21

viewed his impressions in a televised address to the nation, with these conclusions:

A Middle East Organization is a future rather than an immediate possibility. Many of the Arab League countries are so engrossed with their quarrels with Israel or with Great Britain or France that they pay little heed to the menace of Soviet communism. However, there is more concern where the Soviet Union is near. In general, the northern tier of nations shows awareness of the danger.

There is a vague desire to have a collective security system. But no such system can be imposed from without. It should be desired and grow from within out of a sense of common destiny and common danger.

While awaiting the formal creation of a security association, the United States can usefully help strengthen the interrelated defense of those countries which want strength, not as against each other or the West, but to resist the common threat to all free peoples.

So ended the MEDO dream. It was replaced by the Northern Tier concept which was to take form as the Baghdad Pact.

SARSANK TALKS

Foreign affairs figured prominently in the program announced by Nuri on August 4, 1954, the day he returned to power. He had been following closely the Turkish-Pakistani Agreement of April 2, 1954,[2] and the preliminary agreement of July 27, 1954,[3] between Britain and Egypt on the Suez Canal base. He looked forward to the replacement of the Anglo-Iraqi

[2] An explanatory paragraph and the text of this treaty appears on pages 345–46 of J. C. Hurewitz's *Diplomacy in the Near and Middle East*, Vol. II (Princeton, N.Y.: Van Nostrand, 1956). This treaty constituted the first step toward making the Dulles Northern Tier concept a reality, and served as the basis for the Baghdad Pact.

[3] Article I of the agreement deals with the withdrawal of British forces from Egyptian territory and Article IV lays down the conditions under which British troops might re-occupy the Canal Base area. For details on the negotiations leading to the agreement and for the text of the agreement see pages 383–84, Hurewitz, *Diplomacy.*

Treaty of June 30, 1930, by a broader alignment of states interested in the defense of the area. There were other indications that much of his thought and effort during his thirteenth prime-ministership would be devoted to Iraq's relations with her neighbors and the West.

A few days after Nuri took office the Foreign Office announced that Major Salah Salim, Egypt's Minister of National Guidance, would arrive in Baghdad on August 13 for a five day visit. He would have with him a party of twenty. The group would visit King Faisal and Crown Prince Abdul-Ilah at their summer home at Sarsank in northern Iraq, and after two or three days, they would return to Baghdad.

The British-Egyptian Agreement on Suez had been initialed on July 27. It may have been this action which prompted Cairo to suggest a meeting to review inter-Arab relations. Just how the Egyptians put the matter to the Iraqis is not clear, but the Foreign Office let it be known at the time of Salim's arrival that Nuri would use the occasion to review fully Iraq's foreign policy, not "Arab policy." Nuri attended the talks at Sarsank and had further contact with the group in Baghdad. The joint communiqué covering the talks stated that the talks were characterized by "frankness" and a "fraternal spirit." Understanding was reached on "inter-Arab co-operation" and on Arab attitudes on "international issues." No details were included nor would Salah Salim elaborate on the communiqué at a press conference held shortly after it was issued. Newsmen asked him to identify the topics that had been discussed with Nuri but he declined. Nothing further could be said, he insisted, until there had been talks with other Arab leaders. Nuri's summary, as given out by the Foreign Office, revealed that the Egyptians had opposed both the Turkish-Pakistani Agreement of April and any possible multilateral arrangements based on Pakistan as the key, which he was considering at the time.[4] The Egyptian position was that Pakistan did not have anything in common with any Arab state, either militarily or

[4] Nuri, we were told, felt at that time that Pakistan as the cornerstone would be more acceptable to Iraqis than Turkey, their former ruler.

geographically. When Nuri was asked whether he had any alternative proposal, he suggested that the Arab Collective Security Pact be brought into harmony with Article 51 of the United Nations Charter and then be used as the basis for a defense pact, with membership open to non-Arab states like Turkey, Iran, Pakistan, Britain, and the United States. This proposal, Nuri maintained, was welcomed by the Egyptians.

Nuri shed further light on the Sarsank talks during a speech he made before the Chamber of Deputies on February 6 of the following year, when he reviewed the exchanges which had preceded the announcement that Turkey and Iraq would enter into a security pact. At Sarsank, he reported, agreement had been reached on the following points:

1. Both would reconsider the ACSP with a view to strengthening it.

2. The parties would co-operate in combating "destructive principles" and that Egypt, with this in view, would send a mission to Baghdad for the exchange of information with Iraqi experts.

3. It was agreed to reconsider the machinery of the Arab League secretariat general.

4. Army chiefs of staff of the two countries would exchange visits.

5. In order to raise the standard of living there would also be an exchange of information in economic, social and cultural fields.

Whether Salim and his group were really enthusiastic about Nuri's plan to expand the Arab Collective Security Pact or whether Nuri, in his enthusiasm, read too much into their polite reception of it, is hard to say. What was made clear to Nuri on Salim's return to Cairo was that Nasser would have nothing to do with it. Nuri persisted, however. In September he went again to London for health reasons, but probably also to make soundings on the termination of the 1930 Anglo-Iraqi Treaty. He decided to stop on the way in Cairo to see Nasser and on his way back to Baghdad to stop in Istanbul to see Prime Minister Menderes for discussions on regional defense. His talk with Nasser led him to think he now had Nasser's support. He believed that because of Iraq's proximity to the border of the Soviet Union, Nasser was in agreement with Iraq's proceeding with a collective security arrangement, even outside the Arab sphere if necessary, which would include Turkey, Iran, Britain, and the United States. Nuri regarded such an agreement as comparable to the British-Egyptian Suez base agreement which provided for British reoccupancy of the Canal base in the event of a Soviet attack on Turkey. But in this instance, too, it developed later that there had been no meeting of the minds. Nuri's talks with Menderes, fortunately, took a far happier turn.

MENDERES–NURI TALKS

On November 1, 1954, a few days after Nuri's return from Istanbul, he was interviewed by a correspondent of the Sunday *Times*. On November 2 the Baghdad press quoted Nuri as having told the correspondent: "We are not strong enough to be able to assist others, but we are trying to find a means to correlate our foreign policy with the provisions of the Turkish-Pakistani Pact. All that we can do at the present is organize the defense of Iraq through co-operation with neighboring states."

Fortunately our Embassy in Baghdad was able to get details of the Istanbul talks about the same time that Nuri gave out this general public statement. Nuri himself generously furnished the Embassy with a summary of the minutes of the talks. Their substance follows: The minutes begin with observations on Iraq's position in the field of Middle East security. Iraq's security, it is stated, is tied to that of Turkey and Iran. Egypt's agreement with the United Kingdom on the Suez Canal base, which is designed to ward off aggression against the Arab states or Turkey, means that Egypt too is on the way to co-operate with Turkey. As a matter of fact he, Nuri, had repeatedly pointed out to the Arab League states the necessity for co-operation between them and Turkey. During his visit in Cairo he had emphasized the same thing to the government of Egypt and was glad to find Egypt agreeable to this proposition. He had also made it clear to Egypt during this visit that great harm would be caused Iraq by delay in realizing co-operation with Turkey. He had likewise called attention to the benefits that would flow from Iranian and Syrian participation in such co-operation. Syrian participation, for one thing, would encourage other Arab states to co-operate with Turkey.

Menderes was pleased to hear these views from Nuri. Turkey, he said, wants to demonstrate her sincere feeling for the Arab states. If she has not done so earlier it is because she did not know what the reaction would be. Menderes was of the opinion, too, that if co-operation could be realized between the countries of the region, the United States and the United Kingdom would be more inclined to extend aid. He was glad to find that Nuri was of the same opinion.

The points on which Nuri and Menderes had reached agreement were then listed in the minutes and were described as follows:

1. The security of Turkey and Iraq calls for the establishment of co-operation with their neighbors. The best solution is for all Arab states to join in this, along with Iran and Pakistan.

2. Attempts will be made in discussions which Iraq and Turkey are planning to have with Egypt, to get Egypt to join this grouping too.

3. Iraq and Turkey will keep in constant touch in the hope of arranging talks with Syria, Iran, and Pakistan.

4. Nuri explained that Iraq's role in the scheme of defense would be: (a) to safeguard the eastern passes against enemy land forces; (b) to defend her oil wells from air and atomic

attacks; and (c) to facilitate and insure arrival of aid destined for Turkey via Iraq.

5. Nuri made clear to Menderes that measures should be taken to check Communist and Zionist propaganda aimed at preventing *rapprochement* between Arab countries and Turkey. Menderes not only endorsed this but added that measures already taken against the Communists, particularly in Iraq and Egypt, had caused great satisfaction in Turkey.

6. Finally, there was agreement on the need for making mutual assistance in the economic field more effective for implementing the provisions of both the economic and cultural agreements concluded in 1946.

One of the deductions to be drawn from Nuri's version of his October talks with Menderes is that his earlier fears of possible Turkish Irredentist intentions had been considerably allayed and that, although his future course of action had not been worked out in detail, an early bilateral agreement with Turkey was in the making. These minutes I believe also bear out that Nuri, in spite of mentioning Zionism and communism together, regarded the Soviet threat the greater and more immediate. He had been heard to say that ninety-five percent of the Iraqi public regarded Israel as a greater menace than the Soviet Union. He was to take his stand, though, among the few who thought otherwise. In this, as in many other respects, he had the courage of his convictions.

In his August 4 announcement, Nuri mentioned the Turkish-Pakistani Agreement, the preliminary British-Egyptian Agreement, and the 1930 Anglo-Iraqi Treaty in that order. The Turkish-Pakistani Agreement, as events bore out, had encouraged Nuri to exchange views with Menderes. He regarded the British-Egyptian Agreement, as revealed in the minutes of his talks with Menderes, also as an encouragement to approach Turkey in the interests of regional defense. With Egypt in the process of placing her relations with Britain on a more realistic basis, he felt the moment opportune for Iraq to do the same. So, on December 15, he announced in Parliament that his government would terminate the treaty with Britain prior to its expiration in 1957. He promised to inform Parliament in February, or at the latest in March, how this would be brought about and the basis on which future relations with the United Kingdom were to be conducted.

Shortly after this announcement Nuri made a more detailed statement before the Financial Affairs Committee of Parliament. The British government, he said, had been notified that Iraq did not intend renewing or prolonging the 1930 Treaty, nor would Iraq be prepared to replace the treaty by another bilateral agreement as was customary before World War I. In any negotiations Iraq would be guided by Articles 51 and 52 of the United Nations Charter which contain principles for defense and the maintenance of peace as exercised by sovereign, independent countries throughout the world. At the same time Iraq would take into account the safety of neighboring countries like Iran and Turkey, as their safety embraced the safety of Iraq and vice versa. It was likewise necessary for Iraq to take into consideration the Arab Collective Security Pact because of the threat of Israel to Arab countries. But in any event Iraq would not undertake commitments or responsibilities beyond her boundaries except as stipulated in the Collective Security Pact.

The treaty in question was known as the Treaty of Preferential Alliance and had been signed in 1930. It provided for its coming into force on the date of Iraq's admission to the League of Nations, and remaining in force for twenty-five years. Iraq had become a member of the League on October 3, 1932. The treaty, therefore, was due to expire in the autumn of 1957. Even though it provided for Iraq's membership in the League of Nations and for the termination of the British mandate, the treaty was not popular with the Iraqi public. Iraqis resented the British retention of air bases at Habbaniya and Shu ayba and the right to use Iraqi facilities for the transportation of troops and arms across Iraqi territory. They regarded these provisions as infringements on their sovereignty. Nuri, sensitive to this, discerned when he returned to office in August, 1954, that it was time for a change. He felt those agreements between Turkey and Pakistan and between Egypt and Britain, reached earlier in the year, had paved the way.

These developments in the field of collective security were followed by the announcement, about the first of December, that Menderes would visit Baghdad early in January, 1955, to continue the talks begun with Nuri in Istanbul in October. Between the time we received that word and the arrival of Menderes and his party on January 6, I had three talks with Nuri devoted almost exclusively to the problem of security. I wanted to get as full and clear a picture as possible of his thinking before Menderes arrived.

During the first talk Nuri asserted that he found working with the Pakistani as satisfactory as working with the Turks with whom he had had long experience. It was evident that Turks and Pakistanis were on an equal footing in his planning. He confirmed that Menderes would arrive in Baghdad about the first week in January. After Baghdad he would go to Cairo, a wise move, as he would be just the man to give Nasser a needed "push" in the direction of co-operative planning. Nuri hoped that King Faisal would visit Egypt after Menderes had been there and give Nasser a second push in this direction.[5]

Asked what he thought the effect might be on Iraq's relations with other Arab states if Iraq were to sign a bilateral pact with a non-Arab state, Nuri replied that he would not hesitate to make such an agreement because several Arab states were already party to such agreements. He cited Jordan and Saudi Arabia. In the case of Jordan he had in mind the Treaty of Alliance of March 15, 1948, between Britain and Trans-Jordan,[6] and in the case of Saudi Arabia, the Agreement of June 18, 1951, and subsequent ones, with the United States,

[5] These visits of Menderes and King Faisal to Egypt did not materialize. In a speech delivered in Parliament on February 6 Nuri explained that "internal developments" in Egypt had made "postponement" necessary.

[6] The text of this treaty, which is identical to the text of the so-called Portsmouth Treaty rejected by Iraq in January, 1948, appears on pages 296–99, Hurewitz, *Diplomacy*.

on the use of the Dhahran airfield, and on military assistance.

During my next talk with Nuri on the subject of Menderes's visit I found that he was not optimistic about an agreement being reached in January. There were still too many questions requiring "clarification." Perhaps the way could be cleared for an agreement in February. Briefly, what he would like to see would be a regional pact based on Articles 51 and 52 of the United Nations Charter. But before he could make much progress he would have to know how far the United States and the United Kingdom were prepared to go beyond their NATO commitments. Those commitments covered Turkey, but what about Iraq?

As our conversation continued, he expressed deep concern over the vacuum existing in the North between Turkey and Pakistan. He wished he felt free to do something about it. He was reluctant to enter into an agreement with Turkey unless the United States and the United Kingdom were parties to it. He feared the force of Egyptian reaction were Iraq alone to sign an agreement with Turkey. He was also disturbed by the political instability in Syria which was caused by leftist propaganda and agitation. He said he needed more time to reflect and plan.

On the occasion of the third talk I had with Nuri in preparation for the Menderes visit we discussed the needs and capabilities of the Iraqi army. I told Nuri that we felt Iraq could maintain an army of its present size, and perhaps even a larger one, with her own resources. We agreed with him that if any considerable expansion were to take place, and Iraq herself were to meet the increased costs, the funds would have to come from money earmarked for the Development Program. Such a diversion of funds was bound to slow down the program and we would regret that as much as he. We were, therefore, reviewing the current needs of the Iraqi Army with the British in an effort to establish to what extent we could meet Iraqi requirements through our offshore purchases in the United Kingdom. I hoped to be able to give him a picture of the situation before too long. It should be understood, however, that any decision on the amount of aid we would be prepared to extend would be influenced by how much was done locally in building up regional defense and to what extent local facilities would be made available for the common defense of the free world.

Nuri had no quarrel with this. He acquiesced in the rules we laid down and lived up to them. Whether we kept faith with him will be weighed in a later chapter.

During this exchange Nuri gave more details about the kind of defense pact he had in mind. Earlier he had said that he wanted a pact based on both Articles 51 and 52 of the United Nations Charter. His mention of Article 52 was puzzling as it deals with the peaceful settlement of disputes. He explained that he hoped ultimately to achieve a pact between Iraq and her neighbors, along with the United States and Britain, based on Article 51 and "in the spirit of Article 52." In this, he said, he was thinking of the Soviets. He was taking a long view. As the rearming of West Germany gained momentum, the Soviet Union might become less belligerent and more interested in the pacific settlement of disputes, the subject of Article 52. The mention of it in a regional pact would hardly go unnoticed and might even some day, in this context, have an appeal for the Soviets.

In the course of the discussion Nuri said that staff talks with Iran were desirable at an early stage but that Iraq could not take the initiative in this. Iran was delicately situated, and her northern frontier was exposed to the Soviet Union. The initiative and timing for staff talks would have to be left to the Iranians; he did not want to embarrass Iran.

Relations with the Soviets were referred to again. The day before, Nuri had announced that the Iraqi Legation in Moscow was being closed for "reasons of economy" and that he had asked the Soviet government to close its Legation in Baghdad within a reasonable time. Diplomatic relations with the Soviet Union were to be "suspended." He called my attention to this action and asked gleefully: "Did you see what I did to the Russians?" Placing my hand beneath the coffee table in front of us, I asked: "But what will be left underground after the Russians have gone?" Nuri promptly put both his hands under the table, and answered lightly: "We are in touch with developments." This reply demonstrated Nuri's complete confidence in the police. It was characteristic of him that he never doubted the loyalty of the police or the army.

Menderes and his party arrived on January 6. The city had been profusely decorated with flags in their honor. Menderes, on arrival, gave out a statement saying that the visit had been arranged in an atmosphere of friendship during the recent stay in Turkey of the Crown Prince and Nuri. He believed that the close relations now being inaugurated with Iraq would be of major importance in the relations of Turkey with the other Arab states. He regarded it as propitious that his visit coincided with Iraq's Army Day, and he extended warm congratulations to the Iraqi Army.

The Baghdad press carried the statement without comment.

The reception of the Turkish delegation was marred by two incidents of egg throwing which took place between the airport and the government guest house. The security police blamed "leftists" and promptly made twenty arrests.

Some days after the arrival of the Turkish delegation Nuri and Menderes began their exchanges. I learned from Menderes that he, like Nuri, did not anticipate an immediate agreement but did not think an eventual agreement impossible. He felt, however, that some form of association by the United States and the United Kingdom would be necessary to assure it.

The next day members of Menderes's party told me that the Turkish delegation was convinced that Iraq seriously wished to explore the problem of regional defense. Turkish delegates would, however, avoid putting pressure on Iraq. Emphasis was to be on common danger and the need to counter with common defense measures. It was hoped in Turkish quarters that

Nuri would not delay long in making a public declaration of Iraq's intentions.

At dinner at the Turkish Embassy the following evening, I found Menderes optimistic. He felt the exchanges were going well, and they were to be continued. Nuri had at first taken the stand that he was handicapped by not knowing the United States' position. Menderes pointed out that there was nothing obscure in the position of the United States. It had been the experience of both Turkey and Pakistan that where initiative is taken in behalf of common defense, American support and aid are forthcoming. Nuri was still talking in general terms of a pact based on Articles 51 and 52 of the United Nations Charter, but the talks were helping him to clarify his position.

The next day considerable progress was made. At the close of the talks on that day a communiqué was issued announcing that Turkey and Iraq, in the exercise of the right of self-defense as proclaimed in Article 51 of the United Nations Charter, had decided to conclude a treaty expanding co-operation for the stability and security of the Middle East in keeping with the principles of the United Nations Charter. The necessity for such a treaty, the communiqué continued, had been recognized during the talks that had taken place in Istanbul the previous October. Participation in this treaty was considered expedient and necessary for states that had shown determination to serve the goals outlined; that were geographically situated to do so; or that had the means at their disposal to help. Consequently, during the short period intervening before the actual drafting of the treaty was undertaken, Turkey and Iraq would keep in close touch with states that expressed a desire to act in concert with them. Turkey and Iraq would hope that such states could sign the treaty along with them. If not, Turkey and Iraq would continue their efforts in the hope of obtaining later signatures.

The next day, January 14, Acting Foreign Minister Bur-

hanuddin Bashayan gave the press the following amplifica-
tion of the communiqué:

1. Nuri's affirmation, made on previous occasions, that Iraq
would not send her forces to fight outside Iraq still holds good
and was accepted by Turkey.

2. Iraq had obtained assistance from the United States without any obligations or commitments, even before any agreement had been reached with Turkey on the maintenance of
stability and peace in the Middle East.

3. The agreement between Turkey and Iraq gives the lie
to Zionist propaganda that Iraq has offensive designs.

4. It is necessary, and it would be beneficial, for all Arab
countries to join the agreement, with Egypt taking the lead.
Egypt's participation would be welcomed by all peace-loving
countries because of her strategic position and capabilities.

5. The proposed new agreement has no connection with the
Turkish-Pakistani Alliance. It is an entirely new arrangement.
There is nothing in the way of Pakistan, or for that matter
Iran, joining it.

That evening, I dined again at the Turkish Embassy. Menderes, while admitting that the talks had been only in general
terms and that all details for an agreement remained to be
worked out, was nevertheless in good spirits. Nuri appeared
full of enthusiasm and energy. He told me that he was not
going to wait until the proposed treaty had been drafted and
signed before approaching some of Iraq's neighbors about possible adherences. He was going to start soundings at once.
Then, looking around the room he spied the Saudi Arabian
minister, Sheik Abdullah al-Khayyal, off in a corner. His mood
sobered, and with a premonition that was soon proved well
founded, he said: "Those are the people who are going to cause
trouble."

Acting Foreign Minister Bashayan's explanatory statement
on the January 13 communiqué was designed primarily for
Iraqi consumption. Menderes, as he was leaving for Ankara,

handed the press a statement intended for Arabs generally. Turkey and Iraq, he explained, were not interested in achieving just bilateral co-operation. Their objective was multilateral co-operation, and there lay the proof of the importance attributed by the two countries to the entire Arab people. Those who do not now give to Turkish and Iraqi efforts the value they deserve, will come to appreciate these efforts in the light of future developments. After all it is only the short-sighted and ill-willed who have evinced dissatisfaction and apprehension.

A singular honor was bestowed on Menderes on the eve of his return to Ankara. The Iraqi Parliament invited him to address it. He was the first foreign statesman to have been asked by Parliament to do this in the thirty years of its existence. He was enthusiastically received, as were his remarks. Through a common religion, a long common history and a common frontier, Menderes said, the two countries were closely bound. Happily, he concluded, the prevailing atmosphere augured well for close co-operation in furthering their common interests.

On January 19, after a special cabinet meeting and two meetings at the Palace attended by the King, the Crown Prince, and former prime ministers Tawfiq Suweidi, Jamal Madfai, Salih Jabr, Nuraddin Mahmud, Arshad al-Umari, and Fadhil Jamali, a further communiqué was issued in justification of the course Iraq was taking. The high lights of this communiqué were:

1. Since its establishment as a state, Iraq's foreign policy has been based on the twin principles laid down by King Faisal I, (a) to promote vital Arab aims through the unification of Arab ranks, and (b) to insure that Iraq remains an independent, sovereign and useful member of the Arab community.

2. In pursuance of (a) Iraq's endeavors have covered Syria, Lebanon, North Africa, and Palestine. Iraq also participated in the establishment of the Arab League and the Arab States

Collective Security Pact. In pursuance of (*b*) Iraq has continuously sought to organize and consolidate relations with her neighbors and with major powers whose interests are bound with those of Iraq. As a result of this endeavor Iraq has concluded treaties of friendship and good neighborliness with Turkey, Iran, and Afghanistan, and participated in the Sa'dabad Pact.[7] In addition, Iraq entered into a treaty of alliance with the United Kingdom.

3. Iraq, moreover, has never ignored the natural right accruing to any Arab state to take any step in the international field which it found private circumstances made necessary. For example, Iraq welcomed the Anglo-Egyptian Agreement, even though its full details were not known by her until after it had been signed. As a complementary step, Iraq embarked on an understanding with Turkey in the interest of peace and security in the Middle East.

4. Special circumstances also play a role in Iraq's relations with Turkey. Iraq has a long common frontier with Turkey. There are common resources as well.[8] And Iraq is bound to Turkey by the treaties and agreements of 1926, 1937, and 1942.

5. Finally, the projected agreement with Turkey is based on Article 51 of the United Nations Charter in the same manner as the Arab Collective Security Pact.

Iraq's case seems to have been well put to the public at home and abroad in these three communiqués. The final one, a resumé of Iraq's objectives in the foreign field carrying with

[7] Treaty of Nonaggression signed by Afghanistan, Iran, Iraq, and Turkey on July 8, 1937, at Sa'dabad Palace, the Shah's summer residence in the northern suburbs of Tehran.

[8] Exactly what common resources the authors of this communiqué had in mind is open to speculation. Water might have been one of them. As a matter of fact, during Menderes's visit some members of his party discussed with the Development Board the possibility of jointly building dams at the headwaters in Turkey of the Tigris and Euphrates rivers. The dams would be designed to provide hydroelectric power and to help in flood control and the promotion of irrigation schemes. The project, however, never got beyond this preliminary discussion stage.

it the endorsement of six former prime ministers, had particular merit. Unfortunately the communiqués were unable to avert a storm of protest from abroad. Before it broke, however, Secretary Dulles expressed to Nuri and to Menderes his satisfaction with the intention of Iraq and Turkey to conclude a treaty designed to insure the stability and security of the Middle East. He offered both warm congratulations and best wishes for early success.

THE STORM

At this time Nuri often revealed how sensitive he was to criticism of his foreign policy by other Arab states, particularly Egypt. Repeatedly he justified his policy in private conversations, in statements to Parliament, and in interviews with the press.

Answering the Egyptian charge that Iraq had violated the Pact of the Arab League and the Arab Collective Security Treaty, he maintained that Iraq's action was in keeping with both the Charter of the United Nations and of the Arab League. Moreover, Iraq had not moved in haste but had first fully discussed her intentions with the Egyptian government and other Arab League governments. There had been talks at Sarsank. In Cairo there had been a meeting of foreign ministers of the Arab states. In addition, as early as December 12, 1954, Iraq's Foreign Minister had sent an explanatory note on the relation between Iraq, Turkey, and Iran to his Arab foreign minister colleagues. Iraq's special geographic situation necessitated a pact with Turkey. Iraq's action was no different from Egypt's signing an agreement on Suez with Great Britain.

Editorial comment in the Baghdad press on the proposed Turkish-Iraqi agreement was uniformly favorable. The concensus was that Iraq's decision was justified; that Arab states had been informed in advance and had accepted Iraq's views on her special defense requirements; and that Egypt herself had done the very thing for which she was now attacking Iraq. Keen interest in the proposed agreement was sustained into February when editorial comment was almost exclusively devoted to the proposed pact. Iraq's position continued to be enthusiastically defended and Egypt continued to be strongly criticized.

Observing Nuri during the talks I had with him at this time I became convinced that the force and fury of Cairo's attack really surprised him. Charges that he had deserted the Arab camp wounded him deeply. What else could he have done to explain the necessity of Iraq's course to her Arab neighbors? "I have done no wrong," was an expression he used often. He stoutly maintained that during the exchanges he had with Nasser, in Egypt the previous September, it had been agreed that if Egypt could not at this time proceed with a regional defense scheme, Iraq, being the more exposed to the Soviet threat, should feel free to proceed on her own so long as the door was left open for later association by Egypt and other Arab states. He would usually conclude that in the last analysis he was responsible only to the people and Parliament of Iraq.

The extremes to which the Cairo radio went during these days is well illustrated by its broadcasts of January 26 and 27. The former date marked the seventh anniversary of the Portsmouth Treaty riots.[9] Implicit in the villification of Nuri in that broadcast was a thinly veiled incitement of the Iraqi public to repeat the Portsmouth riots and cause the rejection of the proposed Turkish-Iraqi Agreement and the downfall of Nuri.

Another feature of this particular broadcast was a tape

[9] This treaty was negotiated and signed while Nuri was out of office. Salih Jabr was prime minister at the time. Even though the treaty contained a number of provisions favorable to Iraq which were later incorporated in the special agreement between Britain and Iraq of April 4, 1955, Nuri advised against signing until political leaders in Iraq had been consulted. Jabr rejected the advice, signed, and was then faced with riots that forced withdrawal of the treaty and his resignation.

recording of an attack on Nuri and his government by the prominent Istiqlalist Siddig Shanshal, information officer in the Rashid Ali cabinet of 1941 who later became a member of Qasim's first cabinet as minister of news and guidance. How the recording got to Cairo was the subject of lively speculation for days. A source close to Nuri said it had been smuggled out in the Saudi Arabian diplomatic pouch.

The objective of Cairo radio's broadcast of January 27 was to divide Nuri and the Palace. The call to the King and to the Crown Prince was in these words: "In the name of millions of Arabs and of all countries of the Arab homeland we appeal to you, just as they appealed to your grandfather, to save Arabs from the menace of military alliances." The King and the Crown Prince were reminded of "anti-Arab actions" undertaken by the Turks in the past and present. The broadcast concluded: "We pray God to assist you in rescuing the Arabs from the calamity of the Nuri-Menderes alliance."

In the final blast in this series, Cairo radio accused Nuri of having left the Arab bloc to tie his country to Israel and the imperialists. Since Nuri is apparently so adamant, it asked, what purpose could be served by the rumored Nasser-Nuri meeting? Can Egyptians succeed where the united Arab world has failed?

In the midst of this radio campaign against Nuri, the Revolutionary Command Council of Egypt called for an emergency meeting of prime ministers and foreign ministers of the Arab League states. The meeting convened in Cairo on January 22, 1955. Nuri, as might have been expected, did not attend. As he said privately, he was not going to appear in Cairo "to be put on trial." The official reason given for his failure to attend was "illness." He was in fact at the time suffering from a chest congestion, and his physician thought that he was too ill to travel to Cairo. Nuri had been known to leave the sickroom against his doctor's advice when he thought situations required his personal attention. I think that if there had been an abatement of the Egyptian press and radio campaign, and he could have appeared in Cairo with dignity, he would have gone regardless of health.

THE COUNTERATTACK

Baghdad was prompt in taking measures to counteract Cairo's attacks. In connection with the efforts of the Palace on Nuri's behalf I was asked on January 20 by the Crown Prince for our help in arranging a meeting between Nasser, Menderes, and King Saud. He also asked that we make clear in Cairo our support of the proposed pact with Turkey. Having learned earlier that Nuri wanted Nasser, Menderes, and Saud to meet, I was able to tell the Crown Prince that I had already informed Washington of Iraqi wishes in this respect. As for the second request, I told him that our views in support of the proposed pact had been explained to Egypt's Foreign Minister Fawzi three days before. Abdul-Ilah seemed relieved that we were acting so promptly. Shortly after this exchange I was told that the feeling in Washington was that a meeting between Nasser and Menderes would be helpful, but that Saudi participation would not. Ill feeling between Nuri and Saud was of too long standing.

On the same day that I saw the Crown Prince, former Prime Minister Fadhil Jamali and the Iraqi minister to Syria, Abdul Jalil al-Rawi, left Baghdad for Damascus and Beirut to explain Iraq's position to officials in those capitals and to try to reassure them. Jamali alone made another visit to Damascus and Beirut in February. The evening before he left he explained to me that his visit to Beirut was to enlist President Chamoun's friendship. In Damascus he would give President Atasi the latest information the government of Iraq had on French and Israeli "intrigues." It was difficult to gauge how well Jamali succeeded with Chamoun, and no appraisal of this was given me by any Iraqi official. In Syria his efforts were unproductive. Shortly after this second visit to Damascus, the Prime Minister of Syria announced in Parliament that Syria was not interested in the proposed Turkish-Iraqi Pact. In fact, Syria was opposed to it. When an Iraqi official close to Nuri told me how very disappointed the government was over this statement, he explained that it had been hoped that if Jamali could not win Syrian support for the pact, he could at least succeed in keeping Syria from commenting adversely on it. He added a word about the Syrian Army. It was feared, he said, that most officers of the Syrian Army, as the result of French, Saudi, and more recently, Egyptian bribes, were now anti-Iraqi.

The government and army of Syria were constant preoccupations of the government of Iraq. Syria lay across Iraq's lifeline, her main petroleum pipeline. An unfriendly Syria constituted a threat to the line's normal operation. During the uneasy period in 1955, Damascus's propaganda had the same flavor as Cairo's. This increased the concern of Nuri and his government.

Jordan, too, gave the Palace and Nuri concern during the critical early months of 1955. Unfortunately, much of this time King Husayn was out of the country. Nuri was very suspicious of the incumbent Foreign Minister of Jordan, insisting that he was in Saudi pay. On February 17, shortly after King Husayn had stopped briefly in Baghdad, Crown Prince Abdul-Ilah told me that the King and he now understood why Husayn had complained that he had not been kept informed of developments leading to the decision of Iraq and Turkey to join a defensive pact. Abdul-Ilah said that information given representatives of Jordan in Baghdad and Ankara on the Turkish-Iraqi exchanges had not been brought to Husayn's attention.

But the King and the Crown Prince received encouragement from Lebanon and Syria during the days when they were so concerned about Jordan. On February 12 I was called to the Palace and received by the King and the Crown Prince, who wished to inform me about a letter President Chamoun of Lebanon had sent to Nasser, and about an interview between President Atasi of Syria and al-Rawi, the Iraqi minister in

Damascus. I had previously met with the King and the Crown Prince separately but this was the first time I had seen them together. Present also was the Chef of the Royal Divan. He was to do the translating of the Chamoun letter and of al-Rawi's record of the interview.

The young King's bearing throughout my call was composed, dignified and friendly. The Crown Prince, while friendly enough, was on the stiff side. His attitude toward his nephew, the King, while not deferential was, I felt, intended to convey the impression that they worked together as equals. The King opened the interview with some pleasantries. He asked about my wife's health and mine, and expressed the hope that we would be able to stand the heat of a Baghdad summer. When I reminded him that we had both experienced Washington summers, he laughed and said that during his visit to the United States he had been in Washington in August. After this light exchange, the Crown Prince took over. He moved briskly.

He said he knew that I was familiar with the developments arising from the announcement that Iraq and Turkey would enter a defensive pact. He had two documents bearing on these developments, the substance of which he wanted to pass on to me. He then handed the papers to the Chef of the Royal Divan and told him to translate them. The Chef appeared nervous and his translation was at first slow and fumbling. The Crown Prince made no effort to hide his impatience. He paced up and down the room, smoking all the time. After two or three puffs on a cigarette, he would toss it into the fireplace and light a fresh one. By interjecting words to speed up the translating, he only added to the Chef's confusion. At one point he snatched one of the documents from the translator's lap, saying it seemed to be in the way. He tossed it on the desk where the King sat all this time, composed and attentive. When the Chef had difficulty finding a word, he would turn for help not to the Crown Prince, but to the King who patiently and kindly supplied the word. When

I took my leave, the contrast between nephew and uncle again stood out. Abdul-Ilah was cordial in a way, but stiff in manner. The King's bearing was gracious, relaxed and decidedly friendly.

THE CONTENTS OF THE DOCUMENTS

In his letter to Nasser, Chamoun appealed to Nasser to call an immediate halt to Egypt's campaign against the Turkish-Iraqi Pact. The Arab world, he emphasized, could not live by itself. Egyptian propaganda was isolating the Arab world and causing dissension within it.

During the interview between President Atasi and al-Rawi, which made up the other matter the King and the Crown Prince wished to discuss with me, Atasi had expressed concern over French and Saudi intrigue in Syria which he felt was playing into Communist hands. He would rather resign than face the disaster the Communists would inflict on Syria. There was no provision, however, for resignation in the Syrian Constitution. He would have to remain in office and accept any prime minister who had a majority in Parliament. Actually, Atasi continued, sentiment in Syria was overwhelmingly friendly to Iraq. There was no real opposition to the proposed Turkish-Iraqi Pact but Communists, played upon by the French and Saudis, could wreck not only the good relations with Iraq but the country itself.

The nature of Nasser's reply to Chamoun, the Crown Prince told me, was not known. Merely having such friendly sentiments from Lebanon expressed to Nasser was good in itself, and he wanted us informed. He and the King hoped that in learning about Atasi's sentiments the United States would bring pressure to bear to halt French and Saudi intrigues in Syria.

Parliament, too, was the scene of activity during this critical time. On February 6 the Chamber of Deputies was called in special session on short notice. Ninety-six of the 135 members responded and adopted the following resolution presented by seven pro-government members: "This Assembly, cognizant of the government's policy which aims at securing Iraq's strength through co-operation with her neighbors and in accordance with its traditional policy, which is in conformity with the Arab Collective Security Pact and with the Arab League, and the United Nations Charter, fully supports this policy."

At this session Nuri spoke for an hour and a half. It was not a well-organized speech but a rambling recitation. He said two basic principles governed Iraq's traditional foreign policy. These were close relations with all Arab states and good relations with non-Arab states which, because of their geographic position, were of particular importance to Iraq. Then he spoke of the Sarsank talks and his later discussions in Cairo and Istanbul.

"The first chapter," Nuri said, "begins with Sarsank and ends with the visit of the Turkish mission to Baghdad and its departure for Damascus and Beirut. The second chapter covers the visit of the Turkish mission to Damascus and Beirut." At Sarsank he had given his objections to the Anglo-Egyptian Agreement. The evacuation of British troops was a matter solely between Egypt and the United Kingdom. Not so the question of the return of British troops for defense against an attack on Turkey or the Arab countries. This was not solely Egypt's concern. Situated between Turkey and the Suez Canal there were Arab countries whose views on this aspect of the agreement had not been sought. Egypt had acted behind the backs of the Arab countries and Turkey.

On the subject of his September talks in Cairo with Nasser, Foreign Minister Fawzi, and Salah Salim, Nuri said:

> I told them that the part of the treaty dealing with other Arab countries should not be retained unless agreed to by the other Arab countries through the machinery of the Arab Collective Security Pact. But the Egyptians said they could not change the agreement. Anyway, no Egyptians believed

that evacuation would take place. The British had been promising to evacuate for seventy years but nothing happened. If after some time had elapsed and it appeared that evacuation would take place, then it was time enough to change the agreement.

I explained to them that we could not ignore our relations with Turkey and Iran. I assured them that I was not going to Turkey to conduct discussions that would conflict with Egyptian plans.

After the Istanbul talks of October, he explained, he had a communiqué issued, but before it was made public he had copies given to all Arab representatives in Ankara. He continued:

I heard nothing from my Egyptian brothers nor from any of my other Arab brothers after the publication of this communiqué in Istanbul. I heard no complaint or dissatisfaction, nor did I receive a request for any kind of explanation. October and November passed and when December came, the Arab foreign ministers met in Cairo. But no one asked about the Iraqi-Turkish discussions. In Baghdad, the discussions followed the same lines as in Istanbul. The Turkish mission then went to Damascus and Beirut. In Beirut, a UP correspondent was told that the discussions with Menderes had been fruitful, frank and friendly. Then came the attacks. Iraq, it was charged, had taken the Arab countries by surprise!

After an hour and a half of this, the deputies gave Nuri a 96–0 vote of confidence.

We also helped to bolster Nuri during these trying days. The view in Washington on the Turkish-Iraqi intention was, briefly, as follows:

1. We looked with particular favor on any increased collaboration in the Middle East against possible Communist aggression.

2. We thus viewed the Turkish-Iraqi declaration of intention as a constructive step.

3. We were, moreover, prepared to assist Turkish and Iraqi efforts to achieve a realistic and effective defense arrangement.

4. We believed the Arab states should welcome this development as an important step contributing to their own security.

Messages explaining our position in these words were sent from Washington to our Embassies in the Arab states and Israel as a guide in answering inquiries about our stand.

Then at a press conference in Washington on January 18, when Mr. Dulles was asked whether he cared to comment on the proposed pact, he said:

> The United States considers this a very constructive development. It is a move toward building up the so-called "Northern Tier" of which Turkey and Pakistan are already pioneers. In between Turkey and Pakistan lie Iraq and Iran and as those countries take their place to close the gap in between Turkey and Pakistan, we believe the security of the area will be greatly improved.

This public statement from Dulles, blessing what Nuri and Menderes had thus far accomplished and encouraging them to go on to rally their neighbors, did much to bolster Nuri's determination to stay the course.

CAIRO DELEGATION VISIT

Shortly after the Cairo conference which convened on January 22, some of the delegates to it, including a number of Egyptians, visited Baghdad. For reasons explained above Nuri had not attended the conference. He was however represented by former Prime Minister Jamali, Acting Foreign Minister Bashayan, and the Director General of Information and Guidance, Sayyid Khalil Ibrahim. Just before the delegates arrived in Baghdad for their meeting with Nuri, we received from an official Iraqi source the Iraqi version of what had transpired at the Cairo conference. Nasser, our source said, did little talking, letting Salah Salim carry the ball. Salah Salim suggested that Iraq had fallen in line with the proposed Turkish-Iraqi Pact in return for promised military aid from the United States. He claimed, too, that Iraq had promised not to sign an agreement with Turkey until Egypt also was willing to sign. When the Iraqi delegation denied that Nuri had given such a pledge, the Egyptians hedged and said they had got this second-hand from the Turks. The Saudi Arabian delegation, led by Amir Faisal, was uniformly hostile to Iraq. When reminded by the Iraqis that Saudi Arabia was associated with the West through the Dhahran Air Base agreement, the reply was that Saudi Arabia could ask the Americans to leave at any time. Syria, on the other hand, led by Prime Minister Faris al-Khouri, had been helpful. While Jordan, led by Prime Minister Taufiq Abdul Huda and Foreign Minister Walih Salah, did not take a strong line, her attitude was patently anti-Iraq, and both these Jordanians were suspected of being in Saudi pay. The Lebanese delegation, headed by Prime Minister Sami Suhl, was the greatest disappointment. Lebanon had been kept fully informed and it was thought favored the course Iraq was taking. Here was another prime minister suspected of being in Saudi pay. There was no question where President Chamoun stood. He was well disposed toward Iraq. So ran the Iraqi version of the Cairo meeting.

The Cairo delegates arrived in Baghdad on February 2. Disorders took place shortly before their arrival, and there were some bombings and two small demonstrations in protest against the proposed pact. The bombings caused little damage but unfortunately three deaths occurred during the demonstrations. The government said leftist agitators from the former National Front were responsible for these disorders. The demonstrations were quickly and effectively brought under control. While the atmosphere was by no means relaxed, there were no signs at any time of a breakdown in public order.

Talks with the conference delegates lasted only one day. On the evening of February 2 a communiqué was issued which, though brief, contained one bit of information that seemed of more than passing interest. After an exchange of views, the communiqué read, it had been decided to accept the suggestion of President Chamoun that Nuri and Nasser meet in Beirut to resolve their differences, the date to be fixed later.

On February 3 I called on Nuri at his home. I opened our discussion by assuring him that, in spite of the attacks on him, we continued to look upon the course outlined in his and Menderes's communiqué of January 13 as very constructive and as constituting a real contribution to area defense. Then, referring to the communiqué of the evening before, I asked him when his meeting with Nasser might take place. His answer was: "Perhaps never." He had made Iraq's position clear, privately and publicly, and did not attach much importance to a further meeting with Nasser. Looking back over the past few weeks, and particularly to the recent Cairo conference, he had been much encouraged by the Syrian attitude but felt that the Lebanese, with the exception of President Chamoun, had been acting badly. This applied particularly to Sami Suhl, prime minister of Lebanon. He thought it might be helpful for our representatives in Damascus and Beirut to know how he felt about the Syrians and Lebanese. He also wanted them to know that in spite of everything that had happened recently between Egypt and Iraq, he still very much wanted Egyptian association with any defensive pact. And he also hoped that Iran would, at a time of her choosing, come in. "After all," he said, "I sacked the Russians to give the Shah courage." Then he launched into an account of his meeting with the Cairo conference delegates. What he had to say, it turned out, was meant primarily for the Egyptian ears of Salah Salim.

Nuri told me with some delight that he greeted the delegates with these words: "In Cairo you gave me hell. Now here in Baghdad I'm going to give you double hell." He started with some advice. "Come down from the stars to the earth." Face the fact that the Communist threat to common security is real and immediate. "Tomorrow the Communists might be in

Formosa and the next day in our midst." Referring to the proposed pact with Turkey, he told them: "We will leave the door open to all to join but the drafting and signing will not be put off because of current attacks." At this point he mentioned Cairo specifically to them. He found Cairo's reaction and behavior inexplicable, he said, considering how recently Egypt herself had signed an agreement with Britain providing for co-operation between their armed forces in case of danger.

As I was leaving, Nuri said that his doctor thought he was rundown and had ordered him to stay at home and rest for some days. I told him that I would be saying some prayers for him in the hope they might speed his recovery. His response was typical. "Thanks a lot for your prayers, but how about some big guns too?"

By February 4, the Cairo delegates were on their way home. The Lebanese prime minister, Sami Sulh, told the press on his departure that he was leaving with "restrained optimism." Salah Salim, I learned privately, left feeling that he had been let down by the other delegates. In fact, he had at one time during the Baghdad stay openly berated them for failure to support him in the face of Nuri's counterattack.

Right after the delegates left, Nuri met with his cabinet, and later on the same day with the King and the Crown Prince. They discussed the bombings that broke out on the eve of the arrival of the Cairo delegates. So general was the concern over this threat to public order that the imposition of martial law was broached. Nuri vehemently rejected the idea. As was his custom, he insisted that police and army morale were high and both forces loyal to the government. He was confident the government could cope with the situation without imposing martial law, and his confidence won the day. But the continuing radio attacks from Cairo were something else.

He approached me with a plea for assistance in getting as quickly as possible, from the United States, radio equipment powerful enough to match radio Cairo. The Baghdad equipment was inadequate. He was turning to us, rather than the British, because he thought delivery from the United States would be quicker than from Britain, and he was in a hurry. He wanted the equipment in a matter of days, or a few weeks at the latest. He would pay cash and would meet the cost of shipment by air regardless of how much this might be. He sent the Director General of Radio, to the Embassy with the required technical information. What he wanted was a transmitter of at least 100 kilowatts for both short- and medium-wave broadcasts, and the help of an American engineer to supervise the installation. In return for helping him get the equipment quickly, Nuri promised that the facilities would be made available to the Voice of America to use as it saw fit.

I sent his request to the State Department immediately, urging prompt action as this was so clearly to our advantage. To my surprise and chagrin, days and weeks went by, with Nuri pressing me constantly, without any word from Washington on what was being done. Finally, Nuri turned in despair to the British and in time, but much later than he had hoped, he got some new equipment from them. In time, too, I got an explanation from Washington. Nuri's request, instead of receiving priority treatment at a high level in the State Department, as it deserved and as I thought it would get, fell into the hands of some petty bureaucrat who did no more than pass it on to the Department of Commerce for routine treatment as just another "trade opportunity." Commerce put it "in channels" but there were no takers. The "trade" it seems was too busy with domestic demands to bother about such an opportunity from abroad.

Bad as this disappointment was, there were even bigger ones in store for me. Our treatment of Nuri during the following years was destined to be halting, and even bungling at times.

SIGNING OF THE TURKISH-IRAQI PACT

While working out the details of the pact with Turkey, Nuri never lost sight of his accompanying objective, a new

Nuri, host to the Kuwaitis at a reception in October, 1955, honoring the half-brother of the ruler of Kuwait, Sheik Fahad (facing the camera). (Photo presented to the author by Nuri.)

Nuri, with the Iraqi delegation, presiding at the organizational meeting of the Ministerial Council of the Baghdad Pact, November 21-23, 1955. Seated at his left are Foreign Minister Burhanuddin Bashayan; Foreign Office Undersecretary Sayyid Yusuf al-Gaylani; and chief of staff, General Rafiq Arif. Photo courtesy of Iraqi Foreign Office.)

Nuri relaxes at an evening reception which took place at the close of the Baghdad Pact Ministerial Council meeting. Left to right: Tahsin Qadri, master of royal ceremonies; Nuri; Harold Macmillan, then foreign secretary; and the author. (Photo by Elias Jamoua, courtesy of Foreign Office.)

Centurion tanks, with crews, on parade ground at Rashid Military Camp where tanks were presented by U.S. and U.K. at a special ceremony, January 3, 1956. (Photo courtesy USIS.)

King Faisal II, Crown Prince Abdul-Illah, Prime Minister Nuri, and Minister of Development Dhia Ja'Afar arrive for the dedication of the Ramadi dam on April 5, 1956. (Photo courtesy USIS.)

Public reaction to the dedication of the Ramadi dam on the Euphrates, April 5, 1956. (Photo courtesy USIS.)

Aerial view of the Wadi-Tharthar dam at Samara, dedicated on April 2, 1956. (Photo courtesy USIS.)

Nuri (and his beads), with the author at his right, at the presentation ceremony on March 27, 1957, of the Atomic Energy Library, which was a gift from the U.S. to Iraq. (Photo courtesy USIS.)

The author calling on Prime Minister Qasim, November 1, 1958. (Photo presented to the author with the Prime Minister's compliments.)

agreement with the United Kingdom to replace the Anglo-Iraqi Treaty of June 30, 1930, and open the way for British adherence to the proposed pact. As the time approached for Menderes to return to Baghdad to formalize the treaty, Nuri pressed the British for staff talks. He wanted to take part in them personally and did so. They began at Habbaniya airfield on February 22. Nuri was insistent that they either be completed within forty-eight hours, or at least be well advanced by the time of Menderes's arrival on February 23. He found the British receptive and co-operative. He was able to show Menderes substantial progress in his negotiations with the British for a new agreement when the time came for signing the Turkish-Iraqi Pact.

Menderes arrived shortly after midday. Washington and London had both made their attitude toward the projected pact clear. Both wanted to see it signed. Washington preferred, though, that the pact itself contain no reference to the Palestine question.

During the afternoon of February 23 I met with Fatin Rustu Zorlu, deputy prime minister and foreign minister of Turkey, at the Turkish Embassy. He told me the text of the pact had been agreed on and would be signed the next day and submitted to the Iraqi Parliament on February 26. He then made a strong plea for our early adherence. With the United States in the pact, he explained convincingly, the attitude of the Arab states toward it would be quite different. Opposition would be blunted. Besides, Iraq and Turkey would be in a stronger position in their approaches to the Arab states, and the future of the pact would be brighter.

From that day on, over the next four years, I saw Zorlu often at conferences of the Baghdad Pact, usually in company with Menderes. They complemented each other and as a team worked tirelessly to strengthen the defenses of the free world. Menderes's warm personality, ever-ready smile, and slow but steady flow of words, contrasted sharply with the rather dour looking, taciturn, and massive Zorlu. Sitting side by side at

the conference table, Menderes gave the impression of reason-
ableness personified and Zorlu of ingrained toughness, if not
stubbornness. Despite their very considerable efforts to rally
the free peoples of the world against the Communist threat,
they, like Nuri, eventually met death at the hands of their
own people.[10]

I saw Zorlu again on February 24. He showed the British
ambassador, Sir Michael Wright, and me, the pencilled drafts
of letters bearing on the Palestine issue which were to ac-
company the pact and be exchanged at the time of signing.
Nuri in his letter observed that it is "our" understanding that
the pact would enable the two countries to co-operate in
resisting any aggression directed against either party and that,
in order to insure peace in the Middle East, the two parties
would co-operate to make the United Nations resolutions on
Palestine effective. Menderes, in replying, simply stated that
he wished to confirm his government's agreement with the
contents of Nuri's letter. In keeping with instructions I had
received, I expressed the hope that the exchanging of these
letters would not take place until some time after the signing
of the pact. We wanted no reference to the Palestine question
in the pact itself, nor close association between the pact and
any accompanying documents mentioning Palestine. Ambassador Wright inquired whether there was not still time to
change the wording somewhat, but Zorlu took a firm stand.
Nuri, he maintained, could not be induced to accept any
changes in wording, or postponement in effecting the exchange.
Nuri hoped to appease Arab opinion by linking the letters
closely to the pact. Menderes, Zorlu explained, agreed that
Nuri needed the letters as worded and needed them right away

---

[10] The Menderes government was overthrown by a military coup on
May 27, 1960. Menderes and Zorlu were tried by a revolutionary court,
found guilty of crimes against the Turkish Constitution, and sentenced to
death. Zorlu was hanged on September 16, 1961, and Menderes on the
following day.

in order to strengthen his position. Menderes feared, however, that they might cause trouble for his government.

The pact was signed late on February 24, and early the next morning a member of Menderes's party gave me an advance copy of the text with Menderes's compliments. He also commented on the letters concerning Palestine, giving them added significance. The letters, he pointed out, constituted the crux of the agreement between the two countries. Only in them did Turkey and Iraq agree to co-operate in resisting aggression. The pact itself merely obligated the two countries to "co-operate for their security and defense."

Shortly after Menderes's arrival in Baghdad, Abdullah Bakr, Chef of the Royal Divan, called on me at the Embassy at the request of both Nuri and Menderes. He explained that French and Syrian "machinations" were disturbing them greatly. They feared that the French were working through Syria's foreign minister, al-Azm, to effect a coup. They hoped the United States would take steps to curb the French. I told Bakr that we had already expressed to the Government of France the hope that it would support such indigenous defense arrangements as were implicit in the Turkish-Iraqi Agreement. Apparently this did not reassure Nuri and Menderes because Zorlu followed Bakr in calling. He told me that the Turkish Chargé in Damascus had been approached by Adnan Atasi, son of the President of Syria. Speaking for his father, Atasi said a French supported coup was expected. Zorlu was more specific in his request for help than Bakr had been. Zorlu asked that we, with the British and his government, ask the French government not to back a coup but to influence the government of Syria to assume a neutral attitude. I told Zorlu also that we had already urged the French to back indigenous defense undertakings. Nevertheless, uneasiness and suspicion persisted.

The Pact of Mutual Co-operation between Turkey and Iraq was based on Article 51 of the United Nations Charter. Article 5 of the Turkish-Iraqi Agreement provided for adherence by other states. Great care was exercised in wording this article because of Iraq's relations with her Arab neighbors and the Arab position on Israel. The first paragraph of this article read as follows:

> This pact shall be open for accession to any member of the Arab League or any other State actively concerned with the security and peace in this region and which is fully recognized by both the High Contracting Parties. Accession shall come into force from the date on which the instrument of accession of the State concerned is deposited with the Ministry for Foreign Affairs of Iraq.

It was the phrase limiting accession to states "fully recognized by both the High Contracting Parties" which isolated Israel, and placated Iraq's Arab neighbors.

In effect, the Turkish-Iraqi Pact replaced the Agreement of Friendly Co-operation which had been signed between Pakistan and Turkey on April 2, 1954, as a basis for the Northern Tier defense. The Turkish-Pakistani Agreement, in its Article 6, provided for the accession of other states but Nuri felt that its wording was too broad. He wanted a pact with an article which while permitting additional adherences clearly excluded Israel, and this he got in Article 5 of the new pact.

Article 6 of the pact provided that when at least four powers had become parties to it a Permanent Council, at the ministerial level, was to be set up to carry out its aims.

As soon as the text of the Turkish-Iraqi Pact was made public Egypt's Salah Salim warned his fellow Arabs that the Permanent Council mentioned in Article 6 would undertake supervision of "our armies, economy and policies." In reply the government of Iraq issued a communiqué explaining that the Permanent Council was intended to be only advisory, and that its deliberations would be referred to the various interested governments for review and action.

On February 26 the pact was submitted to Parliament for ratification. It was approved by the Chamber of Deputies by a 112 to 4 vote, and by the Senate by 26 to 1.

During the debate on the pact in the Chamber, Nuri again spoke at length. Iraq's co-operation under the pact would, he said, be based on three principles. First, Iraq would not accept commitments outside her frontiers or the frontiers of members of the Arab League Collective Security Pact. Secondly, the government of Iraq alone was responsible for the defense of Iraq and no other government could dictate to Iraq the conditions under which she was to co-operate. Thirdly, Iraq's foreign policy would be based on full sovereignty and on equal rights between the contracting parties. He said again that the pact was in line with Iraq's traditional foreign policy and in no way ran counter to the charters of the Arab League and of the Arab Collective Security Pact. Iran and Pakistan would be welcomed into the pact, and he hoped that the United States and the United Kingdom would join. He placed special significance on the fact that adherence by the United Kingdom would mean the termination of the Anglo-Iraqi Treaty of 1930.

The objections to the pact voiced in the Chamber were few but pointed. Those who attacked it did so on the grounds that Turkey's obligations to assist the Arab states against Israel were not clearly defined; the pact had been hastily drawn up and negotiated; and it was bound to alienate Iraq from other Arab states.

In the Senate, the lone dissenter, the venerable Mahammed Ridha al-Shabibi, explained his opposition on the ground that he favored "neutralism" for Iraq. To this Nuri replied that Shabibi was not representative of the people of Iraq, "99.75 per cent" of whom were in favor of the pact. Salih Jabr, Nuri's strongest political rival, retorted that it was "nonsensical" to think that a policy of neutrality was possible under existing world conditions. Another strong opponent of Nuri on domestic matters, Senator Abdul Mahdi, agreed with Salih Jabr. He described the futility of a neutralist policy and called on the government to take whatever steps it thought necessary for the defense of Iraq's interests. He welcomed the pact, he concluded, as a defensive measure. A further voice was raised against neutralism, that of the independent, Nasrat al-Farisi, who said he saw no possibility of Iraq protecting her interests through a policy of neutrality.

Not many days after Nuri had won this impressive Parliamentary endorsement, a party of guests came from abroad to help him celebrate. President Celal Bayar of Turkey, with his wife and twenty-one Turkish officials, arrived in Baghdad on March 5 for a five-day visit. Among the officials were the minister of defense, Ethren Menderes; the commander in chief of the Turkish Navy, Vice Admiral Sadid Altuican; and the chairman of the foreign affairs committee of the national assembly, Cehad Baban. The days were filled with ceremonial visits, luncheons, dinners and receptions, with no apparent interruptions for substantive policy discussions. Elaborate security arrangements prevented unfortunate incidents and a trip to the holy city of Najaf, where secondary school students chose the day of the visit to demonstrate against the pact, was prudently cancelled.

Nuri enjoyed the festivities and a few days after the departure of his guests I was able to prove to him that the initiative I had urged on him in January had paid off. Washington had decided that some "tangible evidence" of appreciation for Nuri's "forthright stand" was in order. He was to receive, as a gift, twelve 120 millimeter guns with a thousand rounds of ammunition for training purposes. He reacted with boyish delight to this news. He did so want some "big guns."

SECOND STORM

After the signing of the pact, Cairo radio received reinforcements in its continuing attack on Nuri. A new voice took to the air with daily programs. It called itself "Radio Free Iraq." It matched Cairo radio in vituperation and called on the people of Iraq to revolt against Nuri. After three months of this repetitive exhortation, the public lost interest and gradually the voice of "Free Iraq" faded away, but not before some Iraqi authorities claimed that, through a process of "triangulation" and with the help of "friends" from abroad, they had located the source of the broadcasts. They came, the Iraqis insisted, from two stations in Egyptian hands, one in Cairo and the other in the Gaza strip.

While "Radio Free Iraq" died down, Cairo radio Sawt al-Arab kept on with its attacks with varying degrees of force. Nuri had become inured to the steady attacks on him, but when the campaign was extended to the royal family, he reacted at once. He told me that if this "vilification" did not stop, he would withdraw the Iraqi Ambassador from Cairo, but he was quick to add that he was not contemplating breaking diplomatic relations with Egypt, and he did not withdraw the Ambassador.

On October 20, 1955, Egypt and Syria, not content with radio attacks on the Turkish-Iraqi Agreement, entered into a Mutual Defense Agreement.[11] The Foreign Office in Baghdad was quick to discuss it with us. The treaty provided for a Higher Council, made up of the ministers of defense and foreign affairs of the two countries, as the supreme authority, with a War Council consisting of the chiefs of staff of the two countries serving as a consultative body. This agreement, as Foreign Minister Bashayan said to me with no little self-control, "injects a new element into the situation." Nuri had hoped to be able to work with President Quwatli and Foreign Minister Ghazzi of Syria. Now these two had obviously yielded to the extremists in the Syrian army, which caused Nuri much concern.

ADHERENCES

Two weeks after Turkey and Iraq signed their Pact of Mutual Co-operation, I urged our early adherence upon the State Department for the following reasons:

[11] On October 27 Saudi Arabia became party to a similar arrangement with Egypt.

1. We were the originators of the Northern Tier concept and gave the inspiration and encouragement which led to the Turkish-Iraqi Pact.

2. Our adherence, along with Britain's, would give the Middle East proof that we and the British were co-operating in the defense of the free world.

3. Our adherence would enhance our overall influence in the Middle East.

4. Adherence would not materially enlarge our commitments. Through membership in NATO we had already assumed certain commitments and had extended military aid to Iraq.

5. If we joined, Israeli fears that the pact might be used to her detriment would be allayed.

6. Our joining might also help quiet the fears lingering in the minds of Nuri and other Iraqi leaders of Turkish Irredentist designs on Mosul.

7. Nuri had shown great courage in aligning Iraq with Turkey and the West, risking not only much at home but also much in his relations with his Arab neighbors, and had earned our full support.

8. We had already publicly endorsed the pact and privately shown our disapproval of the Egyptian-Syrian-Saudi alignment as an ineffective and ill-contrived defense arrangement.

During the next few years I repeatedly urged our adherence to the Pact as did the American ambassadors in Ankara, Tehran and Karachi, but we were unsuccessful. The United States never joined the Baghdad Pact. Nor have we joined CENTO, as it became known after Iraq's defection.

Nuri constantly sought our adherence. During a call I made on him with Senator Theodore Green and Congressman Bow in 1955, he pointed out that U.S. adherence would show Moscow clearly how the United States felt about Moscow's efforts to cause disruption in the Middle East; U.S. adherence would give encouragement to Iran to join and would give a lift to those who had already joined; it might well have a decisive effect also on waverers like Jordan and Lebanon; and finally, U.S. adherence would not call for any real increase in U.S. commitments or material aid. When Senator Green asked how Egypt would react to U.S. adherence, Nuri brushed this aside with the observation: "The Communist threat is the over-riding, immediate issue. Every other consideration is secondary."

While we were stalling, Britain moved briskly.

Nuri's sudden, surprising willingness to sign a treaty with Turkey caused much speculation in Baghdad. Was Turkish salesmanship the explanation, or was this rather evidence of Nuri's political acumen? Turkish salesmanship as practiced by the persuasive, likeable Menderes no doubt played a part but I attribute his swift action largely to political shrewdness. He was quick to see that an agreement with Turkey could provide the ideal medium through which the unpopular Anglo-Iraqi Treaty could be replaced by something more acceptable to the Iraqi public, while at the same time retaining for Iraq the military benefits derived from close association with the British. That he had judged correctly was demonstrated by the reception given his announcement on April 1 that the 1930 treaty was to be terminated.

He told Parliament on that day not only that the treaty was being terminated, but also that a new agreement was to be signed with Britain on April 4, to be followed on April 6 by British adherence to the Turkish-Iraqi Pact. On May 2 the airfields at Habbaniya, Shu ayba and Margil were to be turned over to the Iraqis.

On April 1 all Baghdad morning newspapers carried the announcement of the termination in banner headlines. Also featured in heavy print was the British intention to join the Turkish-Iraqi Pact and to begin the following month with the evacuation of British troops from Iraq. The stories themselves averaged twelve columns. The only story which had received equally extensive treatment since King Faisal's coronation in 1952 was the story of the signing of the Turkish-Iraqi Pact in February. While there were no street demonstrations, habitués of the coffee shops received the news with evident pleasure and pride.

On April 6 Nuri broadcast a speech to the nation. Now that the long sought termination of the 1930 treaty with Britain was accomplished, greater responsibilities than ever rested on Iraq. She could now work more fully for her own people and Arabs everywhere. Iraq was fortunate in having both independence and money. But there was need for men "who knew how to spend money wisely." Iraq's hope lay in the patriotic efforts of her educated young people.

The terminated treaty, Nuri continued, had been amended and reamended since 1922. With its passing, "sweet aspirations," so often dreamed, were finally realized. Independence was now complete, and Iraq was free from every restriction. The period in which this was achieved was not long in the life of a nation. For once the whole people of Iraq were grateful to Nuri.

The Special Agreement between Britain and Iraq, signed April 4, stipulated that Iraq assumed full responsibility for her defense.[12] This provision was followed with details on how the two countries would co-operate in the defense of Iraq.

On April 5, the British instruments of adherence to the Turkish-Iraqi Pact of Mutual Co-operation were deposited with the Iraqi Foreign Office, thus formally terminating the 1930 treaty, bringing the April 4 agreement into force, and making Britain the first state to join the Turkish-Iraqi Pact.

While in Washington in the late summer and early autumn of 1954, preparing for the Baghdad assignment, I was given the impression in the State Department that London was not particularly keen about seeing the Dulles Northern Tier concept realized. When, however, shortly after my arrival

[12] The text of this agreement appears on pages 391–95, Hurewitz, *Diplomacy.*

in Baghdad the Menderes-Nuri exchanges foreshadowed an alignment of states giving real substance and meaning to this concept, I found the British taking notice and following the talks closely. Even before the signing by Iraq and Turkey in February, 1955, of the Pact of Mutual Co-operation, there was evidence of something more than casual interest among the British in Baghdad; there were signs of real activity. Article 5 of the agreement held great appeal for them, as it opened the way for their adherence. They were quick to see that this would enable them to place their relations with Iraq on a more realistic and popular basis, and increase their influence.

The rapidity with which the Baghdad Pact came into being caught both London and Washington by surprise. I think that until late in 1954 both capitals thought it would take years to formalize the Northern Tier concept. That may account for the apparent lack of interest, originally, in London. The British may have felt that there was no urgency for defining their attitude in detail. London's realistic acceptance of the situation, and readiness to make use of it promptly to safeguard and promote British interests, made an impressive demonstration of flexibility and acumen on the part of a Western power and rivaled Moscow's envied speed and competence in political maneuvering.

The ceremonies marking the transfer of control of Habbaniya to the Iraqis took place there on May 2. They did full justice to this historic occasion. May 2, 1955, was also King Faisal's birthday and the second anniversary of his coronation. It was also the fourteenth anniversary of the outbreak of the Rashid Ali revolt and open warfare between British and Iraqi forces at Habbaniya.

During the ceremonies, speeches were exchanged by the British ambassador, Sir Michael Wright, and the Iraqi foreign minister, Musa Shabandar. They recalled to me a talk I had had with Shabandar in the Iraqi Embassy in Washington just before I left for Baghdad. Ambassador Shabandar knowing that my previous post had been the Union of South Africa asked me about my life there. In closing, I asked him if he knew that part of Africa. He was amused by the question. "I was a resident in Southern Rhodesia for a time," he said, smiling broadly, "but I did not get about much. I was a prisoner of the British."

Shabandar, as I should have remembered, was "banished" for a time to Southern Rhodesia by the British after they had crushed the Rashid Ali revolt. This was the price he had paid for being associated with Rashid Ali.

Jordan, Syria, Lebanon, Sudan, Libya, and Turkey sent special delegations to the May 2 ceremonies, but Egypt was represented by its ambassador in Baghdad.

Sir Michael Wright, in his remarks, took note of the changed relationship between the United Kingdom and Iraq by pointing out that Iraq was now an equal partner with the United Kingdom and Turkey in an agreement under the United Nations Charter for the promotion of security in the Middle East. "Iraq knows," he continued, "that she has the resources of the West behind her in building up her forces to protect her independence. She knows too that if she desires it, Britain will come to her immediate assistance if her freedom is in danger."

In responding, Minister Shabandar said the ceremonies marked the beginning of a new era for Iraq. Her aims were twofold, self-defense and co-operation with her neighbors.

At the conclusion of the speeches, the Royal Air Force ensign was solemnly lowered. An Iraqi guard of honor then replaced it with the flag of Iraq. The ceremonies closed with a parade of Iraqi and British contingents past reviewing stands, with the Iraqi army band lending an American touch by playing its two favorite tunes, "Swanee River," nicely balanced by "Marching Through Georgia."

On the same day, a ceremony following the pattern at Habbaniya took place at the Shu ayba airfield near Basra. The acting consul general in Basra, J. Wright, represented the British, and the mutasarrif of the Basra Liwa, Muzahim Mahir, the Iraqis. Nuri, always the thoughtful and genial host, made personal calls on all visiting delegations.

Pakistan joined the pact five months after the British. However, as early as May 9, Nuri told me that he anticipated Pakistan's joining before the end of the month, and then asked when we would join. When I had to tell him that our joining was not under consideration, he expressed regret but recovered quickly enough to add as encouragement: "When you sign I'll arrange an even bigger ceremony than was held last week when the Iraqi flag went up over Habbaniya."

But while we held aloof, we did not hesitate trying to get others to join, even resorting to the old stick and carrot technique. To our Embassy in Karachi the department explained that so far as possible our aid to Middle East countries would in the future be based on how plans for regional defense developed, rather than on separate country-by-country estimates of individual needs. This principle would hold good whether or not the United States itself became a member of the regional organization.

On September 23 the Pakistani ambassador in Baghdad, Qureishi, deposited Pakistan's instruments of adherence with the Foreign Office. When doing so he explained Pakistan's understanding of the pact in these words: "This is a defensive alliance aimed at stabilizing the peace in the area and at creating active means to protect it from hostilities. It is not directed against any country, but designed to make real the desires of the people of the area for peace and for raising their material and moral standards."

The third and last country to join was Iran. Her adherence became effective on October 25.

As far back as January 14, the day following Nuri's announcement that a Turkish-Iraqi Treaty was in the making, Ghods-Nakhai, Iranian ambassador in Baghdad, told me that he was relieved to hear of the plans. Nuri had shown courage and wisdom, he said. When I commented that an early declaration by Iran of her intention to adhere would advance the cause of common defense, he replied that he was sensitive to the danger facing his country. He would like to see Iran line-up promptly with Iraq and Turkey. Perhaps, he added, after the Shah's return from his trip abroad, light would be thrown on Iran's intentions.

The Shah passed through Baghdad on March 12 on his way back to Tehran. His stay was short but Nuri told me he had a good talk with him. He found the Shah happy about his visit to the United States and the United Kingdom. Iran, the Shah told him, wished eventually to adhere to the Turkish-Iraqi Pact, but Iran was too weak militarily to do so. He would first like staff talks between Iran, Iraq, Turkey, and Pakistan, with British and American participation, to prepare a defense plan for the Persian Gulf area. When such a plan had become a reality, Iran would be prepared to join.

On May 9, Nuri again spoke of the Shah and staff talks. It seemed that the United States, he commented, did not want the talks in Washington, and the United Kingdom did not want them in London. To suggest that they be held in Baghdad without American or British participation would be un- realistic. Middle East defense planning, without the United States and Britain, did not make sense. What the area needed was an overall defense plan under a single command, with a logistics plan assuring uniform arms. "For example," he slyly interjected, "if Pakistan gets American tanks, then Iraq should have American tanks too."

On May 31, Nuri again touched on the staff talks in which he said the Shah was so interested. Even though the United States and Britain were not prepared to participate, he said, nor even have someone in attendance, the talks should be held. To keep shying away from them might dampen the spirits of the anti-Communist element in Iran. That element should be given every possible encouragement. These talks could turn out to be the prelude to Iran's joining the pact, but Iran's adherence just then was not as important as it was to give encouragement to the anti-Communist groups in the country. The presence of Americans and British at such talks, if only as observers, would give the encouragement needed.

That was the last I heard of staff talks from Nuri. The next news from Iran came on October 12 when Iran informed the government of Iraq of her decision to join the pact. There were now sufficient adherences to proceed with the establishment of the Permanent Council mentioned in Article 6, and on October 17 Nuri told me that on or about November 20 the signatories would meet in Baghdad for that purpose.

Only eight months had passed since the signing of the Turkish-Iraqi Agreement, a fine tribute to the energy of Nuri and Menderes.

V

THE
BAGHDAD PACT

INAUGURAL MEETING, NOVEMBER, 1955

The inaugural meeting of the Permanent Council of the Pact of Mutual Co-operation (later known as the Baghdad Pact [1]) opened in Baghdad on November 21, with Nuri, prime minister of the host government, presiding. Prime Minister Adnan Menderes led the Turkish delegation, Prime Minister Chauri Mahamad Ali the Pakistani, Prime Minister Hasain Ali the Iranian, and Harold Macmillan, then foreign minister, the British. A week before the opening, I was instructed to tell Nuri that we would establish some form of political and military liaison with the council. Vague as this was and far as it was from adherence, the news cheered him considerably. I was designated special political observer for the United States, for the meeting, with Admiral John A. Cassady and Brigadier General Forrest Caraway as military observers. These desig-

---

[1] For a concise account of the preliminaries leading to the signing of this pact and for the text see pages 390–91, Vol. II, *Diplomacy in the Near and Middle East,* by J. C. Hurewitz (Princeton, N.J.: Van Nostrand, 1956).

nations were made even before we were invited to participate as observers. We had anticipated such an invitation, and were not disappointed. Shortly after the formal opening, the delegates voted unanimously to invite the United States to participate through observers. Delivery of the invitation was effected in a matter of minutes. I was waiting for the call, with the Admiral Cassady and General Caraway, in an anteroom only a few paces from the conference chamber. The three of us promptly repaired to the conference room. There I thanked the delegates for the invitation, reviewed the various public statements we had made in support of the pact, and finished by saying that "our presence here this morning serves as still further evidence of the continuing interest of the United States in the pact and its objectives."

At this first meeting, it was decided that in the future the Pact of Mutual Co-operation between Turkey and Iraq was to be known as the Baghdad Pact. A permanent Ministerial Council was established. Two committees were to be set up, one military and one economic. The seat of the pact was to be Baghdad. Between sessions of the Ministerial Council the business of the pact was to be carried on by the ambassadors of the member states resident in Baghdad, as deputies. The American Ambassador was invited to attend these deputy meetings as an observer.

At the second session, heads of the various delegations spoke in turn. Each one mentioned points which especially interested his own country. Macmillan stressed the importance of the Economic Committee. Hasain Ali dealt with the desire of Iran to work out border problems with Turkey, Iraq and Pakistan. Mahamad Ali mentioned Afghanistan's "hostility" to his country. Menderes, with his friend Nuri in mind, urged all members to join in a search for a solution of the Israeli problem. All their speeches at some point emphasized the Communist threat and the resultant need to strengthen the Pact as quickly as possible. Mention of this turned all eyes to the little group of American observers.

While Nuri was not at all times the most businesslike chairman, he was throughout the meeting an attentive and considerate host. He entered freely into all the discussions, and much that he said bears repeating here.

At the second session, Nuri spoke extemporaneously at length on the disruptive effects of Communist propaganda. The spread of Communist propaganda throughout the Middle East, he pointed out, antedated the founding of the Baghdad Pact by some years. In fact, it had reached threatening proportions as far back as World War II. Means had to be found without delay to counteract and arrest it. Means for doing this through the Baghdad Pact machinery should be explored. The longer the delay, the greater the danger of sparking a conflagration. Korea was a case in point. There vicious Communist propaganda had free play for years, and eventually set off a war which cost the United States dearly in lives and money.

He returned to this theme in a later session. Unless the Communist propaganda were stymied, he said, there could be no stability in the area. It was designed to mislead those with little education and knowledge of world conditions. This had to be considered in planning countermeasures. The Baghdad Pact had begun well but needed strengthening, and its membership should be enlarged. Here he obviously had in mind adherence by at least one more Arab state and formal, full participation by the United States. A solution must be found of the Israeli problem. He did not elaborate on this except to repeat what he and other Arab spokesmen had said so often. The U.N. resolution on the partition of Palestine of November 29, 1947, would have to serve as the basis for a solution.

During the November 22 session, Macmillan made a suggestion which was warmly received by all and immediately put into effect. This was that at this inaugural meeting of the council, and at all subsequent ones, time be allotted for the heads of delegations to speak off the record. This was done and was manifestly a success. Each head spoke freely of what troubled and interested his country most. A free, helpful discussion followed each presentation. In subsequent council meetings, those held in Tehran, Karachi, and Ankara, I came to feel that this practice was the most valuable feature of the meetings.

In the final communiqué of the meeting special mention was made of Iraq's relations to the pact. It was declared that her responsibilities under it did not conflict with her defense obligations as a member of the Arab League, nor with her obligation to co-operate economically with other members of the League. Note was also taken in the communiqué of the "generous and valuable" military aid that had been extended to each member of the pact by the United States, and of the offer of the United Kingdom to share its experience in the application of atomic energy to peaceful purposes.

Our Embassy felt that this first meeting justified optimism as a workable organization had been formed. Most helpful reviews and appraisals had been given by each delegation. Many clarifying exchanges had taken place. Menderes's contribution stood out. He had obviously given much thought to what might be done by the Baghdad Pact and he sought throughout in his quiet, earnest way to make sure that the initial momentum would not be lost.

Thanksgiving Day, 1955, fell on November 24, two days after the first meeting of the Baghdad Pact. That morning I went to the Anglican Church in Baghdad, which was generously made available to the American community for its annual Thanksgiving service, to read the President's traditional Thanksgiving Proclamation. During the service, I received an urgent request from Nuri that I meet him at the airport. Hurrying there, I found him with Menderes, and we were joined shortly by the British Ambassador. Menderes was about to leave for Ankara. Earlier, he and Nuri had met with the Jordanian minister to Iraq, Farhan al-Shubailat. They had discussed with him Jordan's possible adherence to the Baghdad Pact.

I was told that Minister al-Shubailat would soon be leaving for Amman with a message for King Husayn to the effect that if Jordan were to join the pact, Turkey and Iraq would provide her with arms and economic aid. It was anticipated that the United Kingdom, too, would extend some arms aid. Nothing was said to me about our giving aid but it was intimated that if the United States assured President Chamoun of some arms and economic aid, Chamoun might bring Lebanon into the pact.

These maneuvers and soundings did not bring Jordan or Lebanon into the pact. Rather they set off, in Jordan, so violent a nationalist reaction that within a period of a week three governments were in turn overthrown. My purpose in reporting this airport meeting is to reveal Nuri's deep feeling of isolation from the rest of the Arab world and his characteristic impatience to attack and try to solve the problems which faced him, at times without first doing some prudent preparatory work.

Before his departure, Menderes made this statement about the United States:

> The United States took part in our deliberations. This ally of two members of the Pact, the United Kingdom and Turkey, although not yet legally a member, has strongly supported it since its inception and has for years been extending valuable economic and military aid to all its members. It has virtually joined in collaboration within the Baghdad Pact organization. It not only sent observers to meetings of the Permanent Council but it has officially established liaison in the political and military fields. Obviously, its participation will be beyond sending observers and being kept informed. It is not wrong to assume that the legal accession of the United States is only a matter of time. It is only right and natural that this should occur at a time when the United States itself deems it convenient and appropriate.

And Harold Macmillan sent a message to Secretary Dulles in which he referred to my contribution to the discussions of the council in most gracious terms, adding the qualifying statement: "although he had to limit himself to observations." Dulles, in relaying Macmillan's message to me, added a word of congratulation of his own.

DEPUTIES' MEETINGS

There were three more meetings of the Baghdad Pact Council before Nuri's death in 1958. These took place in Tehran in April, 1956, Karachi in June, 1957, and in Ankara in January, 1958. The Karachi meeting was originally scheduled for January, 1957, but because of strong anti-British feeling prevailing in Iraq over Suez, it was postponed until June. Nuri attended all these meetings as head of the Iraqi delegation.

Baghdad Pact work was, however, not done just at these council meetings. It received continuous attention in Baghdad on the deputies' level. I attended these meetings as "observer."

The first deputies' meeting was held within a week after the establishment of the Permanent Council, with the Iraqi foreign minister, Bashayan, presiding; Ambassador Hossein Ghods-Nakkai representing Iran; Ambassador Goksenin, Turkey; Ambassador Qureshi, Pakistan; and Sir Michael Wright, Britain. The deputies wasted no time. A permanent secretariat was established, subjects for which the Economic Committee was to be responsible were studied, and it was agreed that at an early date the deputies would submit recommendations on ways to counter Communist subversion. Three further meetings of the deputies followed in quick succession. At the fourth, held December 23, 1955, there was present for the first time the secretary general of the pact's secretariat, Awni Khalidi, formerly a member of Iraq's permanent delegation to the United Nations. At this meeting the deputies received the first report from the pact's Security Organization which, in the years to follow, dealt with the problem of security in an admirably calm, detached way. As time went on, the deputies widened their field of activities. They studied highway and railroad communications, and telecommunications. Pest control figured high on the agenda, as did the exchange of scientific information.

By mid-January, 1956, the Baghdad Pact appeared firmly established and well along with the work assigned it. Despite this auspicious start, Nuri was still on the defensive about the pact, particularly in regard to its effect on Iraq's relations with her Arab neighbors. He felt obliged to defend Iraq's association with the pact twice during January before the Chamber of Deputies, and once before the Senate in February. On January 7 he told the Chamber that the pact was concluded to realize a number of objectives, the first of which was the termination of the 1930 Anglo-Iraqi Treaty. There was, he continued, always present the need to repel both Zionism and communism, and in this respect Iraq's foreign policy was in accord with that of other Arab states. But Iraq's proximity to the Soviet border made her more aware of the Communist danger. That helped to explain why Iraq was in the pact. The pact, however, did not place Iraq under any obligations beyond her borders. Then, on January 9, during the budget debate in the Chamber, Nuri again repeated the refrain that the pact did not bind Iraq to any obligation other than self-defense in accordance with Article 51 of the United Nations Charter. He added somewhat irrelevantly: "Attacks on Iraq, of course, were being made long before the Baghdad Pact came into existence."

On February 13 Nuri made this statement before the Senate:

I want to reiterate once more that Iraq has not undertaken any responsibilities outside her frontiers and that she will not incur any further responsibilities unless Parliament approves the same.

I consider the dispute between Iraq and the other Arab states a temporary one, which will disappear because it is unnatural. Iraq has never thought of injuring any Arab state in any manner. Despite all the abuse, Iraq will not hesitate or falter because she considers the interests and importance of the Arab nation no less important and vital than those of the Iraqi people.

COUNCIL MEETINGS

As the April, 1956, meeting of the council in Tehran approached, pressure on us to join the pact was intensified. On April 1, Bashayan made an especially strong plea that we become members before the council convened later in the month. This he felt would have a "salutary" effect on Moscow, Cairo, and Jidda, the seats of the strongest and most persistent attacks on Iraq and the pact. I told him I could hold out no hope that we would join then or in the near future.

In February our relationship to the Baghdad Pact had been discussed in Washington between President Eisenhower and Prime Minister Eden. This was followed by a meeting in the State Department with the ambassadors in Washington of pact member states. We admitted to them that from a psychological and practical point-of-view a good case could be made for American adherence. But, the need for the United States to retain maximum influence in the face of current Middle East problems precluded our adherence "for the present." In this ambiguous way the State Department was saying that joining the pact would only arouse Israeli misgivings and sharpen Egyptian opposition. The atmosphere in the Middle East was already overcharged. Better avoid any action that might further complicate matters. Better remain on the side lines, with a free hand. This statement that we were not prepared to join was balanced in the communiqué on the meeting with a repetition of "solid" United States support for the purposes and aims of the pact and a promise that United States "observers" would play constructive roles in the pact's committees. This reliance on observers gave me serious concern, and several

times before the council met in Tehran, I sent warning messages to Washington.

In these messages I pointed out that planning in both the
economic and military fields was moving briskly. Our presence
as "observers" could commit us in the minds of the pact members. We were getting involved without having a voice. Joining the committees, but not members of the pact, we had a
voice in the committee meetings but still did not have a vote
on the council where final decisions were made. I pleaded with
Washington that we guard against being stampeded by pressures from member states into giving more stopgap aid; that
we either join or disentangle ourselves; and that we avoid
making further commitments without an equal voice.

At the Tehran meeting we did no more than become a full
member of the Economic Committee.

SUEZ CRISIS

Between the council meeting in Tehran and the next meeting in Karachi in June, 1957, Nuri and Iraq's membership in
the pact were subjected to the heaviest attacks of all, both
inside and outside the country. These attacks were due to the
British, French, and Israeli military action against Egypt. The
Suez crisis came close to being Nuri's undoing.

Israel began the attack on Egypt on October 29. On October
30 the British and French governments delivered ultimatums
to Israel and Egypt telling them to keep their forces at a dis-
tance of ten miles from the Suez Canal. British and French
forces, the two governments were told, were going to occupy
the Canal Zone, by force if necessary. This they undertook to
do, but they met resistance from the Egyptians, and the war
was on.

When I called on Nuri on November 1, I found him more
worn and preoccupied than ever before. He professed not to
have known in advance the real nature or extent of British

action. He had thought, he said, that there was only to be some kind of restraining action by the British against Israel. "I thought the aggressor was to be punished," he explained. The turn of events had shaken him badly. He was at a loss, he said, how to deal with the increasingly strong anti-British feeling.

The same day martial law was decreed and approved by the Council of Ministers. Some five hundred students demonstrated in midmorning in Baghdad in support of Egypt, but they were quickly and peacefully dispersed. Public sentiment against Britain was mounting fast. The reason was a widespread conviction that the joint British-French action was part of a plan prearranged with Israel to eliminate Nasser. Subordinate government officials began asking whether this was not a good time to get rid of Iraq's "pro-British" government. Senior officials, while not unhappy over Nasser's predicament, were deeply concerned over the difficult position in which Iraq had been placed. They felt that the British had let the Arab world down badly, and Iraq was being forced into a position of opposition to the British. Iraqis were also acutely aware of Israeli military superiority over Jordan and Syria, and this added to their concern.

On November 3 Nuri left for Tehran to attend a meeting of the Moslem members of the pact, called by President Mirza of Pakistan. Two meetings in Baghdad, on November 9 and 19, followed. These were held to deal with the problems created by the British attack on Egypt.

On November 10, following the Tehran Moslem meeting and the first of the Baghdad Moslem meetings, the government of Iraq issued a statement containing an ingenious formula for meeting the crisis. It showed Nuri's imagination and courage. France was to be dealt with by breaking diplomatic relations. With the backing of her Moslem friends, Iraq was able to announce that Britain was to be excluded from deliberations of the Baghdad Pact. "In view of current circumstances," the statement explained, Iraqi attendance at the pact meetings was to be confined to meetings with the three other Islamic states.

This announcement posed some problems for us. We were not members of the pact but we were members of the Economic Committee. If a deputies' meeting of the pact were called while the British were still ostracized, I felt it would be in order if I attended, as always, as observer, and I told the State Department that it was my intention to do so. If, however, a meeting of the Economic Committee were called, should we as members fall in line with our Islamic friends, or abstain in deference to our old friends the British? I favored the former course, but before the State Department got around to answering, the British solved the problem for us. They informed the Iraqi Foreign Office that they would be attending all committee meetings as usual. British nationals on the pact secretariat continued, too, attending to their duties as usual.

While the Moslem members of the pact were meeting in Baghdad, I was summoned twice late at night to join the group at the Rose Palace.

At the first meeting the chief participants were Crown Prince Abdul-Ilah, Nuri, General Rafiq Arif, the Iraqi chief of staff, Menderes and Sir Michael Wright. I particularly noted at the time Menderes' calm bearing. Nuri looked very distraught. General Rafiq was "grimly serious." The British Ambassador was "glum." Menderes filled me in on the Moslem talks that had just taken place in Tehran. The main topic there had been whether, in view of the unsettled state of affairs, Soviet military intervention might not be imminent. It was felt Soviet intervention could not be ruled out. At the Tehran meeting the consensus had been that the Baghdad Pact could be put on a firm foundation only if the United States joined it. Nuri spoke next. What, he asked me, was the latest word from Washington? My answer that we were strengthening our Mediterranean Fleet and that the President had sent a message to Ben-Gurion relieved Nuri and eased tension all around. Just as the group was breaking up, we received word of a BBC announcement that Israeli troops would be withdrawn from Egyptian territory. "There," Menderes said, "we have the results of President Eisenhower's timely approach to Ben-Gurion."

Before I left, Menderes told me privately that he was pleased with the Tehran talks, as they had considerably cleared the air so far as relations with the British were concerned.

Shortly after this meeting Menderes returned to Ankara, but was back in Baghdad about a week later. This time President Mirza and Prime Minister Suhrawardy of Pakistan and the Iranian foreign minister, Ardalan, also came to Baghdad. On the day of his arrival, Menderes asked me to call. He told me that he had already talked with Nuri, the Pakistani President and Prime Minister, and the Iranian Foreign Minister. He was working for Britain's early return to active participation in the pact, but this was not easy to arrange. The crucial meeting would take place that evening at the Rose Palace. In this connection, I thought it helpful to remind him of President Eisenhower's statement a few days before in which he had explained that the United States wanted to maintain ties with old friends, while working in the United Nations toward a solution of the problems arising from Suez and the military action against Egypt.

When I returned to the Rose Palace shortly before midnight, substantially the same group was there as at the first meeting with the addition of the Pakistanis and the Iranians. Pakistani Prime Minister Suhrawardy did most of the talking. The burden of his long discourse, addressed for the most part to me, was that now, more than ever, the United States was needed in the pact as a full member. I could only remind the group that the United States government was pledged to work out a solution of the consequences of the British-French-Israeli action within the framework of the United Nations. Nuri interjected the suggestion that it might be timely for a ship or two of the United States' Sixth Fleet to pay a "friendly visit" to Beirut. President Mirza informed me that the group had decided to ask Crown Prince Abdul-Ilah to go to Washington to present its case, and this visit did actually materialize several months later.

On November 21, Menderes asked me to see him at the Turkish Embassy. He said that the four Moslem delegations were having difficulty in drafting a communiqué on their deliberations in Baghdad. They wanted to say something that would bolster Nuri. Could something be said about our joining the pact, or at least that we had again been requested to do so? I told him that as there was no chance of our joining then or in the near future, there had better be no reference at all to the United States and the pact. The following day the Crown Prince and Nuri called on me at the Embassy to discuss the communiqué and our relationship to the pact. Nuri wanted no mention of this made unless we were prepared to follow up the communiqué with an announcement of early adherence. When I said that was out of the question, he replied somewhat testily that he hoped we would then at least avoid making more public statements that raised false hopes.

Nuri's Moslem friends were justifiably concerned about his future. Popular agitation for his resignation was rampant throughout November and December and into the New Year.

During November there were serious riots in Baghdad, Najaf, and Mosul, and ones of lesser violence in Kut, Samawa, and Kirkuk, in most cases sparked by students inspired by Communist and Ba'athist (Arab Renaissance Society) propaganda. They were encouraged by the ceaseless din of the Cairo and Damascus radios. The deaths and bloodshed were caused mainly by clashes between the police and armed mobs. In Mosul and Najaf, however, the army had to be called in to reinforce the police. Official tally placed the number of persons killed in these riots at twenty-five. The actual figure was generally believed to have been higher.

When the Suez crisis broke, Nuri had been in office for two

years, and had developed a system of control based on management of the police, army, press and, to a large measure, of the political life of the country. It was well designed to resist mob pressures. At the start of the disorders he had the colleges and secondary schools closed indefinitely. Martial law was stringently applied, including military censorship of the press. Parliament was suspended. A number of known leftists and ultra-nationalists were arrested and temporarily detained. Nuri's firmness and courage helped maintain the morale of the less confident members of the government. His political rivals had no wish to assume the responsibilities of government under such unsettled conditions.

During a talk I had with the Crown Prince toward the end of November he referred to the pressures on the Palace to dismiss Nuri. But, he said, as a "change of policy" was out of the question, a change of government would mean no more than a "change of faces." It seemed best, therefore, to "stick with Nuri."

By January, 1957, it was evident that Nuri had weathered the storm. He reopened the schools but not before he had three hundred students suspended from academic life and inducted into the army for their normal military service. This increased opposition to Nuri among intellectuals, although many teachers and officials welcomed the return of normal academic activity.

His survival of the long crisis thus brought Nuri increased prestige in spite of his diminished popularity.

THE EISENHOWER DOCTRINE AND
THE RICHARDS' MISSION

Calm having been restored, superficially at least, the British resumed attendance at the deputies meetings, and at the June council meeting in Karachi they were fully reinstated.

During this time the Eisenhower Doctrine was proclaimed

in Washington, and the Richards' mission visited Baghdad.

The 1956 crisis caused Washington to review our Middle East policy, and it was concluded that something more, if not new, should be done to impress upon the world the determination of the United States to support the independence of the countries of the Middle East. The Eisenhower Doctrine was the result. It originated in a special message President Eisenhower sent to Congress on January 5, 1957, and was given the force of law by a resolution passed by Congress in March. It authorized the President to use the armed forces of the United States to secure, on request, the independence of any nation or group of nations in the Middle East against overt aggression from any nation under the control of international communism; to extend military aid to any nation or group of nations requesting it; to co-operate with any nation or group of nations in building up economic strength to further the maintenance of independence.

Nuri at once expressed warm approval of the doctrine. He hailed it not only as a guarantee against direct Communist aggression, but also as a guarantee of help against any Arab state that might have Communist leanings. He looked upon the doctrine as supporting his known international policies and thus as strengthening his position within the Arab world.

Shortly after Congress approved the doctrine, former Congressman James P. Richards was appointed, with the rank of ambassador, to head a delegation to the Middle East which would make a survey of the needs of the region. Fifteen countries were visited, including Iraq. Before the delegation left Washington, Nuri expressed the hope that it would have broad enough authority to permit consideration of United States support for some of the economic activities of the Baghdad Pact.

The mission arrived in Baghdad early in April. As a result of its study, Iraq received some direct military and economic aid, and the Baghdad Pact some support for its nonmilitary projects, all on a grant basis. The army received artillery and electronic equipment. The police force also received some modern equipment. Telecommunications equipment for the government of Iraq was authorized to enable Iraq to play her part in a regional communications system. Authorization was also given to engage the services of consulting engineers to supervise the construction of a Baghdad-Kut-Basra railroad.

With reference to Baghdad Pact projects, Ambassador Richards announced at a press conference in Baghdad on April 8 that the United States was prepared to take the necessary legal steps to make available, through the Secretary General of the Baghdad Pact, up to $1,000,000 to cover the cost of railroad, highway, and telecommunications surveys, as recommended by the Economic Committee of the pact; and $11,500,000 for the four regional members of the pact, for engineering studies and equipment in support of these projects.

Press coverage of this largess was limited and coldly factual. Three newspapers used the occasion to address an "open letter" to Richards, warning that the way to secure better U.S.-Arab relations was to withdraw United States "support" for Israel.

KARACHI COUNCIL MEETING, JUNE, 1957

The Karachi meeting of the Council of Ministers had been postponed from January to June because of the Suez crisis. As the time for the meeting approached Washington, as usual, studied how it could strengthen the Baghdad Pact without joining it. At Tehran we had become members of the Economic Committee. The Military Committee remained. Why not join it? I had already made my position clear. I was opposed to our assuming more responsibilities unless we had a vote in the council, which only membership could give us. My fear that Washington would continue on its vacillating course was soon confirmed, not by the State Department but by the British Embassy in Baghdad, which early in March

informed us that the British Ambassador, on advice received
from the British Embassy in Washington, had told Nuri that
we had decided to join the Military Committee. Nuri replied:
"If that is so, we can hold a council meeting the end of the
month." But it was not until the end of the month that I was
told by the State Department that we had decided to join the
Military Committee, and that I could now tell Nuri. When I
did so, anticlimactic as it was, Nuri showed pleasure, but could
not refrain from observing that "joining yet another committee still does not give you a vote on the council," and adding good-naturedly: "Tell Mr. Dulles that under the circumstances I would be glad to do the voting for him, if requested."

The council met from June 3 to June 6. The presiding
officer was Prime Minister Hassan Suhrawardy, the East Pakistan political leader. He was every bit as loquacious as I had
found him at the midnight meetings in Baghdad in November. But he did not do all the talking for the Pakistanis. Several times he summoned General Ayub Khan, then chief of
staff, and had him answer questions. Today, their roles are
reversed. General Ayub, who seized power in the bloodless
coup of October, 1958, is now field marshal and president.
On January 30, 1962, he had Suhrawardy arrested and impris-
oned. On his release on August 19, 1962, the government
issued a communiqué explaining that he had been detained
"to prevent him from acting in a manner prejudicial to the
security of Pakistan" and added that "the Government is now
satisfied that Mr. Suhrawardy will not henceforth participate
in any disruptive activities." [2]

As in previous council meetings, we "observed" at this one.

Two days after the Karachi meeting closed, June 8, Nuri
resigned. He had been in office since August 4, 1954. They
had been demanding years, climaxed by the Suez crisis and
its nerve-racking aftermath in Iraq. A confidant of both the
Palace and Nuri, when asked by me why Nuri resigned, replied: "He's tired. On the advice of his closest friends he is

[2] *New York Times,* August 20, 1962.

going to get some rest. But he'll be back in office in a few months."

ANKARA COUNCIL MEETING, 1958

The next and last meeting of the Baghdad Pact Council opened in Ankara on January 27, 1958, and continued through January 29. There were no more committees left for us to join. This time our contribution was of a far different kind. To the great joy of all member states, Secretary Dulles himself came to see for the first time what these meetings were like.

Nuri had been succeeded on June 18, 1957, by Ali Jawdat, a former prime minister and one time Iraqi ambassador in Washington. Jawdat had been in office six days when I saw Nuri off at the airport for London, where he was going for another physical check-up. One of his chief preoccupations as he was preparing to leave was the future of the Baghdad Pact. During our farewell chat he remarked that Jawdat was a trusted friend of his of long standing, had supported him in bringing Iraq into the Baghdad Pact, and had consistently supported the pact. But the days were passing, and Jawdat still had not publicly come out in support of it. He was beginning to feel uneasy about this. That was the mood he was in when he left the country.

It was not until July 6 that Jawdat gave his policy statement to the press. Its principal emphasis was on Iraq's ties with the Arab world. While reference was made to some of Iraq's commitments, no mention was made of the Baghdad Pact by name. Neither was there any reference to the danger of Communist aggression nor to the favorable aspects of Iraq's relations with the West. There was no implication that Iraq might not continue participating in the pact but at the same time the statement made no endorsement of the pact. It must have come as a disappoinment to Nuri in London.

The Jawdat government lasted only until December 11, 1957. It was succeeded by the government of Abd-al-Wahhab Murjan, a protegé of Nuri. Although Nuri was not in office when the council met in Ankara, he attended as head of the Iraqi delegation, just as he had at Tehran and Karachi.

Late in the afternoon of the closing session at Ankara a report was received that Egypt and Syria had decided to form a union. Members of the pact, especially Turkey and Iraq, had been closely following the trend that culminated in this decision. Word that a union was to be formed did not therefore come as a surprise, but it disturbed the group nevertheless. The Iraqi delegation naturally showed particular concern, and no member of that delegation was more visibly disturbed than Nuri. The council meeting adjourned with only expressions of concern about the worsening of conditions, but before many days the lines between Cairo and Baghdad became sharply drawn. On February 1, 1958, the formal announcement of the establishment of the United Arab Republic was made. On February 12, less than two weeks after Nuri's return to Baghdad from Ankara, the governments of Iraq and Jordan announced that they had formed a federation. Its name was the Arab Union. Shortly thereafter Nuri was back in office as prime minister of Iraq and then as prime minister of the Union. During the remaining months of his life, although preoccupied with trying to forge the Arab Union into an effective counterweight to the United Arab Republic, he still found time for the Baghdad Pact. When I last saw him on July 12, three days before his death, he told me of his plans to leave for Istanbul with the King on the fourteenth of July, to attend talks with the Moslem members of the pact before the next meeting of the council which was scheduled for later in the month in London.

Nuri's attachment to the Baghdad Pact never wavered. He gave much thought to how it might be strengthened. At the council meetings his observations were listened to with respect. Often he gave evidence of his honest fears of Soviet military action. Even more often he called attention to the unstable political situations in Syria and Lebanon, which, he maintained, were caused by Communist or Communist-inspired propaganda. Occasionally, when discussing inter-Arab relations, he sorrowfully made note of Iraq's isolation within the Arab world. On these occasions he would plead for "full backing" of the pact, meaning formal adherence by the United States. He firmly believed that our joining the pact would have a sobering effect on Moscow and a healthy effect on other Arab states.

IRAQ'S WITHDRAWAL

On the day of Qasim's coup, July 14, 1958, the Baghdad Pact headquarters were sealed and occupied by Qasim's troops. No member of the secretariat re-entered the building. No further meeting of deputies or of any other group connected with the pact took place in it.

At a press conference on July 26, Qasim was asked what policy his regime would follow with reference to the Baghdad Pact. He gave no direct reply. He said: "The countries of the Baghdad Pact have not yet recognized the new regime, and so this is not the time or place for discussing the matter." The new regime's feeling toward the pact, however, was made clear to me by Foreign Minister Jumard during a talk I had with him on August 2. Jumard claimed that the Baghdad Pact had been signed on behalf of Iraq with the authority and knowledge of no more than twenty people. It lacked popular support, and the majority of Iraqis had been kept in ignorance of the obligations assumed by Iraq under it.

It is true that the pact never enjoyed wide popular support. Its implications were never clearly put before the public, and consequently it was never understood by the public. No adequate campaign was conducted within Iraq to counteract Nasser's strong and persistent campaign of distorted interpretations. Nuri himself was chiefly to blame for this failure to educate the public. Unfortunately, he had no appreciation of the importance of public relations. This shortcoming of his and its consequences will be dealt with in detail later.

Jumard was right in saying the pact did not have the backing of the Iraqi public. He was wrong, however, in asserting that it had been signed with the authority and knowledge of only a handful of Iraqis and that the obligations assumed by Iraq had been kept from the public. On the contrary, the record shows that Nuri, through his many public statements and announcements and his speeches in Parliament which subsequently appeared in the press, made all essentials dealing with the negotiations leading to the signing of the pact and Iraq's obligations under it available for all to see.

But Minister Jumard's views on the pact were mild compared to those of Siddiq Shanshal, minister of information in Qasim's first cabinet. Shanshal maintained that the pact was no more than an instrument through which the West imposed its control over Iraqi affairs without regard for the wishes of the people. In fact, the United States and the United Kingdom, he insisted, had an agreement with Nuri under which Nuri, in exchange for Iraq's membership in the Baghdad Pact, was allowed to continue his "corrupt control" of the country.

In view of these opinions it is no wonder that Qasim withdrew Iraq from the pact. But why did he wait until March, 1959, before formally doing so? Perhaps he was too preoccupied with consolidating his hold on the country to spare time for anything else. He certainly was preoccupied with that problem, but I am sure that in spite of this he did not lose sight of the pact. I think that just because he was so worried in the early months about how firm his grip on the country was, he saw some advantage in only holding aloof at first and not breaking completely. He may have felt that this continuing link with the pact and its member states, however tenuous, had a certain "protective" quality which was helpful to

Iraq in her relations with the outside world at a time when so much uncertainty prevailed at home.

Without Nuri's Iraq, the Baghdad Pact became known as CENTO, with its seat in Ankara. With the move we went along as "observers," and "observers" we are to this day.

VI ᓚ

NURI'S DOMESTIC POLICY

Nuri's early education, military training and army service under the autocratic Ottoman Empire set his character and determined his course as a public figure. He was disciplined, loved order, and had a calculated approach to public issues.

As he grew older and acquired the reputation of a "strong man," Nuri was usually in office at moments of particular stress. He relied on the support of the Palace, army, and police; control of the press; and maneuverability among political parties and leaders to remain in power and follow his program. The public entered little into his calculations. He had confidence in his ability to determine what was best for his people. Once, during a press conference, when he was questioned about land reform, he described the sheiks as "the fathers of their tribes." In the latter years of his life he looked upon himself as "father" to the people of Iraq. Admirers and detractors alike called him "The Pasha."

PALACE

Nuri's loyalties were intense and one of the strongest was his loyalty to the Hashimite dynasty. It began in the days of the revolution against Turkish rule and with his close association with Sherif Husayn of Hejas, founder of the dynasty and father of Iraq's first king, Faisal I. It was still strong in the days of Iraq's last king, Faisal II, grandson of Faisal I.

My only opportunity to observe Nuri and the young King together was on ceremonial and social occasions. Nuri was always respectful and friendly. During our talks, whenever he referred to the King, it was with unquestionable loyalty and devotion.

Devoted as Nuri was to the Hashimites as a family, his feeling for the Crown Prince was unmistakably reserved. When the Crown Prince and Nuri called on me to discuss the communiqué on the conference of the Moslem members of the Baghdad Pact, the Crown Prince did practically all the talking. Nuri sat quiet and ill-at-ease. Abdul-Ilah's attitude toward him was rather contemptuous. He seemed to be saying: "Here is an old man, but one who must be tolerated."

Four days after this joint call, Nuri came to the Embassy alone to see me. He came to advocate a visit by the Crown Prince to Washington as spokesman for the four Moslem members of the Baghdad Pact. Despite their strained relations, he pleaded eloquently, without bitterness, and successfully.

Nuri had a fine sense of humor and did not hesitate to use it even where the Crown Prince was concerned. One story he enjoyed telling concerned an incident that took place in Washington in the summer of 1952, during the Truman administration. Nuri had accompanied King Faisal and Abdul-Ilah, who was at that time Regent. The Crown Prince, as Nuri would remind one, was fond of clothes and proud of his knowledge of them. Nuri told how he and Abdul-Ilah took a stroll along G and F Streets in Washington one afternoon, doing a little window shopping. It was the day before the party was to call on President Truman. All the windows they passed had displays of seersucker suits. Nuri liked them very much and wanted to buy some, but Abdul-Ilah would have none of it. These were cheap, popular products meant only for the working class. No one of standing would be seen in such attire. So Nuri, having always respected Abdul-Ilah as an authority on clothes, reluctantly gave up his plan to buy some. The next day when they were ushered in to see President Truman, to Abdul-Ilah's chagrin and Nuri's great delight, they found the President cool and neat in one of the seersuckers they had seen so widely displayed.

During the summer and early autumn of 1955 one heard criticism in Baghdad of King Faisal for his long absence from the country. It was, I was told, the first criticism openly made of him since his coronation in 1953. It was customary for the young King and his uncle to absent themselves from Iraq during the summer. In 1955 they left in June. As September neared and they were still abroad, resentment was outspoken. It seemed to stir the public particularly that the royal pair should be absent at a time when the Algerian situation seemed especially critical. Iraqis, like Arabs everywhere, were highly emotional where Algeria was concerned. Up to this time, the public had been inclined to make liberal allowances for the King's youth. Much of the acclaim that had been given him publicly, I surmise, was given him as grandson of the highly revered Faisal I, rather than as King in his own right.

Soon after my arrival in Iraq, I came to feel that the King should begin to assert himself. He had admirable qualities, an alert mind and a warm, appealing personality. He was handicapped by the constant presence of his undiscerning and unpopular uncle, the Crown Prince, and an entourage of courtiers. As Regent, Abdul-Ilah had gained a reputation for petty political maneuvering and intriguing, and he did not change for the better with the years. The atmosphere of the Palace was unwholesome and it was not surprising that despite its authority to name and recall prime ministers, it had little influence on government. This state of affairs was not serious so long as a man of Nuri's stature was on hand, but in the absence of a strong man as prime minister, the ship of state floundered distressingly.

Nuri's closest friends, if not Nuri himself, felt the Palace should show him deference, even when he was not in office. One of these friends complained to me one day in the winter of 1957, when Nuri was for a time out of office, that the Palace was ignoring him. "Nuri," he said, "is too great a man to be ignored whether in or out of office." He contrasted the cold treatment being given him by the Palace with the way he had just been received in Washington by President Eisenhower and Secretary Dulles. "That," Nuri's friend said, "moved him more deeply than anything he has experienced in years."

ARMY

With the termination of the mandate in 1932, and for some ten years thereafter, the army played a dominant role in Iraqi politics. From then on, although it had the power to control political developments, it kept more and more aloof from politics. By 1954 it had become the main bulwark of the government in office against seizure of power by the opposition. Nuri no doubt had a lot to do with this relationship between army and government. As a professional soldier who had the interests of the army at heart, he was generally acceptable to the rank and file. He was careful, as he proved during the parliamentary and public debates on the Turkish-Iraqi Treaty and the Baghdad Pact, not to commit the army to tasks beyond the frontiers of Iraq or those of the member states of the Arab League Collective Security Pact. He always strove to get the latest and the best equipment for the forces. The army could feel easy with him in power.

Another reason why the army at this time protected the government from the opposition was the fact that senior army officers such as the chief of staff, General Rafiq Arif, and the assistant chief of staff, General Gazi Daghistani, were dedicated supporters of the Crown and firmly believed that the army should be kept out of politics. They were intent on keeping aloof from partisan struggles unless one group or another should threaten action which might cause deterioration of the position of the army itself.

This helped Nuri considerably during the uneasy years he held office between 1954 and 1958. He felt confident that he could rely on the army to keep aloof and give him a free hand to deal with the problems of the day as he thought best.

About ten months before the coup the Embassy prepared a study of the army's role and position. We noted that while the army had played little part in politics, its officers and men shared the opinions and emotions of the civilian population from which they were drawn. They, too, were Arab nationalist, anti-Israel, and to some extent anti-British. Dislike of the United States was somewhat mitigated by our arms aid. We concluded that a situation which stirred deeply any of these emotions might cause the army, like any other group, to react so violently that even loyalty to the Crown would be abandoned. This was proven correct when Qasim's coup destroyed the Monarchy.

POLICE

Nuri was passionately devoted to public order. He knew that nothing permanent could be built without peace and security. He was quick to react to any threat to public order and was ready to call on the police or even in extreme cases impose martial law when he thought it necessary to forestall or suppress disturbances. He reacted most sharply to threats from leftist quarters which he feared especially because he thought they were inspired and largely directed from Communist centers outside the country. While his record shows frequent, and often prolonged use of police and troop forces, he never attempted to impose himself on the country as a dictator. He always held office at the bidding of the Palace, often in times so trying that none of his political opponents, who frequently accused him of highhanded methods, could be induced by the Palace to assume the responsibilities of high office.

During the unsettled months preceding Nuri's return to office in 1954 leftist activities had increased, reaching their peak in June of that year when ten deputies from the National Front were elected. When Nuri assumed office in August he promised to curb "the handful of men endeavoring to direct the public into the wrong paths with the aim of serving the foreigner and creating political disputes and propagating anxiety and chaos among the public under the guise of serving democracy, liberty and peace." Early in September he began to keep this promise. He had the Penal Code amended so as to outlaw Peace Partisan and Democratic Youth activities as well as Communist activities. Daily clashes between police and Communists so disrupted the Communist party that in less than a year it became impossible for it to carry on a co-ordinated campaign against the government. Arrests were followed quickly by court action which imposed sentences of up to two years at hard labor.

Known and suspected Communists were not the only persons to receive police attention. As students often responded to Communist agitation with riots, demonstrations and strikes, the police kept close watch on them. Some teachers and junior government officials also received attention.

Usually in the case of students, teachers and junior government officials the price for having engaged in "Communist and Peace Partisan" activities was expulsion from school and loss of jobs. The extent of police and court action was revealed by the government from time to time by the publication of lists

of those involved. For example, on October 24, 1954, 119 persons were listed, fifty-four of them junior government officials
and the rest students. On three subsequent lists the majority
that appeared were students, with a sprinkling of teachers.
These lists had thirty-one, sixty-nine, and forty-four names
respectively.

The government, loath to sentence students to prison terms,
at first proposed to have them inducted into the military
service, but this met opposition from the military authorities
on security grounds. The problem was resolved by establishing
special training units, isolated from other military personnel.
Inductions, however, were not fully applied. Expulsion from
school and work had a sobering effect, and gradually many
of the students and teachers found their way back into the
classroom. Some of the Communists were eventually pardoned.
The end of March, 1956, the Ministry of the Interior announced the release of about fifty convicted Communists from
prison, all of whom had signed statements "disavowing" communism. Of the 180 still serving prison terms, it was anticipated about fifty-four would receive a royal pardon as soon
as they also signed "disavowal" statements.

Police and leftists played a game of seesaw during these
years. Periods of arrest were followed by periods of quiet, and
then pardons. Opposition and disgruntled groups constantly
watched for an opportunity to find out whether the government was inclined to adopt a more lenient course. To do this
they resorted to strikes.

For twenty months there had been no strikes of any conse-
quence. Then early in June, 1956, a number of strikes broke
out, some lasting as long as three weeks. One was for higher
wages. Two were in protest against legislation raising rental
ceilings on commercial property. One was against the introduction of modern laborsaving machinery. But the government was not coerced. It easily contained the situation, and
the rash of this particular type of protest soon subsided.

Not many months before Nuri's death, I checked with a

friend of mine in the Ministry of the Interior on Communist strength. I asked how many avowed, recognized Communist agents there were at that time in all Iraq. His answer was "250 with brains," the majority concentrated in Baghdad. The next largest concentration was in the Basra area, with Sulamaniya following, and then Najaf. Of the four centers of strength, Basra was the most difficult to keep under control because of the ease with which agents could pass the frontiers between Iraq, Iran, Kuwait, and Saudi Arabia.

The population of Iraq was estimated by the United Nations at close to seven million in 1959. The threat of communism in Iraq did not lie in numbers. The Communists were a relatively small group but they were well disciplined and organized. Given the opportunity, they could move quickly to exploit the grievances of the masses. A number of their grievances were well-founded. The government recognized this. Hence the eternal police vigilance.

Nuri was as solicitous of the police as he was of the army. He wanted both equipped with the best that was available and took every opportunity to get it for them. Right after the Suez crisis he saw an opportunity to put in a plea for the police force and thought so well of it that he came to the Embassy to put his case before me there. This was early in January, 1957. The police, he began, had done a commendable job in containing demonstrations and maintaining public order during the tense weeks of the crisis. They managed somehow to do this in spite of their inadequate equipment. The next time things might not turn out so well. To be on the safe side they should have more modern radio equipment, transport equipment, and small arms. It would not be fair to the army to draw on its budget to pay for this equipment. He hoped the United States would foot the bill. That was not asking too much. After all, he shrewdly pointed out, it had been in the interests of the United States that internal order had been maintained during the Suez crisis. A similar situation might well recur. If help for the army was justified, help for the police was too. They were complementary, he said. It will be recalled that as a result of the Richards mission to Baghdad in April, 1957, we gave Nuri some modern equipment for the police.

Any account of how Nuri tried to maintain public security and order would be incomplete without a picture of Said Qazzaz, Nuri's minister of the interior, on whom he relied implicitly.

Qazzaz, a Kurd, started his career as a civil servant in 1924. The highest post he held before being minister of the interior was that of director of the port of Basra. Basra, center of the date industry and the Basra Petroleum Company, had a large group of industrial workers in addition to its dock workers. Labor in the area proved vulnerable to Communist subversion, and often the city and vicinity suffered from strikes. From this environment and atmosphere, Qazzaz moved into the Ministry of the Interior. Having visited the United States in 1950 on a leader-specialist grant, and having returned with admiration and warm feeling for the United States, he was inclined to talk freely and frankly with all of us at the Embassy.

Like Nuri, Qazzaz had genuine fear of the disruptive effects of subversive Communist activity. Coming from the North he was, like Nuri, equally alert to Soviet pressures from the outside. Nuri had in him an utterly courageous, completely honest, and thoroughly trustworthy friend and put heavy responsibilities on him. Qazzaz met them unflinchingly. To him must go the credit for the high degree of internal security and stability that prevailed during Nuri's thirteenth prime-ministership.

Qazzaz was among the first to be arrested by Qasim and among the first of Nuri's associates to be tried publicly by Qasim's military tribunal. I watched his trial on television. He stood erect and strong for hours under a barrage of charges, accusations, and tauntings. He made no apologies. He did not ask for mercy. He maintained throughout the trial that what he had done, he had done from conviction, to save his country and his people from communism, and if he had it to do over again he would do the same. As he and everyone who watched the proceedings anticipated, he was sentenced to death and hanged.

One of the first dinners my wife and I attended after our arrival in Baghdad was given by Lord and Lady Salter. Lord Salter was in Iraq at the time making an analysis for the government of Iraq of the Development Program. It was at this dinner that we first met Minister Qazzaz and his wife. It was a special occasion for them as it was Mrs. Qazzaz's break with purdah, her first public appearance without being veiled. One detected at once that she was shy and sensitive, and this first experience without veil, among non-Arabs, was difficult for her. It was a moving scene, she demure and diffident, and he, either at her side or nearby, trying with words and glances to give her courage.

The day after his trial ended, she was encountered alone by friends in a shop in Baghdad, buying a dress. They were surprised to find her on such an errand at such a time. In answer to their inquiring looks she said, with head high, "I am so proud of my husband. This is my way of celebrating."

PRESS

One of the conditions under which Nuri had agreed to return to power was that he be given a free hand by the Palace to revoke press licenses. In the months preceding his return a marked proliferation of newspapers had taken place along with a sharpening of critical comment generally. Through the Press Ordinance he was given the means to act, and he acted promptly. During his first month in office he revoked licenses on a wide scale.

In justice to Nuri it should be noted that at the time he took office about seventy newspapers were being published.

Most of these had only limited circulation. The majority
relied neither on circulation nor advertising to keep going,
but on blackmail. It is to Nuri's credit that after resorting
to drastic suppression, he re-licensed a half dozen of the more
responsible journals on the understanding that they would
exercise self-control. But the power to act at any time remained in his hands, and this eventually rankled the liberally
inclined even among his supporters. Early in January, 1956,
Jamal Omar Madhmi, a deputy from Erbil who was regarded
as a Nuri man, criticized the Press Ordinance before the
Financial Affairs Committee of the Chamber. By retaining
the powers of this decree in his hands Nuri was, he charged,
exercising a constant veiled censorship. Not only should it
be revoked but the prohibition of the importation of various
foreign periodicals should also be lifted.

Nuri's answer, given before the same committee, was that
the ordinance had been issued to meet growing complaints of
the public against the "confusion" that prevailed in the press.
The press had been penetrated by elements which used it as a
tool for propagating subversive ideas aimed especially at the
younger generation. There were also certain persons who had
converted the press into means for extracting money through
blackmail. Previous legislation was inadequate for curbing
these practices.

Authority to act under the ordinance was wide. It extended
beyond newspapers even to leaflets. One such action was
announced on February 8, 1956. On that day twelve persons
were arrested for having distributed leaflets attributed to the
"Liberation Party" in such widely separated cities as Baghdad,
Mosul and Basra. The leaflets were strongly critical of the
Baghdad Pact and also urged internal reform based on "the
principles of Islam."

Between June 8, 1957, when Nuri's resignation became
effective, and June 18, 1957, when Ali Jawdat's term as prime
minister began, no editorial comment appeared on either the
outgoing or incoming governments. Then, on June 21, as if

acting on a prearranged signal, all newspapers broke out with criticism and advice. All pleaded for greater freedom in the political life at home. All expressed the wish that something be done to restore Arab unity abroad. Perhaps the sharpest tones were employed by the independent *al-Bilad* of Baghdad. While it readily encouraged Jawdat's proposed efforts to improve inter-Arab relations, it struck a pessimistic note about the chances of improving things internally. "Deterioration at home," it wrote, "is attributed to the absence of a democratic way of life. At present it is impossible to exercise the major civil rights guaranteed by the constitution. One of the most important of these is the freedom to organize political parties."

Free expression of the press continued and became even more pronounced as the months went on. By July, Jawdat's minister of the interior, General Sami Fattah, a former head of the air corps, began showing concern. During a talk I had with him the end of July he told me that he had warned the press not to be "too free" and threatened some editors with withdrawal of government advertising unless they "behaved." "From one of my agents," Fattah continued, "I learned that one of these editors was heard to say that this general we have now is even worse than the one we had before, General Nuri."

With Nuri out of office, the familiar pattern was repeated. Removal of restraint was followed by ever freer expression, and then a return to repression. Nuri tried to avoid this cycle. His practice was to keep things under constant control by threat of action if possible, and if that proved ineffective, by action itself.

PARTIES

Another condition which Nuri had insisted on before agreeing to resume office in 1954, was the authority to dissolve the political parties. This he did promptly, dissolving all including his own Constitution Union party. Now, he announced, every individual could compete in the elections on an equal basis. This was, to be sure, a departure from the traditional form of parliamentary government, which, in the world at large, had become closely associated with political parties. Iraq had a parliamentary form of government from 1925 when the Organic Law [1] became operative until Qasim's coup in 1958, but in name only. This was not surprising. Parliamentary government in Iraq was not an indigenous growth. It had been imposed on the country from the outside. Few of the essentials necessary for a true and healthy parliamentary government were present. For one thing, political parties at the time were unknown.

Parties in name only did emerge in Iraq along with the succession of parliaments. These were the United Popular Front, the National Democratic party, the Independence party, the Socialist party of the Nation, and Nuri's Constitutional Union party. Besides these five there were the Communists, outlawed as a party but working together for the most part underground. The five so-called parties, even though they professed definite aims and publicized programs of action, in the last analysis functioned more like political clubs with their membership pledged rather to follow and support a particular leader than work for the realization of party programs. Even so, when they were abolished, many voices were heard calling for their immediate restoration. Before very long Nuri yielded to these pressures. He could afford to as the Turkish-Iraqi Pact and the Special Anglo-Iraqi Agreement, two of his immediate objectives, had been concluded. On May 11, 1955, with the nicely balanced words of the politician, he had this to say before the Internal Affairs Committee of the Chamber of Deputies: "No nation can rule and no democratic rule can survive without the assistance of

[1] The Organic Law was approved and signed by Faisal I on March 21, 1925. A detailed discussion of its origin and nature appears in Majid Khadduri's *Independent Iraq, 1932 to 1958* (2d ed.; New York: Oxford Univ. Press, 1960), pp. 13–18.

parties as part of its system. Our country, though, does not have scope for numerous parties in its system. Two are sufficient, one in office and the other in opposition."

This was the first public indication that Nuri thought a two party system might prevent a revival of the many splinter groups that had had a debilitating effect on the political life of the country. He had further reason for wanting to see a two party system established, to which he attached as much, if not more, importance than the prevention of the re-emergence of splinter groups. Nuri and his close supporters, as we learned through talks with them, had been very much impressed by the superior organization and discipline shown by the leftist forces in the election the previous summer. They wanted, above all, to bar this element from getting legal sanction as a party. The ideal plan, as Nuri saw it, would be to revive his own party, and to form one other party, preferably under the direction of his main rival, Salih Jabr, for whom he had great respect. In the summer of 1955, Nuri approached Jabr. He was not encouraged by what Jabr told him. Jabr reportedly said that while he would continue his political activity, he was not yet prepared to reorganize a party of his own. He apparently gave Nuri no reason for not wanting to form a party at that time. It was surmised that he felt that so long as the Association Law, which gave the Minister of the Interior extensive power over groups and gatherings, remained in force, any party would be completely dependent on the Minister's benevolence for its existence. At the time he confided to a member of my staff that with his party having been inactive so long, he had lost all means of patronage and without it he did not see how he could get his party working effectively again.

Despite Jabr's rebuff, Nuri expressed his wish that an opposition party be organized as a prelude to a two-party system. Toward the end of January, 1956, while appearing before the Financial Affairs Committee of the Senate, he gave assurances that he would act quickly on any application for the establishment of a political party, and then expressed regret that up to then none had been received. Shortly after he made this statement an application was received, but not from Jabr and his friends, as Nuri had hoped. It came from a relatively unknown group, none of whom had had a political career. The group petitioned to form a party under the name "Liberation party." Action came quickly as Nuri had promised, but in the form of a rejection, first by the Minister of the Interior and then, on appeal, by the Council of Ministers. Turning down this application, however, did not immediately silence the petitioners. They issued leaflets in the name of the unsanctioned party attacking the government for both its foreign and domestic policies. A dozen of the "liberators" were arrested.

Nuri, however, held out hope for the revival of parties well into 1957. In February of that year, before the Financial Committee of the Chamber, he followed the line that on the lifting of martial law there should be a discussion to determine whether "we shall have two or more political parties" and this time added: "When reconstituted they will be allowed again to publish their own newspapers." Later, in April, when speaking to a group of Sudanese journalists who had come to Iraq to cover Development Week, he again held out the possibility of revival. But June came and Nuri left office without any party revival having taken place. Neither Jabr nor any other public figure showed interest in Nuri's oft expressed wish to see two parties established. This was no doubt due less to inertia than to a disinclination to play the game according to Nuri's own very definite concept of the rules.

In spite of Nuri's repeated public statements that he favored the revival of political parties, at least on a two party basis, I think at heart he was quite content with the situation as it was. As one got to know him, one could see that he preferred to work alone as much as possible. One with his self-confidence could hardly be otherwise. In party politics one is expected to work with others and within a program. Nuri, it always seemed to me, was at his best when working with a few individuals, preferably behind the scenes. That suited his temperament best. In his public appearances he was handicapped in two respects. He was not an effective public speaker and usually gave the impression that he did not much care what the public thought of him. This was misleading. On those rare occasions when he was greeted in public with some warmth and enthusiasm, he showed unmistakably that he welcomed it. I remember well one such incident. It was during Development Week in 1957 when Nuri, rather than the King or Crown Prince as was customary, was asked to inaugurate a public works project near Baghdad. Perhaps it was no more than the holiday spirit that motivated the crowds along the highway and at the scene of the dedication but they did cheer him lustily, and for days he spoke privately of the pleasure this had given him.

The public, however, did not enter into his day-to-day calculations. He was blind to the need for good public relations. This is surprising because, in public life, he was shrewd in many other ways. The explanation is hard to find. It is true that he spent many of his formative years in the medieval atmosphere of the Ottoman Empire, and perhaps that accounts for this particular blind spot in his character. But then, how would one explain the many ways in which he did shed that early influence and adjust himself to the ways and exactions of the twentieth century? His character and personality were bafflingly complex, and his actions were more often than not contradictory.

Nuri's inclination to work without party restrictions and directly with as few individuals as possible was favored by the fact that Baghdad was the center of the country's political power. This fit in admirably with his way of operating. In view of this, he had less territory to watch and check on, and fewer people to contact. And within the restricted area of Baghdad there were seldom more than three or four people close to him on whom he relied to make his program effective. This small group of intimates changed from time to time. The three he worked closely with in the last years of his life were all some twenty years younger than he. There was Khalil Kanna, whose wife is a niece of Mrs. Nuri and who at various times was minister of finance and minister of education under Nuri. His special responsibility was handling press relations. Dhia Ja'far, minister of development in his last cabinet, often appeared as negotiator on the domestic political scene. The third was Murjan, long time president of the Chamber of Deputies and once, for a brief period, prime minister. His specialty was to cultivate the tribal leaders among the deputies. The three differed in intelligence, drive and temperament but Nuri knew how best to use them. Each did effective work in the field chosen for him.

In summary, in carrying out his programs Nuri relied in the first instance on the backing of the Palace, then on the loyalty of the army and police, on power to censor the press, and on freedom to work, preferably behind the scenes, on key individuals. It was fascinating to watch him operate. When I arrived in Baghdad I asked a diplomatic colleague of mine whom I had known at a previous post what kind of man Nuri was. His answer was as colorful as true: "He's as full of tricks as a monkey."

SPEECH FROM THE THRONE

How Nuri proceeded to realize his objectives in the foreign field in accordance with his August 4, 1954 program, has been reviewed in Chapters IV and V. In the Speech from the Throne delivered on December 1, 1954, Nuri's objectives in both foreign and domestic fields were outlined in detail. In this section the latter will be considered.

The objectives in the domestic field which were stressed in this speech were improvement of rural conditions through land reclamation and land distribution to small farmers; increased housing facilities; expansion of medical facilities; improvement of public education; review of the tax structure; elimination of corrupt elements in government; and the strengthening of the army. When mentioning the last objective, the King announced that the government had accepted the American offer of military aid, "without condition." This reference to American military aid was the first public indication that Nuri was in favor of the program.

Government programs announced in Speeches from the Throne, or their equivalent, usually follow a fixed pattern. They are comprehensive and reassuring. They touch on all the obvious problems of the country and, at the same time, hold out hope that solutions will be found. The December 1 speech was no exception. How energetically Nuri attacked the problems posed, and to what extent he succeeded in solving them, will be taken up next.

DEVELOPMENT PROGRAM

One of Nuri's biggest problems when he returned to office in 1954 was how to repair the damage done by the spring floods, and how best to safeguard the country from a recurrence of such disasters. Improvement of rural conditions stood high on his program. Reclamation and land distribution were mentioned specifically. Logically, Nuri insisted on giving high priority to flood control through the Development Board.[2]

Nuri had had firsthand knowledge of the operations of the Development Board. It was established by law in April, 1950. In September of the same year, just as the board was getting under way, Nuri had once again become prime minister. As prime minister he was chairman of the board. He

[2] A discussion of the creation, composition, and areas of responsibility of the Development Board appears on pages 356–58, Khadduri, *Independent Iraq*.

took a close personal interest in it from the start and had, consequently, much to do with the board's early program. It is worth noting that in the board's first program, which covered the period 1951–56, more than one-third of a budget of 155 million *dinar*[3] was allocated to flood control, water storage, irrigation and drainage projects. Thus, some years before the costly floods of 1954, Nuri was already concentrating on flood control and operations stemming from it. By the time he returned to office in 1954, despite the frightening floods of the spring, complaints were growing that there was too much concentration on long-term projects such as flood control instead of on smaller undertakings that would bring a few of the amenities to the masses at once. When I arrived in Baghdad, Lord Salter, who since the previous March had been making a review of the board's program at the request of the Iraqi government, made it plain that he did not at all belittle the board's long-term plans but at the same time thought it imprudent of the government to ignore the ever growing public uneasiness and impatience at the lack of tangible evidence of the board's activities. A month or two before Lord Salter sounded that precautionary note, our Embassy, in evaluating the program had noted the lack of balance in these words: "The Iraqi development effort is good as far as it goes, but it is basically a capital works program and is weak in human support projects." In his final report Lord Salter put it more graphically: "The Board has thought of its task almost exclusively in material terms, in brick and mortar. It has not been influenced by persuasive arguments that there is human capital as well as material, and that capital investment may be suitably and more often beneficially made in improving the quality of human beings."

While Nuri was prime minister the program was steadily expanded, and with this stimulus the economy of the country expanded too. A revision of the five-year program that became

[3] One Iraq *dinar* (ID) = $2.80.

effective April 1, 1955, raised to ID304,306,000, or almost double what had originally been planned for the period. Basically, however, the program remained the same. It was still essentially a long-term capital plan with ID266,181,000 consigned to flood control, irrigation, drainage, roads, and bridges and only ID38,125,000 to small projects like clinics, primary schools, workers' houses and secondary roads and bridges. The final expansion in Nuri's day took place in the summer of 1956 when the five-year program was extended to six years at a cost of ID500,007,327. With such vast sums being spent and allocated for future spending the threat of inflation was ever present. In one of the first talks I had with Lord Salter he had this in mind when he said that he felt at times as though Iraq were building on a mine field. He urged closer co-ordination between the planners and the economists as one means of arresting this danger. Whether this good advice was taken to heart in Iraq is hard to determine. There was in evidence at the time a rapid buildup in supply goods and services, and that may have had a salutary effect. In any event, Iraq was fortunate in coming through those years with a healthy economy on the whole.

The Salter report, while comprehensive in scope, stressed the desirability of a program better balanced between long-and-short-term projects. In May, 1955, the report was referred to a high level committee for study. As a result, the board's program was reviewed. This re-evaluation led to a more general acceptance among planners of the thesis that in the future the board's projects must meet the immediate needs of more people. The program followed during the last months of Nuri's life, when the emphasis was beginning to shift, called for a variety of undertakings. Here is a partial list: a bitumen refinery, a cotton textile factory at Mosul, cement making projects, electric power development projects, sugar refineries, mineral surveys, a sulphur recovery project, building of a pipeline from Kirkuk to Baghdad for transporting natural gas, a fertilizer manufacturing project, construction of paper-making plants, production of animal food from dates, a steel manufacturing project, an atomic energy program, establishment of a laboratory for scientific and technical research, a rayon manufacturing plant, a wool products plant, and five additional textile mills in scattered localities.

With all that in the making or blueprint stage, surely no one could complain of lack of balance.

Nuri ran true to form in his relations with the Development Program. He never yielded to public clamor or pressure if he felt he was right in what he was doing. He had decided on several priorities, the first of which was flood control. He was determined to save the country from suffering and losses such as it had experienced in the spring of 1954, and he was not to be prematurely deflected into more popular fields. It seemed senseless to him to talk about land distribution and better living conditions for the rural population until the threat of floods was eliminated. That had to come first. Reclamation, irrigation, and expansion of cultivable areas could follow, and all this had to precede any land distribution to the small farmer. Twice during those last years, floods, which might have been as disastrous as the one in 1954, threatened Iraq, and twice he had the satisfaction of seeing the control measures he had sponsored and encouraged save the country. It was then, and not until then, that he was ready to broaden the program to bring its advantages to more people, more quickly, as he had been urged for some years to do. When he made the change, he did so impressively.

Nuri had been largely instrumental in setting the pattern of the program of the Development Board in its early years. What was even more important was that he facilitated the financing of the board's projects. It was Nuri who carried through the negotiations with the Iraq Petroleum Company (IPC) which led to the signing on February 2, 1952, of a revised agreement considerably more favorable to Iraq than its predecessor. Nuri timed his move for revision well. In Iran the oil industry had just been nationalized. In Saudi Arabia the Arabian American Oil Company (Aramco) had just negotiated a new agreement based on the 50–50 profit formula. Because of these developments Nuri found the IPC receptive to his approaches. In the final agreement the 50–50 formula was adopted, and the nationalization issue was dropped. It was a mutually advantageous agreement. It was estimated that under it the government would receive at least £30,000,000 in 1953 and 1954, and by 1955 at least £50,000,000. It was also in 1952 that a law became effective earmarking seventy percent of the oil revenues for development purposes. When Nuri left office in July, 1952, the prospects for the Development Board were bright.

During the next few years while Nuri was out of office the oil industry in Iraq prospered. Not long after he returned to power in 1954 he took another look at the 1952 agreement. Favorable as it was to Iraq, he concluded that the time was propitious for still another revision. On March 24, 1955, a new revised agreement was signed. Under its terms the percentage of the revenues going to the government was increased, and pipeline and pumping facilities enlarged. It was agreed that two of the existing pipelines were to be extended to a terminal near Sidon, Lebanon, and the pumping facilities along the thirty-inch pipeline to Banias, Syria, were to be stepped up. Under this latest agreement, therefore, Iraq was to get more revenues at once, and on completion of the pipeline and pumping changes it would be possible to export larger quantities of crude oil. The Director of Mines of Iraq estimated that under this new agreement government revenues from oil in 1956 would rise to £76,000,000. Then came a temporary set-back.

Early in November, 1956, during the Suez crisis when feeling against the British and against Nuri as their "tool" ran high in the Arab world, IPC pumping stations in Syria were blown up. According to an eyewitness, a driver in IPC employ who escaped from station T2, a Syrian army column of a hundred armored vehicles surrounded this station early in the

morning of November 3. All company employees were placed
under arrest and driven off into the desert. Then the station
was blown up. That same day an IPC plane made a recon-
naissance flight over Syrian territory and found that in addition to station T2, stations T3 and T4 were also in flames.
The demolition, the flight established, had been carefully
planned and expertly executed. The pipelines affected by this
destruction had been carrying about 25,000,000 tons annually,
or three-fourths of all of Iraq's oil exports.

Faced with this curtailment of three-fourths of the oil exports and oil revenues, Nuri lost no time in turning to IPC
for help. He must have felt rebuffed in his first soundings.
During a talk I had with him on December 13 on the oil
situation he made the only derogatory remark about the IPC
that I ever heard him make. The IPC, he said curtly, is "out
of date." This he amplified by adding that the company
should operate and market its supplies "on the same basis as
the consortium in Iran."

The IPC was not long in meeting Nuri's wishes. He had
asked for an advance of £20–25,000,000 over a twelve-month
period. Under the loan agreement that was reached in February, 1957, Iraq was to get the difference between six million
dinar, the anticipated quarterly share of oil revenues, and the
actual receipts from the exports through Basra and the partially restored lines through Syria. Repayment was to begin
when, and to the extent, the Iraqi share exceeded six million
dinar quarterly.

These promised advances greatly relieved Nuri. How necessary they were was open to question. At the Embassy we were
of the opinion that if substantial increases in petroleum exports took place before April 1, 1957, Iraq's monetary reserve
was adequate to sustain the level of government spending
through six months of 1957. Actually, the pumping of oil
across Syria was resumed on March 11, 1957. By the end of
the first quarter of the year, petroleum exports were already
about forty percent normal. By the end of the third quarter,

recovery had reached the point where the Development Program could again go forward at a good rate. By May, 1958, it appeared that exports through Syria would soon reach the pre-Suez level of 25,000,000 tons annually. Nuri had come through the crisis with the program and relations with IPC in a satisfactory state.

As Nuri had seen, the first step to arrest the threat of floods was to construct a series of dams. When the spring waters began rolling down from the mountains in Kurdistan into the Tigris and Euphrates rivers, the dams would then divert and disperse the increased flow. The dams would funnel this mass of water into basins in the Wadi-Tharthar and Habbaniya areas, transforming these depressions into artificial lakes. From these reservoirs the water would then be parceled out in a systematic way over the flat countryside, adding to the fertility of the land already under cultivation and reclaiming vast stretches that had bloomed hundreds of years earlier, before just such a succession of dams and canals had been destroyed in the thirteenth century by invading Mongol hordes from the north.

During Development Week, beginning April 1, 1956, the first in an annual series organized by the Development Board, Nuri had the satisfaction of witnessing the dedications of the Samara dam of the Wadi-Tharthar flood control project on the Tigris and the Ramadi dam flood control project on the Euphrates. One of the main items on his domestic program had been achieved, to the immense benefit of the people of Iraq. It was also a happy occasion for the American community in Iraq. Through the United States Operation Mission (USOM), the agency operating under our Technical Co-operation Agreement with Iraq, much needed publicity was given to the accomplishments of the Development Board. The initiative in this was taken by Nuri's minister of development, Dhia Ja'far, who was more sensitive than Nuri to the need of keeping the public informed of the progress of the program. At Minister Dhia Ja'far's request, with Nuri's concurrence, USOM produced an illustrated brochure describing the projects dedicated during Development Week; provided full photographic coverage of the ceremonies that took place; and finally, for countrywide distribution, planned and produced a ten minute colored documentary film of the week's events. As the first Development Week ended it could be said that Nuri, through his Minister of Development, had made a good, if belated, start in educating the public on what the Development Board was trying to do for it.

By the time the 1957 Development Week arrived, the program had become more diversified. It seemed an appropriate moment to present to Iraq a gift which Washington had had in mind for some time. On March 24 I presented the government of Iraq with an Atomic Energy Library as a token of the interest of the government of the United States in the peaceful use of atomic energy. When accepting this gift on behalf of Iraq, Minister Dhia Ja'far felicitously quoted President Eisenhower to the effect that the task ahead for mankind "is to find the way by which the miraculous inventiveness of man shall not be dedicated to his death but consecrated to his life." Nuri cut the ribbon and declared the library ready for use under the direction of a well-qualified scientist, Dr. Kashif al-Ghita, a former Fulbright grantee who had studied at the Argonne National Laboratory of the Atomic Energy Commission in Lemont, Illinois.

It was not only during Development Week that USOM made itself felt. This was the operating agency for our entire technical aid undertaking in Iraq. Its work brought me often into contact with Nuri for Nuri's interest in all phases of the Development Program never flagged. He wanted the help of American technicians and his requests under the aid agreement were frequent and varied. The technicians, supplied only on request, served without cost to the government of Iraq. With many of them we also provided equipment for training purposes without cost. While I was in Iraq there were about a hundred American technicians helping develop the country.

Among them were engineers, public health and public administration specialists, and agriculturists. The engineers, in whom Nuri had special interest, were mainly experts in dam construction, flood control, irrigation development, and highway construction.

LAND

Nuri, the land, and the sheiks are closely related. One can hardly deal with Nuri and the land without a word first about the sheiks. Nuri came in close contact with them at the start of his public career and remained in close touch with them throughout his life. He understood them and they revered him. As a result, their support of him as a political leader was solid and steadfast. This relationship, beneficial as it was to Nuri's political fortunes, unfortunately was not always in the best interests of the country. The sheiks, as tribal leaders, control and claim personally to own vast stretches of land. Until this monopolistic control is broken, substantial land reform will be blocked. Nuri, I am afraid, so valued his personal relationship with the sheiks that he was blinded to this. He would rationalize. To him the sheiks were kindly, attentive "fathers" looking after the every want of their tribesmen. While they held title to large estates, he maintained that these estates would gradually be broken up and divided among the sons of the sheiks as they died. His theory was that time was bringing reform. But here Nuri fell victim to some superficial generalization. He failed to differentiate between the law of inheritance in effect in northern Iraq and that in southern Iraq. In the North, where the former Ottoman code was honored, all heirs shared equally with a resultant division of the estate, as Nuri liked to remind the public. In the South, in accordance with local tribal custom, the eldest son inherits all, and the estates remain intact. Nuri conveniently overlooked this contrast in Iraq's law of inheritance.

At the age of eighteen Nuri received his commission as lieutenant in the Turkish Army and was assigned to an infantry unit in Iraq charged with the collection of taxes from the nomadic tribes. These were taxes on livestock, for the most part sheep, and were largely in arrears. Roaming tribesmen do not make the most willing or prompt taxpayers. I do not know how good a tax collector Nuri was. But I know that good or bad, tax collectors are never very popular. Nuri seems to have managed, however, to satisfy his Turkish masters and at the same time to establish his enduring popularity, if not with the ordinary tribesmen, definitely with their leaders. And while Nuri was making a place for himself among the tribal chiefs, he was at the same time becoming acquainted with the countryside and tribal ways. He used this knowledge and experience profitably for the rest of his life.

How the sheik, traditionally merely the chief representative in law of the tribal lands, acquired title to them is an interesting story. It is reminiscent of the story of the camel which began with only his nose inside the tent of his master but pushing farther and farther in, eventually dispossessed him completely. It took only thirty years for the sheiks to accomplish an astounding transformation with profound sociological implications.

Under Ottoman law, the state was regarded as the ultimate owner of the tribal lands which the tribes held as tenants in occupation. Use of the land was essentially communal, with only limited parcels marked for individual cultivation. The sheik, a member of the paramount family, customarily approved by acclamation of the tribe and confirmed by the government, served as the link with the authorities. He transacted, on behalf of the tribe, the business that had to be done with the government. He was responsible, for example, for collecting the taxes from the individual tribesmen and passing them along to the agent of the central government. He was responsible, too, for maintaining and leading an armed force for the protection of the tribe. He acted on behalf of the whole tribe as host to visiting officials or neighboring tribal chiefs. He also provided for tribal social activities.

No doubt one important factor that contributed to the breakdown of this tribal system which left absolute power and title in the hands of the sheiks was the growing emphasis on cultivation, rather than on grazing. With that, of necessity, came a shift from nomadism to permanent habitation. Cultivation, in turn, got its boost from a combination of new markets, improved communications, and technical advances. In the latter field better irrigation and farm implements, particularly tractors designed to increase grain production played a vital role. With this more sophisticated way of life developing and with hitherto unheard of skills and techniques required of tribal spokesmen, the sheik's position naturally became more important and demanding.

Land registry, or Tapu as it is known in Iraq, also played a part in the metamorphosis of the sheiks from mere tribal spokesmen to virtual owners of the tribal lands. It was a Turkish official, Midhat Pasha, who became governor of the province of Baghdad in 1869, who initiated the Tapu system. Tapu, which opened the way for registration of tribal lands in the name of the sheiks, was originally intended as a stabilizing means among roaming, quarrelsome tribes. Under this system, tracts of land could be bought for a small periodic payment. The title deed did not in fact confer actual ownership, but it did offer security of tenure. It was hoped that this opportunity to obtain a form of title to land would stimulate interest in a fixed agricultural way of life and thereby reduce tribal frictions. Actually, it did not work out that way. Many sheiks were distrustful of the plan, regarding it as a disguised step by the government to restrict their freedom of movement. In instances where sheiks took advantage of the offer and had title to the land in question registered in their names, bitter relations between sheiks and tribesmen often flared up. By the time the British arrived on the scene during World War I, disputes were widespread. To stabilize the situation, British political officers adopted the policy of recognizing a single sheik for each tribe and confirming his possession of the land. "Stabilization" greatly enhanced the power and position of the sheiks.

By the time the sheik was directing the large estates as virtual owner, the government obligingly stepped in and regularized his position. Not only was his title to the land confirmed by law, but he was simultaneously given representation in Parliament. Here the sheiks constituted a formidable bloc, always on the alert to safeguard their privileged position. Until their power is broken, the great mass of rural workmen will exist in virtual feudal serfdom. Meanwhile, some alleviation of the problem is possible in spite of the sheiks. A start has been made by converting quite considerable tracts of public land (*miri sirf*) into small holdings and allotting them to the landless peasants. This program had Nuri's enthusiastic support. Our Embassy was pleased that in this instance he drew on American technicians for help. Particularly impressive progress had been achieved while I was still in Iraq in the settlement at Latifiya, only thirty miles from Baghdad. This locality had been well chosen and as a community of small landowners has good prospects of survival. The soil is fertile and well suited to the growing of vegetables and fruits. There is a steady market in Baghdad for such products.

I think Nuri honestly believed that with the passage of time most of the big estates, through inheritances, would be divided, and other essential reforms would then follow more or less automatically. But he was too good a politician to let matters rest there. Moreover, land reform had been promised in the Speech from the Throne. Nuri acted quickly. On November 16, 1954, three months after assuming office, he had a Land Ordinance issued replacing the Law of 1952 which had proved to be full of loopholes. Nuri had it put in effect at once administratively, while still awaiting Parliament's approval. In trying to bring about general improvement in rural living conditions, it was hoped also to arrest the steady flow of people from the countryside to the cities. This trend was particularly alarming in south-eastern Iraq where from the province of Amara alone fifty thousand persons had migrated to the cities in the previous ten years. The ordinance itself, in a word, aimed at an increase in *miri sirf* land, the settlement of some tenant farmers as small landowners, and reduction of the big estates. It soon became apparent that this ordinance required tightening up. It was in turn repealed and replaced by Law No. 66, published on June 6, 1955. This law fixed the terms under which government lands granted to settlers under varying degrees of provisional ownership [4] could be changed to outright ownership. The law also provided the much needed authority for recovering government land situated near cities which had been held under long terms of provisional ownership and which the Government wanted for its housing, hospital, and school projects.

Thus Nuri had succeeded, and quickly, in getting the aims of his government on land reform down on paper. To execute them, however, called for time, concentration, and zeal. Time ran out for Nuri before much was accomplished, and besides, during those last few years of his life he had to give his attention and energy to a host of pressing problems. And finally, he was I think always torn between the need for reforms and his feeling of loyalty to the sheiks, and that perhaps more than anything else slowed down the process. As a result, life on the land and in the towns continued to be mean and miserable for thousands and produced all too often an explosive atmosphere. Our Embassy was fortunate in ob-

[4] The two most common forms of provisional ownership are *lazma* and *tapu*. The former can be converted to outright ownership by payment of one-half its cash value, provided it has been kept under cultivation. The latter can be registered in outright ownership after ten years' cultivation.

taining rather detailed firsthand accounts of how country and town life looked in the southern half of Iraq during the last years of Nuri's life.

In late 1957 a local official from the Kut Liwa paid a farewell call on us just before leaving Iraq for a visit to the United States. He talked freely about conditions in that province. It was in the town of Hai, Kut, that during the Suez crisis one of the most violent Communist inspired demonstrations occurred, causing a number of deaths among the police. Despite stern, repressive measures against the Communists following this violence, Communist activity was not brought to a complete halt, according to the official. The sporadic circulation of hand bills continued. This official attributed the fact that the party was able to remain intact and active to the widely prevalent discontent. He estimated there were twelve to fifteen thousand individuals in the province without any means of livelihood, persons who had been driven off the land partly because of population growth, but also through the highhanded acts of the landlords. He held the two ruling sheiks mainly responsible for the widely unsatisfactory living conditions. They were brothers and one was a member of the Chamber of Deputies. Together they enjoyed a monopoly of the land in the vicinity of Hai. They were notorious for the ruthless way they treated their tenants. At least half the crops grown by the tenants were turned over to the brothers yielding them an annual income of ID500,000 each. Toward officials they were obstructive to the point where they even interferred with government claims to land properly coming under government control.

We are indebted to two foreign anthropologists for a vivid description of life in a small town in southern Iraq. These two observers lived during part of 1957 and 1958 at Da ghara, a town of 1,500 situated in the Diwaniyah Liwa near Baghdad. The town's population was divided into two principal groups. The tribal sheik and his family made up one. The other consisted of the town's officials, some small tradesmen, and a few handicraft workers. Life in this small community was marked by corruption among the police and a deadening outlook on the world. For officials, teachers, and clerical workers there was no intellectual stimulus. From the foreign radio stations came only incendiary broadcasts. Economically the town and its surroundings were suffering from land salinization due to careless use of the water available for irrigation purposes. Some benefits had been brought to the town by the Development Board, but in a gradual fashion. Even so, they might have had a politically stabilizing effect if it were not for the feeling of resentment and frustration ever present among the small educated group in the community. To be sure, a generous portion of the national income was being spent on welfare. What was badly needed in addition was some form of positive political inspiration. Unfortunately for the country at large, such leadership was lacking.

KURDS

The Kurds give the tone and color to life in northern Iraq.

The Kurdish minority comprises twenty percent of the population of Iraq and is concentrated in the northern mountains and plain regions of the country within easy contact with Kurdish groups in Turkey, Iran, and the U.S.S.R. Iraq's main oil deposits lie within the area inhabited by the Iraqi Kurds.

Iraq's Kurdish minority has resisted all efforts to assimilate it in the predominating Arab culture. It has not only retained much of its separate identity, but its hopes of Kurdish autonomy within Iraq, if not of a Kurdish state itself, although dormant at times, have never died. It is, therefore, readily susceptible to propaganda designed to increase Kurdish unity and foster opposition to governmental authority. It, too, suffers from economic ills. The combination of aspirations and dissatisfaction make it especially receptive to Communist propaganda. All these factors, in spite of its relatively small numerical strength, make it a most important, if not the most important, element to be considered in any study of conditions in northern Iraq.

In the early 1920's, not long after the establishment of the Iraqi state, the power of the northern tribal leaders was gradually weakened and replaced by the authority of the central government. This change was made possible when the central government acquired an armed force and the ability to move troops into the northern area. With this visual evidence of power and authority, the government, and not the tribal leaders, became the accepted arbiter of tribal disputes. The aghas exchanged their horses and guns for land rovers and sedans, and looked to the government to maintain their ownership claims to the land. It was the Communists who in time opened the eyes of the villagers to the fact that the aghas no longer had the power to enforce the feudal concept that had so long governed their relationship. Agitators went to work. When the stage of violence was reached, troops and police would step in. This was the established cycle when Nuri came to power in 1954. He made it clear at once that he would take a firm stand against communism. There would no longer be a period of waiting until violence occurred. No agitation would be permitted, and agitators were arrested. Police vigilance put a stop to open proselytizing. A warning went out to the villagers that the aghas' right of ownership would be respected and that violence would be met with drastic action. The lid was on and was forcibly kept on by Nuri.

Nuri was loyally assisted in maintaining public order in northern Iraq by the forceful, intelligent mutasarrif of Sulamaniya Liwa, Brigadier Omar Ali. Our staff in Kirkuk kept in close and friendly contact with him. Twice I myself had the pleasure of visiting him and talking at length with him.

Brigadier Omar Ali fully appreciated how much emphasis

Nuri placed on public order. This he preserved with a firm hand. But he went beyond that. He was not content with just repressing Communist activity. He had tracts exposing Communist methods and views distributed among the literate. He had the village mullahs brought to his headquarters in Sulamaniya periodically for anti-Communist briefings. He felt that in the long run only substantial expenditures on public works could assure peace in the area. He wanted money for public works to relieve the unemployment situation. He also wanted to see many more schools built. He got some funds for these purposes, but always felt they were insufficient. Sometimes in his discouragement he would tell his friends that he wished he could be relieved of the burdens of the mutasarrif's office and return to active army service.

When Nuri was killed, Iraqi Kurdistan was enjoying public security and order, but many of the social problems that had long plagued the area remained unsolved. One of Nuri's last public acts, however, showed understanding of Kurdish racial pride and sensitivity. It occurred when the Arab Union between Jordan and Iraq was formed. This merger with another Arab state was viewed by many Kurds as a growing threat to their separate identity. When the question of the Arab Union's flag was finally resolved by the decision that each country would have its own flag, Nuri insisted that Iraq's flag remain unchanged with its two stars, the one representing the Arab element and the other the Kurdish. Kurdish anxiety was momentarily relieved by this gesture and by the appointment of a Kurd, Ahmad Mukktar Baban as prime minister of Iraq to succeed Nuri.

TAXATION

It was not until early in May, 1955, that Nuri was able to come to grips with the promised tax reform. He relied heavily on Khalil Kanna and Dhia Ja'far for help in this. Kanna, a previous minister of finance, was minister of education at the time. Dhia Ja'far was an engineer by profession. The three began, in the spring of 1955, to work out a plan covering both land and income taxes. At the time there was no tax on agricultural property. These deliberations led to a recommendation for a land levy based on ability to pay. It was also planned to use the new law as a means to induce large landowners either to cultivate all their holdings or dispose of their unworked portions. In tackling income tax revision, there were two old problems that had to be faced. How was the necessary income data to be obtained? And how was any income tax law going to be effectively enforced? At first it was thought simply to apply a lump sum tax on such categories as merchants, doctors, and lawyers. Eventually a more scientific approach to the problem was decided on. At this point Nuri requested me to provide, through USOM, the services of an American income tax expert to help draft a law. We met his request.

On June 20, 1956, the new income tax law was passed by Parliament. Under it some exemptions, including those for married couples, were raised. While tax rates generally were reduced, the number of categories subject to the tax was increased from four to six. On paper at least the country had been given a fairer and better balanced law.

It was not until March, 1958, however, that Parliament passed the new land tax law. Through it the gap between government and people could be narrowed. But would the law be enforced?

Nuri was killed before he could do much about the application of these laws. But he kept faith with his promise when he assumed office to do something to improve the country's tax structure. He did get Parliament to enact the laws. Responsibility for enforcement passed on to others with his death.

HEALTH AND EDUCATION

Nuri was interested in public health and education, and placed equal emphasis on them. Invariably when he discussed these fields he linked them. Several times he said to me that he would never sanction a cut in the appropriations for public health and education to meet unanticipated needs elsewhere, not even if the army were involved. Nuri, with his known devotion to the army, could hardly have emphasized his interest in these two fields more eloquently.

I had closer contact with Nuri in matters related to public health than in those pertaining to education. Through the Technical Aid Agreement we put at Iraq's disposal a number of our public health specialists on leave for that purpose from the United States Public Health Service. Nuri showed a lively interest in them, their qualifications, and their methods.

In the field of education Nuri was well served in my time by two successive ministers of education, Khalil Kanna and Dr. A. H. Kadhim. Kanna was an especially energetic administrator. Kadhim was the more experienced in pedagogy. He had done graduate work in this field in the United States and had had years of experience in teaching. One of the posts he had filled was that of dean of the Higher Teachers College. Both men had a thorough understanding of Iraq's needs, and both brought intelligence and energy to the solution of the problems that were troubling the country.

Kanna, early in Nuri's thirteenth prime ministership, publicly diagnosed the fundamental weakness in Iraq's educational system and thereby indicated the direction the government was taking. He did this at a press conference in May, 1955. Iraq, he said, was experiencing an industrial and agricultural "renaissance." There was an urgent need for skilled labor, technicians, and trained agriculturalists. But the schools kept right on turning out an over-abundance of lawyers, other professional types, and administrators. The system needed a thorough overhauling with a change in emphasis from professional training to training for industry and agriculture. It will take years to effect such a fundamental change but Nuri's government did point the way.

I had a special reason to remember Dr. Kadhim, Kanna's successor. Dr. Kadhim addressed himself with vigor and imagination to a particularly pressing problem, the relations between students and government. The part played by students in the riots and demonstrations during the Suez crisis had disturbed Nuri. Consequently, when Kadhim began concentrating on "closing the gap between students and government," as he put it, Nuri gave him warm encouragement. Kadhim's plan was to establish summer camps in different parts of the country. The camp program provided for sports, seminars, lectures—including ones on communism—and some participation in public works construction. Nuri became very enthusiastic about the project. On March 28, 1958, he asked me to see him at his home. He said he wanted to establish the camps as quickly as possible. To do so he needed £500,000. He did not want this money as a gift, but as a loan. He was going to ask IPC for an advance, and he hoped the American interests in IPC, Standard Oil of New Jersey and Socony Mobiloil, would be receptive to his request. He would also like to have at least three American camp specialists to help establish and direct the camps.

Nuri got the money and, for a start, one American expert. Just as the camps were being established and students enrolled, Qasim's coup occurred and this well-conceived and far-sighted plan was abandoned.

Nuri's interest in education extended to an undertaking in which all Americans in Iraq took pride. This was the work done at Baghdad College. This institution was founded about thirty years ago by American Jesuit priests. It is not a college as its name implies, but a school of preparatory rank. American Jesuits are responsible for the preparation of the curricula and for the teaching. The priests have always concentrated on teaching. They do not proselytize. They have won converts to Roman Catholicism, but this has been done by example, by living their daily lives in keeping with their religious principles and convictions.

The student body is made up of Iraqis from families of rich and poor alike. Entrance standards are high, and intelligence, not social standing, is the criterion for admittance. The son of the wealthy, well known, and influential father pays his way. The son of the small shopkeeper, clerk, or civil servant is helped with scholarships. The atmosphere in the school and on its playing grounds is democratic. The quality of the teaching is excellent. The product, the graduate, usually an impressive individual, is found frequently in high places in business, government and teaching, or on his way to a high place in one of these fields.

Nuri took a personal interest in Baghdad College and had become familiar with the effective non-sectarian teaching done there. While I was in Baghdad the Jesuits decided, upon urging from graduates and friends, to expand the work to college level. Nuri welcomed this. To encourage and make it possible he generously arranged a grant of public land, assessed at $1,000,000, on which to build the university. Nuri had the satisfaction of seeing the building program started on this site shortly before his death. Today, Al-Hikma University, as it was named, is being eagerly used by hundreds of Iraqis of college age.

PURGE

A fight on corruption in government had also been promised in the Speech from the Throne. By the spring of 1955 plans to attack this evil were taking shape. Parliament, it became known, would be asked to authorize the naming of committees to investigate charges within various ministries, and on the provincial and municipal levels as well. It was not until the following year that the Chamber of Deputies and the Senate approved the "Law for Regularization of Governmental Machinery," commonly known as the "Purge Bill."

The law authorized appointment of a committee composed of three senior judges and two senior government officials, with power to investigate any official receiving a monthly salary of twenty-seven *dinar* or more, who had been accused of "bad conduct."

The committee began work the end of 1956. It set out first to clean up the regular civil service, particularly within the Ministry of the Interior. During November six high-ranking officials in the ministry were dismissed and examination of the cases of four others begun. The investigation included such senior officials as the assistant director general of the interior, two mutasarrifs and a number of commandants of police. By the end of November thirty-four officials had been suspended from two to five years. It was a healthy beginning.

CRITICISM

Nuri faced the critical problems of the period with courage and energy. The problems were varied, and few were given to quick and easy solution. Before his death he could, however, point to a number of beneficial accomplishments in various fields. Nevertheless, criticism of him was sharp and persisted to the end. Typical examples of these attacks follow. They come from a highly articulate political figure of the left who was inclined to play a lone hand; from a group of liberals and leftists who often worked closely together; from a more conservative source, Nuri's chief political rival of his latter days; and one from a nonpolitical, detached observer.

Kamil Chadirchi's National Democratic party, which had joined the National Front in the June, 1954, elections, was suspended by Nuri in August, 1954, along with its widely read newspaper *Sawt al-Ahali*. The following October Chadirchi appealed for re-establishment of his party but was turned down. From then on he and his group were rather effectively muzzled. While he was kept under police surveillance, he was at first left free to carry on his legal profession. During the years he was living in forced political retirement we got in touch with him several times. Each time, in order to forestall any last minute hitch, we informed the Ministry of the Interior in advance of our intention to interview him. The ministry raised no objection.

The first of these calls was made by a member of my staff and took place in the summer of 1955. A word about Chadirchi's political tendencies seems in order before his observations are reported.

Chadirchi, a member of one of Iraq's best known, wealthy, conservative families, was himself extremely liberal in his political views. Attempts were made from time to time to label him a Communist, but he consistently denied being one. Many Iraqis took him at his word, but these same Iraqis felt that he allowed himself to be used by the outlawed and underground Communist party. His comments covered a wide field. These points stand out:

1. The Americans, he cautioned, must not allow themselves to be taken in as in the past by mere lip service to the cause of social and economic reform. He had often before heard Nuri's inaugural promises along that line.

2. Iraq, despite her substantial income from oil, remained a poverty stricken land.

3. The small cultivators continue to be mulcted, first by the sheiks and then by the government itself which has placed the burden of taxation on their shoulders.

4. He was neither a Communist, nor even a Communist

sympathizer, but a "progressive socialist" believing in evolutionary development rather than revolutionary change.

5. Many Iraqis feel that the U.S.S.R. is now the only power actively sponsoring the cause of social reform.

6. Both the U.K. and the U.S. have traditionally supported reactionary elements in Iraq, and they must share the blame for the lack of social progress.

7. The British Embassy and the IPC have always supported certain vested interests and have thus obstructed social reform. The role of the U.S. in this is an indirect one. The U.S. simply supports the British position.

The next call on Chadirchi took place in February, 1956, after Nuri had been in office about eighteen months. Again, it was at his home. He was still under police surveillance, if not by that time under actual house arrest.

With his party not able to function, and with the police constantly keeping an eye on him, Chadirchi during this visit quite naturally launched into a sharp attack on Nuri for his "suppression of personal liberties." Turning then to foreign affairs, he concentrated his criticism on Iraq's adherence to the Baghdad Pact. By that action he claimed that Nuri had estranged Iraq from the Arab world without gaining any benefits for the country. Then, generalizing, he alleged that Nuri was kept in office only through British backing. The incumbent British Ambassador he labeled a "second Cornwallis." (The reference was to Sir Kinahan Cornwallis, British ambassador from 1941 to 1945, who many Iraqis insisted had behaved more like a high commissioner back in the days when Britain administered Iraq as the mandatory power, than as an ambassador to a sovereign state.) Nor did the United States escape Chadirchi's attention. The U.S. had no policy of its own, he said. It simply acquiesced in the British efforts to control Iraq through Nuri.

The collective protest I mentioned was in the form of a petition to the King to remove Nuri. This took place a little over a year after Nuri had formed his government. The petition was signed by three leaders of the dissolved Istiqlal party, Muhammad Mahdi Kubba, Faiq as-Samarrai, and Muhammad Siddiq Shansal, and by three prominent members of the former National Democratic party, Chadirchi, Muhammad Hadid, and Husain Jamil. Colloboration between the leaders of the two opposition groups, as revealed by the protest, was not at all disrupted by the dissolution of their parties. After Nuri's death all six, incidentally, played more or less prominent roles in Qasim's regime, at least in its early days.

The protest covered just about everything. Main targets, in its words, were Nuri's tendency to govern by decree; his failure to provide adequate remedies for economic ills; his encouragement of an educational policy with harmful prospects for the country's future; and in foreign affairs, his pursuing a course which had isolated Iraq from the other Arab states and entangled her in "military blocs and dangerous commitments."

About a month after this group-protest had been submitted to the King, Salih Jabr, head of the former Umma party, presented a memorandum to the King that was highly critical of Nuri's domestic policy. This memorandum, dated November 2, 1955, was not published, but was given some circulation in Baghdad political circles. We obtained a copy from a former official of the dissolved Umma party. These were the points made by Jabr:

1. Nuri's government was without constitutional basis.

2. The existing Chamber of Deputies was a "spurious" body, as it came into being by "appointment."

3. The dissolution of the political parties was unconstitutional, as was also the suspension of newspapers, the "persecution" of students, and the closing of the schools.

4. What Iraq had was "individualistic totalitarian rule."

5. The King should restore to the people the rights guaranteed them by the constitution.

But the most genuine criticism of Nuri to come to my attention did not originate among politicians and public men. It came from a highly perceptive, intelligent woman who had lived most of her life in purdah and at middle age was permitted by her husband no more than a life of semiseclusion. She was the wife of a respected Iraqi who had served his country with distinction in high office in various fields. It was while he was on a mission abroad that she sent a message to my wife saying she would like to see her. She had some things she wanted very much for her to hear. She would come alone and wanted to see my wife alone. She explained that they had met once at a rather big reception at the Embassy on one of the rare occasions when her husband had taken her with him in public. She hoped that on his return from his extended mission abroad he would adopt a more liberal attitude and take her out more often so that she could enjoy freer contact with people in close touch with day-to-day developments.

My wife warmly encouraged her to come, and within a matter of days she appeared at the Embassy. The two talked at length. She had been married at the age of fourteen, she explained, and had been kept in strict seclusion most of her life. She had raised a big family and had accepted the traditional submissive role for Arab women, but never as a desirable one. Through husband and sons she had kept herself informed of what was going on in the country. She had given this much thought. And now an irresistible urge compelled her to talk to someone outside her family circle. It was perhaps presumptuous for her, she added, after having lived in such seclusion, to comment and pass judgment on what was going on in the world.

At this point my wife interjected that there are any number of instances recorded in Arab history when Arab women, though sequestered, had followed public affairs closely and had, through their husbands, exerted great influence on passing events. It was almost as though their removal from the world, with its many distractions, had sharpened their perception.

These words put her at ease. Enthusiastically and vividly

she then poured out her recommendations for Iraq's welfare. The country sorely needed a program of education and enlightenment for the masses. In this connection, vocational training must not be overlooked. There were far too many "white collar" workers, and it was high time the people learned the dignity of working with their hands. The police must be reformed. It was useless to try to suppress communism with brute force. Instead, people must be helped to a better way of life. Fine public buildings and engineering projects were all very good but it was of immediate importance that the people be given security and hope for a fuller life.

As will be seen there was a sameness about the criticism of Nuri regardless of its source. Of all that came to my attention, I thought that coming from this Iraqi woman, asking for nothing but an opportunity to be heard, was the most telling.

EVALUATION

So went the criticism. But what did Nuri give the country? High on the list is his delivery of the country from the floods, and that is something that should last long into the future. And through the energetic and continuous operation of the Development Program, he kept priming the economy of the country and kept it running at a lively, fairly even pace. Through alignment with the free world he obtained for Iraq assurance of help from beyond the Arab world in case of outside aggression. He gave Iraq public security and order, at the expense of some personal freedom, but there were many Iraqis who were willing to pay this price for public order. There were many who felt they had been victims of license long enough. Often the record of Nuri's last years shows that he made a start with reform in this field or that, but did not get very far. Why? The answer is that he ran out of time. His critics would ask why he did not start sooner?

His supporters would retort that he did not start earlier with this or that project because he was busy with something else. This was true; Nuri was never idle. The quarrel was with his list of priorities. His list had been prepared with care and with the conviction that what he was doing was best for the country which he had come to know intimately in the course of a long and active life.

VII

NURI AS ARAB NATIONALIST

INTRODUCTION

Nuri's Arab nationalism was questioned during his last years. This was in part a result of the Baghdad Pact which, because it aligned Iraq with the free world, was deeply resented in such Arab world centers as Cairo, Damascus, and Riyad. The fact that bitter and sustained press and radio attacks on this action were directed from Egypt, the traditional leader of the Arab world, at a time when Nasser was its chief spokesman, added to its effectiveness in isolating Nuri. Much that he had done for the cause of Arab nationalism was conveniently ignored or entirely forgotten. What he was trying to do for Arabs everywhere was widely misunderstood.

It seemed to have been forgotten that Nuri's thinking about Arab independence and unity began in his teens and that he started working actively for them, at considerable personal risk, while the Ottoman Empire was still in existence. He was among the first Arabs openly to espouse the cause and among the first to take up arms in its behalf.

In the Blue Book, one of the very few records that Nuri wrote, he outlined his plan for Arab unity, which came to be known by the more restrictive title, "The Fertile Crescent Plan." This publication was in the form of a memorandum addressed in 1942 to Richard Casey, at that time British minister of state for the Middle East, with his residence in Cairo.

In outlining his plan, Nuri showed understanding of Arab diversities and of the need to respect the historical background, local traditions, and the peculiar ways of life of each separate Arab entity. His approach to Arab unity was wholly practical. Complete unity was to be realized in stages. While Iraq's interests and those of her immediate neighbors got first priority, he never lost sight of the wider issues of Arab nationalism. His main observations and recommendations follow.

To begin with, he wrote, Iraq's relations with the Arabs of historic Syria are closer than with those of the Arab peninsula. While all are bound closely by language, custom and religion, the economies of the two are different. Egypt, on the other hand, because of her large population and her special relations with the Sudan, has problems which put her in a separate category. It can be assumed, therefore, that neither the states of the Arabian peninsula, nor Egypt, would at first be inclined to join a federation or league built on Iraq and Syria. They might join in time, if such a federation proved practicable, and meanwhile consultation between the states of the federation and these other Arab states would be encouraged.

Having thus laid down some strictures on immediate, wide, Arab unity, Nuri's fundamental Arab nationalism reasserted itself in these words: "Many of our problems are the same; we are all part of one civilization; we generally think along the same lines and we are all animated by the same ideals of freedom of conscience, liberty of speech, equality before the law and the basic brotherhood of mankind." [1]

In Nuri's view, the only hope for permanent peace and progress among the Arabs was for the United Nations to call for the restoration of historic Syria, that is the re-unification of Syria, Lebanon, Palestine and Trans-Jordan into a single state. The form of government, whether monarchical or republican, unitary or federal, would be decided by the people themselves. Along with the establishment of such a state there would also be created an Arab League, embracing at the start Iraq and Syria, but open to any other Arab state. The League would have a permanent council responsible for defense, foreign affairs, currency, communications, customs, and the protection of minority rights.

Nuri's plan provided semi-autonomy for the Jews in Palestine within such a state; for Jerusalem to be open to all religious groups for pilgrimage and worship purposes; and for the Maronites in Lebanon, if they requested it, the same kind of privileged regime they enjoyed during the last years of the Ottoman Empire. He added:

> The British Empire is not founded on negations but on positive ideals. Free institutions and free co-operation give it a living force of tremendous strength. Upon this foundation of free co-operation a true union of many diverse peoples and countries has been formed, depending less upon stipulations and statistics, and more upon the nobler and more permanent principles which are written on the heart and conscience of man. If an opportunity is given to the Arab peoples to establish such a free co-operation among themselves they will be prepared to deal generously with all the Jews living in their midst whether in Palestine or elsewhere. Conditions and guarantees there must be, but let them not constitute a dead hand lest they become a dead

---

[1] *Arab Independence and Unity* (Blue Book), p. 11; originally marked "Confidential Not For Publication," but no longer so regarded.

letter, as so many minority provisions in European constitutions became during the past twenty years.[2]

Nuri did play a personal role in bringing about an Arab federation shortly before his death. Ironically it was not the Iraqi-Syrian union envisaged in his Blue Book, but the union of Iraq and Jordan, a union forged to counterbalance one formed earlier by Egypt and Syria.

ARAB UNION

Some years before the Arab Union was formed Nuri had made an attempt to bring the two Hashimite kingdoms closer together. As a means to this end he tried his hand at matchmaking, and appropriately enough in the spring of the year, in April, 1955. Announcement had just been made of King Husayn's engagement to Princess Dina, a distant cousin and member of the Hashimite family who was then living in Cairo. Nuri, the story went, lost no time in suggesting to King Faisal that he should emulate his young cousin. The Iraqi public, he assured Faisal, would welcome his early marriage. He believed the ideal wife would be the daughter of former King Telal of Jordan, sister of Husayn, who made her home in Beirut. But this was not the whole plan. As an intermediary to work out the details, he suggested Muzahim al-Pachachi, a former prime minister. In making this particular suggestion, Nuri was stepping out of the cupid role into the one more familiar to him, that of politician. Muzahim al-Pachachi happened to be in opposition to him, and keeping him occupied outside the country fitted in nicely with Nuri's own plans. The young King, however, was not receptive. Still worse, the Crown Prince, who had not been taken into Nuri's confidence, was considerably annoyed by Nuri's presumptuous behavior. Abdul-Ilah had reserved for himself the privilege of timing

---

[2] *Arab Independence and Unity* (Blue Book), p. 12.

his nephew's marriage, and it was quite generally believed in Baghdad that it would be put off as long as possible. So nothing but a little more strain on his relations with the Crown Prince came out of this attempt of Nuri's to bring Iraq and Jordan more closely together.

Actually, in spite of this attempt to bring Iraq and Jordan together at the altar, there was little if any sentiment in Nuri's approach to Jordan. He viewed the country in a factual, hard-headed way. Jordan, he once said to me, is an artificial political entity, economically unviable, and inevitably bound to become linked in time with a neighboring Arab country. If Jordanians were given a free choice, he maintained, the majority would opt for union or federation with Iraq.

Those words were spoken some years before the Arab Union (AU) became a reality. The years leading up to that union were years of political unrest and economic strain for Jordan and, because of these uncertainties, years of anxiety for Iraq. Nuri, fully realizing that Iraq would be assuming heavy responsibilities through union, nevertheless worked tirelessly toward that end when the Palace, early in 1958, chose him for the task.

It was on January 15, 1958, when I called on Nuri for one of our exchanges on general trends and developments that I found him particularly concerned about Jordan. Saudi Arabia, Egypt and Syria, he insisted, were conspiring to bring to power in Jordan a government linked to them. The intrigue was being financed by Saudi Arabia. Arms were being smuggled into Jordan from Syria for the Jordanian co-conspirators. Saudi troops were deployed along the border of Jordan. Jordan's Arab Legion was simply not strong enough to deal with an unsettled internal situation and at the same time be on the alert to meet possible invasion. Jordan had the right, in case of invasion, both under the Arab Collective Security Pact and the 1947 Iraqi-Jordan Treaty, to call on Iraq for help. Iraq, however, would under no circumstances intervene unless requested to do so by the government of

Jordan. Then, like a true Arab nationalist, he added: "The situation in Jordan is just one more development underlining the urgency of settling the Palestine problem."

In the months that followed, the critical trend continued. On May 13 I called on Nuri at his home to express our concern over persevering instability, and at the same time to impress on him that we felt Iraq was in a position to exercise a constructive influence. If Iraq would extend some economic aid, as we were doing, that would have a beneficial, practical effect, but what was equally important was that it would have a healthy psychological effect. I then told Nuri what I had learned during a recent visit to Amman. By both American and British sources I was told that there was a general feeling in Jordan that Iraq was indifferent to her fate. Some friendly gesture by Iraq at this critical time would give the people of Jordan a much needed lift.

Nuri replied that he had little confidence in Jordan's government. He was nevertheless proceeding with legislation to help Jordan finance potash and super-phosphate projects. This might help some but not much. The trouble was that Jordan needed at least six million pounds for development purposes, to do any good. But economic aid, in no matter what proportions, would be wasted unless Saudi and Egyptian maneuvering and intriguing in Jordan were first curbed. That was how he summed up the situation.

Nuri did, however, get quick action from Parliament on his aid bill. Six days after our talk the Chamber (and thirteen days later the Senate) authorized the advance to the Arab Potash Company, either as a loan or contribution, ID625,000 for the production of potash salts from Dead Sea deposits, and one million *dinar* as a loan to the government of Jordan for financing a super-phosphate project.

In his personal relations Nuri was most generous with whatever means he possessed. In his public relations, where spending Iraq's money abroad was concerned, he was cautious, generally reluctant, and often downright parsimonious. These latter traits were revealed repeatedly during our talks on aid to Jordan. At one point he claimed Jordan herself was largely to blame for her plight. He had repeatedly urged Jordan to desist from any action that might cost her the British subsidy. But she did not follow his advice. She listened to Nasser and King Saud. Glubb and his fellow British officers should never have been dismissed.

During those days Nuri would plead goodwill and poverty interchangeably. There was some justification for the latter right after the interruption of the flow of oil through Syria during the Suez crisis, but he kept on with that argument after the oil began flowing again. Nuri disliked asking Parliament for authorization to do anything and was inclined to avoid doing so, or to put off doing so, if he could. To get aid for Jordan beyond what had already been authorized for the potash and phosphate projects meant still another approach to Parliament. I think he found that too distasteful, and so he clung to the story of poverty. At the same time he watched carefully the extent of our aid. In October, 1956, he showed some impatience about the pace we were setting. It was then that he remarked wryly to me: "I really don't expect you to do much of anything until after your November elections." When in April of the following year I told him that we were extending ten million dollars in aid to Jordan, he was visibly cheered, but could not refrain from checking his enthusiasm with the remark: "Tell Mr. Dulles that up to now he has been working only on the tail and leaving the head, Nasser, intact."

But while Nuri was sparing with his *dinars,* his ideas flowed as profusely as ever. Once while we were on the subject of U.S. aid to Jordan, he produced from his fertile mind a formula based on rather ingenious reasoning. He proposed that we channel our aid for Jordan through Iraq. This was one way of rewarding Iraq for having come out boldly for the West. The credit would be given Iraq for generosity among the Arabs and would go far toward rehabilitating

Iraq in the Arab world. But there was something in this for the United States too. By helping Jordan through Iraq, the United States would in the long run get off easier than she would by giving aid directly and openly. Aid from the United States, publicly scrutinized, had to be substantial. He calculated that direct, public aid would have to be about three times as much as aid passed to Jordan surreptitiously through Iraq.

Nuri could not ignore Parliament. Neither could Dulles ignore Congress. And so this complicated and unorthodox exercise of Nuri's in high finance, whatever its merits, was doomed from the start.

During all these months of exchanges with Nuri on economic and military aid for Jordan, Nuri kept in mind the possibility of Iraq having to intervene militarily in Jordan. On September 20, 1956, he told me that as a precautionary measure he was sending supplies to three points along the route into Jordan, the pipeline stations at H–4 and H–5 in Iraq, and to Mafraq in Jordan. A small force would be assigned to guard the stocks. Iraq's sole aim, in anything undertaken in the military field, was to save Jordan from communism. He wished we would make that clear in Tel Aviv.

Developments came quickly. On October 11 Nuri asked me to see him at the Council of Ministers building. He told me that Iraqi troops would cross into Jordan on October 15. He wanted us to pass the word on to Tel Aviv that he guaranteed not to engage in any aggressive acts. Iraqi troops would remain in the Jordan valley, east of the River Jordan and "away from the frontier." Iraq's treaty with Jordan obligated Iraq to come to Jordan's assistance in case of aggression from outside, as well as in case of an internal upheaval. That was how he interpreted the treaty. He reserved the right to freer and wider movement within Jordan should disorder become widespread.

Through our soundings in Tel Aviv we ascertained that there was no objection to the entry of Iraqi troops into

Jordan provided they remained east of the River Jordan. But these preparatory steps of Nuri's proved premature, and two days later, on October 13, I was told that orders for the troops to move on October 15 had been canceled. Instead, the Crown Prince and the chief of staff, General Rafiq Arif, were flying to Amman. Up to that time only an oral request had been received for military support. Nuri wanted something in writing. The fixing of a new date for the entry of Iraqi troops would depend on the outcome of these talks in Amman.

On October 17, after Abdul-Ilah and Rafiq Arif returned to Baghdad, Nuri came to see me at the Embassy. The plan now was for the Jordanian cabinet to adopt a resolution requesting no more for the present than that Iraq hold one infantry division in readiness near the border in Iraq for entry in case of aggression, as provided by treaty. The government of Jordan hoped, though, that the stockpiling at H–4, H–5 and Mafraq would continue as planned. But, Nuri told me, he had no intention of proceeding with supplies for the time being.

These developments in October, 1956, looked as though Nuri, in his characteristically energetic way, had jumped the gun. Nuri, however, in his talk with me, blamed it all on "faulty co-ordination" between King Husayn and his cabinet.

So matters rested until April of the following year when, I was told, King Husayn personally asked that Iraq take preparatory steps for moving troops into Jordan. A build-up began at H–3. By the middle of May the number of troops there had reached five thousand, according to Nuri. "They are there though for defense, not offense," he emphasized. That was the situation militarily on the Iraqi-Jordanian border when Nuri left office in May.

In the months that followed, the trend of events in Jordan and pressures from Egypt and Syria brought the two countries closer together. On February 1, 1958, Egypt and Syria announced the formation of the United Arab Republic. On February 11, an Iraqi delegation headed by King Faisal went to Amman in response, we were told by a Foreign Office source, to Jordan's known desire to unite with Iraq. On the very next day, Iraq and Jordan announced that they had formed a federation to be known as the Arab Union. The agreement to federate was reached so quickly in principle chiefly because the Jordanians were willing to compromise on the matter of the head of the Union and on Iraq's continuing her membership in the Baghdad Pact. Consultations were to be undertaken at once on the drafting of a constitution for the Union. It was hoped the new constitution could come into force about the middle of May.

After decades of talk about Arab unity, two unions suddenly and simultaneously emerged. Not since the Suez crisis of 1956 had the political rhythm of the area been so affected.

The announcement was received calmly by the public in Iraq. No street demonstrations were organized either for or against the Union. The press played up the news with what might best be described as cheerful restraint. The Palace, Nuri, and all Iraqis who had had experience in public life or followed public affairs, understood what Iraq had taken on and what lay ahead. Much hard work and many sacrifices, material and others, would be required. The Palace and Nuri saw this clearly.

At this point the Crown Prince asked me to call at the Rose Palace. He wanted to bring me up to date on the Palace thinking. For the present, he said, Iraq would take no position for or against the UAR. Iraq would nevertheless be on the alert for any action affecting Jordan. Paperwork, as he called it, was already being done on the possible movement of Iraqi troops into Jordan. Now, once again, Iraq needed a "strong man." The King and he were thinking of asking Nuri to return to office. But a "typical" Nuri cabinet would not be acceptable. Nuri would have to agree to accept some men chosen by the Palace.

On March 3 Nuri became prime minister for the fourteenth and last time. Like the announcement on the Arab Union, word of Nuri's return to power was received calmly by the public. The inclusion in his cabinet of men like Fadhil Jamali as foreign minister and Karim al-Uzri as finance minister gave the government the appearance of a broadly based national coalition, as wanted by the Palace.

I called on Nuri at his home on March 5 to learn something about the program and timetable of his new government. The principal objective, he told me, would be to pave the way as smoothly and quickly as possible for formalizing the Union and establishing its government. He estimated the life of the Iraqi government he was then heading at from two to three months. Within that time he hoped to get through Parliament an amendment to the Iraqi Constitution legalizing the federation with Jordan, bring about Iraqi adoption of the Arab Union Constitution, dissolve the existing Parliament, and hold elections for a new Parliament. With a new Parliament at hand, a new Iraqi government would be formed adapted to the needs of the Arab Union.

Nuri had estimated well the life of his government. On May 12 the proposed constitution for the Arab Union was ratified by Parliament with only one dissenting vote, that of Senator Shabibi, implacable opponent of Nuri. On May 13, when I saw Nuri again at his home, he told me that both King Faisal and King Husayn had asked him to become the first prime minister of the Arab Union (and the only one this short-lived federation was to have).

Four of the portfolios in the Arab Union government cabinet went to Iraqis and three to Jordanians. Tawfiq Suweidi, a former prime minister of Iraq and long time friend of Nuri's became foreign minister of the Union. Another Iraqi, Karim al-Uzri, became minister of finance. While he had previously held a number of public offices in Iraq, he was essentially a professional economist. Sami Fattah, a retired air force general with considerable government experience, became minister of state for defense. The three Jordanians were Ibrahim Hashim, deputy prime minister; Sulaiman Tuqan, minister of defense; and Khulusi al-Khairi, minister of state for foreign affairs.

The first Union Parliament meeting took place in Amman on May 27. Ten days previously the Iraqi Chamber of Deputies had chosen fifteen of the twenty members apportioned to Iraq. The list appeared to have been drawn up by Nuri and, it seems, approved by a mere show of hands. On May 22, King Faisal announced the five additional names.

Nuri, of course, had a hand not only in setting up the Arab Union government, but also in the selection of the new Iraqi government, of which Ahmad Mukhtar Baban, former deputy prime minister, became prime minister. To form two governments at this critical time called for much political experience and flexibility. Nuri, naturally, wanted to get the new Union government off to a good start. For this he needed experienced, dependable men. In making his selections he had to keep two considerations constantly in mind, preferences of the two Palaces and balanced communal representation throughout the federation. And in both countries, whether working on the formation of a government for Iraq or the Union, he was, like any politician in any country, confronted with names of people for whom jobs somewhere, somehow, had to be found. All in all, Nuri did well. Certainly a good basis was laid for the Union. In his policy statement of May 20, Nuri recalled with justified satisfaction the aspirations of his days as a revolutionary forty years earlier. The establishment of the Arab Union, he declared, constituted a major step toward realization of the goals of the Arab revolt.

On May 6, just two weeks before Nuri issued his policy statement, the Arabic press of Baghdad carried Nuri's answers to questions put to him by Associated Press correspondent Wilton Wynn. The desirability of Arab unity was the keynote of this exchange. Unity, Nuri stressed, had always been the main objective of the Arab nationalist movement, and now, if only the United Arab Republic would stop interfering in

Iraq and Jordan, co-operation between the Arab Union and the United Arab Republic could be worked out.

The main provisions of the Union Constitution were as follows: each state retained its individual international status and existing system of government within its own borders; the Union government was to have a Head of Union,[3] along with distinct legislative, executive, and judicial authorities; the Union government was to have responsibility for foreign affairs, treaty making, defense, customs, co-ordination of financial and economic policies, currency, banking, and joint communications. Finally, provision was made for other Arab states to join.

On the whole, the wording of the Arab Union Constitution left considerable freedom of action to the prime minister. He had a choice of an active or passive role. How the Union would eventually emerge, either with a strongly centralized government or as a federation with diffused governmental authority, depended therefore largely on how the first prime minister chose to exercise the prerogatives of his office. It is hard to say what course Nuri would have followed had events spared his life and that of the Arab Union. If he had discharged the duties of Union prime minister as he had always done as prime minister of Iraq, then a union would literally have developed. But Nuri might not have wanted that. He might well have preferred to retain a large measure of influence in Baghdad. When I talked with him on May 21, right after his return from Amman, he gave no indication of the course he intended to follow. It was perhaps still too early for him to make such a decision. When I asked him whether he was satisfied with the way the Union, and specifically, the government apparatus were emerging, he was evasive. It would take time, he replied, to construct the necessary government "machinery" and to get it to "run smoothly."

[3] King Faisal of Iraq became Head of the Arab Union with the title: "His Majesty King Faisal II of Iraq, Head of the Arab Union."

He thought "some" progress had been made toward this end during the talks he just had in Amman. He found himself handicapped, though, by still not having a staff and he saw no prospects of getting one before the middle of June.

In spite of his concentration on the establishment of the new Union, Nuri found time to give thought to problems of his friends. When I told him that President Eisenhower had nominated me as the first United States ambassador to the Arab Union and added, in a light aside, that I was now faced with the problem of finding adequate living quarters in Amman for the period when the diplomatic corps would be in residence there, he told me not to worry. "I will see that you are properly taken care of," he assured me. I knew he meant it and would do that for me, if I permitted him.

Nuri's spirits reached a very low point about the middle of June, 1958. He had for months been struggling with the problem of how to place the Arab Union on a sound economic basis. He began to feel that the response of Iraq's friends to his appeals for co-operation were too slow and indefinite. During one of our talks at that time he remarked, despairingly that he was too old to preside over a non-viable state. What had happened was simply that, through the Arab Union, Jordan's economic and financial problems had been shifted to Iraq. Unless there were guarantees of long-term aid from Iraq's friends to meet this situation he would have to resign.

This proved to be only a passing mood. During the remaining weeks of his life he never talked about resigning. He seemed to have become satisfied with, or at least reconciled to, what we and the British were prepared to do economically for the Arab Union.

I saw Nuri for the last time on July 12, 1958. I found him very disturbed over Lebanon. What was the United States going to do to help save the situation? He kept pressing me for an answer. I had nothing reassuring to tell him.

It must have been shortly after I saw him that Nuri decided

that the Iraqi contingent on the Iraqi-Jordanian frontier should be reinforced. On July 13, two brigades converged on Baghdad, apparently destined for the Iraqi-Jordanian frontier, if not for Jordan herself. Qasim was in command of one of them. Neither brigade went beyond Baghdad. Early in the morning of July 14 Qasim sparked the coup that brought him to power. During the disorders of the day, troops rounded up a group of guests at the Baghdad Hotel in search of Jordanian ministers of the Arab Union cabinet who had just come to Baghdad and registered there. They did actually, in the group herded together at random, get three ministers, along with three Americans and two Germans. The group was forced outside into a truck. There a mob attacked them and killed the three Jordanians, one of whom was the Union deputy prime minister, Ibrahim Hashim, the three Americans and one of the Germans. On July 15, Nuri was killed on a street not far from the American Embassy. On the day of his death, American marines landed in Lebanon. Three days later, on July 18, Qasim informed us that Iraq had withdrawn from the Arab Union.

Just as calmly as the public had received the announcement of the Arab Union six months earlier, it now received word of its dissolution. There was no enthusiasm at its birth and there were no regrets at its death. The public, I fear, at no time cared to face the sacrifices, largely financial, that had to be made if the Arab Union was to become a stabilizing factor.

KUWAIT

On a number of public occasions Nuri stressed the point that the Arab Union Constitution left the door open for other Arab states to join the federation. In private he made it abundantly clear that he had Kuwait in mind especially. In fact, in the talks I had with him on the subject he never mentioned any other Arab entity by name. He made it equally clear why he wanted Kuwait to join. Practical considerations were up-permost. The burden of carrying "unviable" Jordan would become tolerable if Kuwait's oil revenues were added to Iraq's. As a member of the Arab Union, however, Kuwait would be better able to counter subversive propaganda and activities. Moreover, with the addition of a non-Hashimite member, the Union would gain breadth and have greater appeal for other Arab states.

There were two problems which complicated Iraq's relations with Kuwait. Iraq was handicapped in marketing her oil from the Basra area because of the lack of anchorage facilities for deep draught tankers. Kuwait suffered from the lack of fresh water. Iraq was in a position to give Kuwait what she needed. Kuwait could extend the facilities Iraq wanted. Nevertheless, they found it hard to reach agreement.

Under the Ottoman Empire, Kuwait formed part of the Basra Liwa. Kuwaitis feared that the Iraqis had ambitions to "re-absorb" them and the Iraqis did nothing to dispel these suspicions. All the fears, suspicions and ambitions marring the relations between the two were evident in exchanges on a draft treaty covering water facilities which the Sheik of Kuwait presented early in 1955 to the government of Iraq through the British, the protecting power. The draft treaty provided that Iraq would permit Kuwait to draw drinking water from the Shatt al-Arab, to be transported by a pipeline running to the city of Kuwait. To facilitate this, Iraq was to cede the right-of-way, along with a thirty meter strip on either side, and enough ground for erecting the necessary installations.

The draft treaty was not well received in Baghdad. While Iraq was ready to supply Kuwait with water, she was not prepared to cede any land. Nor did Iraq want to become involved in negotiations requiring a demarcation of the boundary. Iraq, while accepting the *de facto* existence of Kuwait, wanted to avoid any move that might be interpreted as according the sheikdom *de jure* recognition. Furthermore, Iraq wanted as a *quid pro quo* for the water, or so it appeared at first, the right to rent certain anchorage sites in the port of Umm-Qasr, with some small territorial cessions to facilitate access to the port. By October, however, when the brother of the sheik of Kuwait, Sheik Fahad bin Salim-al-Sabah, visited Baghdad, Iraq had shifted her position. In a talk with Sheik Fahad, Nuri adopted a more reasonable attitude. Kuwait could have the water without condition. Because what Iraq wanted in the port of Umm-Qasr would benefit both Iraq and Kuwait, he proposed that the construction be done on a 50–50 basis, and that the formality of leasing any territory be waived. The Ruler's brother was favorably impressed, so Nuri told me, and Nuri hoped for a solution on this basis. But nothing came of it, not even when in June, 1956, the ruler himself, Abdullah al-Salim al-Sabah, spent six days in Iraq. The Ruler showed no inclination to discuss the projects, insisting that his visit was one of courtesy only.

The reports, which circulated from time to time while these discussions were in progress, that Iraq was insisting on something in return for furnishing Kuwait water, upset Nuri very much. Whenever one of these reports gained currency he would tell me, with feeling, that it was baseless. It was traditional with the people of the desert who were so fortunate as to have water, to share it freely with their less fortunate neighbors. He would not have Iraq violate this tradition. Iraq would gladly share her water supplies with any of her needy neighbors, without thought of recompense.

But during the last months of Nuri's life preoccupation with efforts to bring Kuwait into the AU pushed the water and port projects into the background.

On March 14, 1958, just eleven days after Nuri returned to power, he spoke to me in some detail about Kuwait's joining the AU. The time had come, he began, for Britain to overhaul her traditional position in the area. She might well start with Kuwait by withdrawing from her "protector's role" and granting Kuwait "sovereign" status. This would pave the way for Kuwait's adherence to the AU. He had suggested this to Foreign Secretary Selwyn Lloyd when he passed through Baghdad some days earlier on his way to Manila. In any event, he hoped Britain would influence Kuwait to join the Union and that we would use our influence on Britain to the same end. The AU needed strengthening and Kuwait could give it the needed strength.

On May 9, al-Uzri, AU finance minister, came to see me at the Embassy at Nuri's request. He stressed Nuri's concern over the need of bolstering the AU financially. He told me then that the ruler of Kuwait, Salim-al-Sabah, would arrive in Baghdad on May 10 for a visit of several days. Nuri, al-Uzri said, was now prepared to offer demarcation of the Kuwait-Iraq boundary and guarantees for maintenance of the Ruler's existing degree of sovereignty in return for Kuwait's joining the AU. Nuri would so inform the Ruler during his presence in Baghdad.

The Ruler arrived as scheduled. At a dinner which was given in his honor, Nuri told me that talks with him were not going well. He had offered demarcation and water, but found the Ruler unresponsive. It worried him still more that the Ruler told him that he would visit Cairo soon after Nasser's return from Moscow.

After Nuri told me this, I talked with the Ruler myself for a time, hoping to draw him out on his views on the AU. Having in mind the adoption of the AU constitution the day before, I remarked that he had come to Baghdad at an auspicious time, just when the AU was being formalized. His response was perfunctory and noncommittal.

So the Ruler came and went and Kuwait was no nearer the AU. I was told that during his stay he had shown concern over UAR-AU tension. His visit opened Iraqi eyes to the fact that the Ruler had a serious problem internally created by the strength of pro-Egyptian public sentiment, and also to the fact that he exercised considerable independence of action, in spite of the British presence.

Before passing on to Nuri's relationship with his bigger neighbor, Saudi Arabia, I have one footnote on Iraq-Kuwait relations to add, a development that occurred after Nuri's death, after the breakup of the AU, and just before my departure from Baghdad. This development turned out to be a harbinger of things to come—Qasim's threatening attitude toward the little, rich sheikdom.

The Ruler visited Baghdad once more, spending five days there in October of 1958. The press headlined his arrival. At the airport he was welcomed by Qasim and five of his cabinet ministers. Then followed a news blackout. No communiqué was issued on his departure. There is a plausible explanation for his having been given this silent treatment. His visit coincided with the announcement in Cairo by the secretariat of the Arab League that henceforth Kuwait would be considered a member of the League. Such status for Kuwait, as we now know, could hardly have been welcomed by Qasim. In June, 1961, after British sovereignty had been withdrawn, he claimed Kuwait as Iraqi territory.

SAUDI ARABIA

In 1954 relations between Iraq and Saudi Arabia were strained, as they had been for years. This distrust between the Hashimite and Saudi dynasties began in 1925 when the Saudis ousted the Hashimite King Ali from Hejaz. Abdul-Ilah, onetime regent and later crown prince of Iraq, was Ali's son. While regent he had refused to send an Iraqi envoy to King Saud's coronation. The initiative in relieving tension, therefore, seemed to lie with him. The twenty-year-old King Faisal was not one to act on his own. The nod had to come from his uncle, the Crown Prince. The nod did actually come from him early in 1957 and led to a marked improvement in the relations between the two countries. Nuri played a part in this.

Nuri's feelings for Saudi Arabia during my early acquaintance with him were far from friendly. In fact, he was bitter. Dynastic rivalry did not concern him. What disturbed and upset him was Saudi opposition to his foreign policy and specifically, Saudi use of "American dollars," as he called the oil revenues paid by Aramco, to make trouble for him among his Arab neighbors. Of course one might say that Iraq was not above using "English pounds," her oil revenue from IPC, to promote her interests. Nuri was not above playing this accepted game of bribery himself, but his complaint was that every time he placed money where he thought it might help, the Saudis would come along and spend twice as much. They had too much money at their disposal. "If their revenues were cut off for only six months, I could stabilize the situation," he boasted to me one time. In a more reasonable frame of mind at another time he explained that what the Saudis did with their money within Saudi Arabia was no concern of his, but when Saudi money was used in Iraq and elsewhere to weaken the defense against communism, and thus expose Iraq and her neighbors to danger, it was definitely a concern of his.

At the November, 1956, meeting in Baghdad of the Moslem members of the Baghdad Pact, it was decided to send Abdul-Ilah to Washington to explain the views of the Moslem powers on the situation in the Middle East as affected by the Suez incident. Washington was not at first receptive to the Crown Prince's visit. It was feared that this was just one more move to bring pressure on us to join the Baghdad Pact. A visit by King Saud was also a possibility. To have the two together in Washington might prove awkward. Nuri, however, insisted to me that the Crown Prince's mission was broad in nature, encompassing the whole field of current problems, and his going as a spokesman of Iraq's Moslem neighbors would be very popular with the people of Iraq. That worked. On January 11, 1957, it was announced in Washington that Abdul-Ilah would visit in February. Three days later we were able to telegraph the department that the Crown Prince had expressed the wish to meet King Saud while in Washington. Now everybody was happy. The meeting between the two did take place and marked the beginning of a decided change for the better in the relations between the two countries.

The meeting in Washington between King Saud and the Crown Prince was soon followed up in Baghdad. Early in March, Nuri sent his close friend Abdulla al-Damaluji on a visit to Saudi Arabia as ambassador-at-large. The choice was a happy one. Damaluji, who came from Mosul, had for years served as adviser to King Saud's father, Ibn Saud. He knew King Saud intimately, and his mission turned out to be rewarding. King Saud promised to visit Baghdad in May, after Ramadhan. Damaluji was also able to get an insight into King Saud's ideas on the problems affecting the area. Since his Washington visit Saud had become sensitive to the Communist threat. For the first time he showed concern over the leftist trend in Syria and the role Egypt was playing there. Hostility to the Baghdad Pact had turned to mere indifference. In this mood, he agreed not to attack the pact publicly any more.

Some comments Nuri made to me in the course of a discussion of Damaluji's visit show how flexible he was. Obviously, he said, Saud's adherence to the Baghdad Pact was out of the question in spite of his anti-Communist feeling. Some way should be found, however, to utilize his very considerable influence in the region. One way of doing so had occurred to him. He would put aside for the moment all thought of gaining further support for the Baghdad Pact and concentrate instead on aligning the countries of the Middle East publicly behind the Eisenhower Doctrine which, he felt, was well designed to help meet the threat of communism.

"I want to break up," Nuri explained, "the Egyptian-Syrian-Saudi joint command. That can only be done gradually. Getting Saudi Arabia into a more or less formal pro-Eisenhower Doctrine alignment would help in that direction." Just the day before, he continued, he had asked President

Chamoun, who had stopped in Baghdad on his way to Riyadh, to try to find out whether King Saud would take the initiative in lining up the governments in the Middle East behind the doctrine.

Chamoun passed through Baghdad again on March 26, on his way back from Riyadh to Beirut. When Nuri asked him how Saud had reacted to his suggestion, Nuri told me Chamoun had said no more than: "Be patient. Move slowly." When I asked Nuri whether this was Chamoun's advice or Saud's, Nuri said that Chamoun had not made that clear to him, and he had not pressed the matter further.

Nuri's behavior in trying to get support for the Eisenhower Doctrine was typical. Often I found him warmly enthusiastic about one of his projects one day only to drop it the next and move on to something new and different. This was explained by his quick, fertile mind and his impatience.

King Saud came to Baghdad in May as promised. There were talks with top Iraqi officials and there was entertaining. The communiqué that was issued at the conclusion of the visit on May 19 was, on its face, no more significant than communiqués usually are. The meeting of the two kings marked the start of a new era, the communiqué began. There followed a statement that the meeting had provided the opportunity for an exchange of views on matters of interest to the two countries, as well as the whole Arab-Moslem world. Then, as was inevitable, the Palestine question was touched on. The peace and security of the area, it was reaffirmed, were dependent on a just solution of that problem. There had been full agreement, too, on the necessity for preserving Arab-Moslem rights in the Gulf of Aqaba which was described as a "closed Arab Gulf connected with the Holy Places of Islam." Finally, the dangers threatening the "Arab nation" were identified as "Zionism, subversive principles and imperialism." This statement calls for some explanation.

From an Iraqi Foreign Office source I learned that Nuri very much wanted specific mention of communism in the communiqué. This was blocked by the pro-Egyptian, anti-Iraqi foreign minister of King Saud, Yusif Yasin. The most Iraq could get was the single allusion to "subversive principles."

But for a real appreciation of what was accomplished by the visit one had to look behind and beyond the communiqué. There one found substantial gain. Major credit for this must go to Nuri, who did an outstanding job in charming Saud. Saud had come expecting to transact business with the Crown Prince but soon found his attention drawn to Nuri, who took over. It was essentially the spell skillfully cast by Nuri on Saud that opened the way for closer co-operation. The decades of animosity between the Hashimite and Saudi families seemed to be dispelled. Saud's suspicion of the Baghdad Pact appeared to be eliminated. Acknowledgment of its value to Iraq was obtained. Tangible evidence of closer relations could be found in the initialing of air and trade agreements during the visit; an exchange of views on oil policy; and agreement for co-operation in the field of education and on aid to Jordan.

One evening during King Saud's stay Nuri gave a dinner in his honor in the gardens of Amanah Hall. As usual, Nuri was the perfect host, thoughtful and attentive throughout. As King Saud is a devout, practising Moslem, only fruit juices were in evidence in his presence. But at the same time, Nuri did not forget his less orthodox Moslem guests, or his friends from the West. They, on entering the garden, were told by the Foreign Office *chef' de protocol* that somewhat removed from the presence of His Majesty, behind a clump of bushes and a row of trees, a bar had been set up where choice whiskies and brandy were available. All evening, before and after dinner, this category of Nuri's guests could be seen dividing its attention between talking with the King and his party, and making trips behind the bushes.

Not long after King Saud's departure Nuri, in one of his light, whimsical moods, made an evaluation for us of the ruling families in Riyadh and Baghdad. In Saudi Arabia, he said, the King is good but the Crown Prince, who happens also to be prime minister, is bad. In Iraq the King too is good and the Crown Prince is also bad, but fortunately in Iraq, the Crown Prince is not prime minister. Iraq has a good prime minister and therein lies the difference.

Much credit for bringing the two "good" kings together and opening the way for closer understanding between these two neighboring Arab states must be given to Nuri. Unfortunately, both King Faisal and Nuri were removed from the Iraqi scene by violence before something more lasting could be accomplished.

EGYPT

From the autumn of 1954 to the summer of 1958 the relations between Iraq and Egypt were strongly influenced by the personalities of their leaders. Both Nuri and Nasser were men of exceptional intellect, character, and gifts of leadership, and it is not surprising that they determined the relations between their two countries.

Nuri was risking his life in battle for Arab independence before Nasser was born. Yet Nasser came to be looked upon as the personification of Arab leadership. The cause of the strained relations between the two was the fact that Nuri brought the Baghdad Pact into being, and made Iraq a member of it. Nasser seemed to feel that Nuri was inexcusably presumptuous in adopting a foreign policy of his own, and even worse, in carrying Iraq with him outside the Arab world. Nasser's reaction offended and shocked Nuri deeply. This was no pose on his part. In recognition of the traditional leadership of Egypt in the Arab world, Nuri had personally and through emissaries kept in contact with Nasser as he developed his foreign policy. He was surprised therefore when he was charged with having moved clandestinely. He maintained that there was no difference between Egypt's coming to terms with Britain on the Suez base and Iraq's joining the Baghdad Pact. Both actions were taken in the interests of defense and both with non-Arab states. Nuri interpreted every act of the government of Egypt as an act of Nasser himself. When the Egyptian Ambassador in Baghdad was called home on consultation, Nuri would say: "Nasser called him to report on me." When Egypt recognized Red China, Nuri characterized it as "one more move by Nasser in his campaign of blackmail against the free world."

By the end of 1956 Nuri had had enough of the vicious attacks made on him by Cairo and Damascus radios in protest against the Baghdad Pact. It was on December 25 of that year that he said to us at the Embassy that only the Soviets were benefiting from "Nasser's campaign of interference in the internal affairs of Iraq." The need to call a halt was urgent. "We are ready to shake hands and place our relations on a basis of co-operation." He made definite mention of the need for a "co-operative solution" of the Palestine question and the need for co-operation in the economic field, but he could not be made to say how the two countries were to proceed. He said he was sending his close friend Tawfiq Suweidi to see the Egyptian Ambassador. If Nasser's reaction to his offer for a new start were favorable, he would consider meeting him for discussions. He recognized that Nasser was "the key to normal relations with other Arab states."

Whether these thoughts of Nuri's ever reached Nasser, I do not know. Unfortunately, the attacks on Nuri continued and relations with Egypt remained critically strained. When Cairo and Damascus formalized their co-operative pressure on Nuri through the UAR, thus making Nasser a next door neighbor, Iraq countered with the AU, and the line of division was firmly drawn.

Nuri invariably referred to the prestige Nasser enjoyed among Arabs, when discussing the subject of Palestine. If Nasser would only capitalize on his position in the Arab world and take the initiative in trying to find a solution for the problem, Nuri said he would support him. During a talk I had with him on January 15, 1956, Nuri remarked that the unsettled conditions in the region pointed up more than ever "the need to settle the Palestine problem." He continued to hope that Nasser would take the lead toward this end. He claimed that he had himself told Nasser earlier that Iraq was ready at any time to fall in line with a settlement on the basis of the 1947 U.N. resolution. Later that year, in August, Nuri again mentioned Nasser to me in connection with Palestine. He had always placed his hopes on Nasser to bring about an amelioration in Arab-Israeli relations. In fact, shortly after Mr. Dulles had announced his proposals on August 26 the year before,[4] for a settlement in the Arab-Israel zone, he had advised Nasser through the Egyptian Ambassador in Baghdad, the Iraqi Ambassador in Cairo, and through British channels that any step that he took toward finding a solution would have Iraq's support. He received no reply however. Nasser did publicly give his blessing to Eden's statement of November, 1955, on Israel. Then, unfortunately, matters took a discouraging turn. Arms and economic deals with the Communists followed. The trend toward closer relations with Moscow culminated in the nationalization of the Suez Canal, and all hope of utilizing Nasser's prestige among Arabs to ease relations with Palestine faded.

Nasser's decision to purchase arms from the Soviet bloc shook Nuri badly. On October 7, 1955, he called on me at the Embassy to tell me about a talk his foreign minister, Bashayan, had just had with Nasser in Cairo. Nuri reported Nasser took the position that he had no choice but to turn to the Soviets. Egypt's dollar resources were too limited to permit buying arms in the United States. When asked whether he was not disturbed about the presence of Soviet technicians in his country, Nasser did not reply directly, but said they would be kept to a minimum. If a settlement on the Palestine problem could

[4] Speech by Secretary Dulles delivered August 26, 1955, before the Council on Foreign Relations, New York.

be reached, he would not expand the arms agreement, but with conditions as they were, he could not retreat from it either. Nuri went on to comment on Nasser's statements: "So long as Ben-Gurion keeps giving Egypt one blow after another to intimidate her with a show of his strength, Egypt must arm herself and arm well." For Egypt to arm herself effectively, he continued, was all to the good, but where she got the arms was a matter of great importance. Inter-area responsibilities also had to be weighed. The long view was essential. A Communist hold, even if only slight at first, as under this agreement, in the long run threatened not only the security of Egypt, but of Egypt's neighbors as well. He wished there could be free area-wide exchanges on that issue.

By July, 1956, according to a report brought back to Baghdad from Egypt by the Iraqi military delegation that had gone there to attend the Evacuation Day ceremonies, the nature and quantity of Soviet military equipment on display were very impressive. Nuri's apprehensions increased. Yet, as the Suez crisis sharpened during the months that followed and I saw Nuri almost daily, he never once even intimated that military force should be used against Nasser. When the British, French, and Israelis launched their attack in October and November, Nuri, despite his years of feuding with Nasser, reacted with shock and sympathy, like every other true Arab nationalist.

SYRIA

In the opening paragraphs of this chapter I called attention to Nuri's proposals for Arab unity, "The Fertile Crescent Plan," and the key position of Syria in his plan for unification. Between 1942, when the Blue Book was written, and 1954, lively discussions and debates on the plan had taken place, but nothing had been accomplished toward making it a reality. From 1954 to 1958, Nuri made clear a number of times that he had not abandoned his ideal of ultimate Arab unity but because of so many pressing problems, the plan had to be held in abeyance.

Early in 1955, the moderate government of Faris al-Khouri in Syria fell. A left-wing group, under the twin Assali-Azm leadership, emerged as the successor government. With a leftist trend in both official civilian and army circles in evidence, the country drew closer to Egypt. Nuri told me that the president, Atasi, viewed this with considerable concern and he, himself, during these early months of 1955, frequently expressed deep concern over the turn of events in Syria. The hope of ultimate union with Syria was not to be abandoned. To press it under circumstances then existing in Syria, would only cause embarrassment to Iraq's friends there. This he would avoid, and he had assured them accordingly. While he was prepared to keep Iraq temporarily from being injected into the Syrian scene, he did not want Syria "harmed" either by Turks or Israelis. He wished for assurances that these two neighbors of Syria would not take advantage of the unsettled political situation there.

There was another obvious reason for putting aside the Fertile Crescent plan for some time, although Nuri never spelled it out in his talks with me: this was the buildup of the Baghdad Pact. For Iraq to do her part in establishing the Northern Tier defense system and at the same time concentrate on Syria, was beyond her capabilities. Something had to be put aside, and close as union with Syria was to his heart, Nuri seems to have decided that it would have to be tabled in favor of the bigger issue of regional defense.

Until the autumn of 1955, Nuri's references to Syria were confined for the most part to charges of French, Egyptian, and Saudi intrigue. He complained and he worried. He did not mention intervention by Iraq, directly or indirectly, militarily or otherwise during that period. Syria needed political stability to prevent a possible Communist takeover. She needed economic assistance, and this Iraq could give. Business interests in

Syria wanted closer relations with Iraq, but France, Egypt and Saudi Arabia were opposed to this. Of the three, France was most at fault for the unsettled state of affairs. France was stirring up officers in the Syrian army against Iraq, and France was sparking the opposition to Iraq among Egyptian and Saudi government officials. If France stopped intriguing, the situation would become calm. Having assigned the role of major villain to France one day, did not stop Nuri from concentrating on Saudi Arabia the next. "Ninety per cent of the trouble in Syria is due to Saudi money," he would say. If revenues and credits to Saudi Arabia were frozen for six months the situation could be stabilized. Why could not Aramco see this? If the situation were not stabilized soon, communism would prevail and Aramco stood eventually to lose all.

That was the way Nuri discussed Syria with me from early February until early October, 1955. Then his thoughts turned more and more to ways and means of intervening. This change coincided with the news that arms from the Soviet bloc had begun flowing first into Egypt, and then into Syria as well.

It was on October 4, 1955, that Nuri mentioned to me the arrival of Soviet arms in Egypt. This, he said, meant that Egypt and Saudi Arabia were getting set to strangle Iraq through the Communists in Syria. The future of Iraq was at stake. He wanted a free hand. He would first talk with Syrian friends of his, urging them to "rid" the country of the Communists. But to approach them without the "backing" of the United States and the United Kingdom was "useless." He could talk effectively only if he knew he had this backing. He would also have to have a "guarantee" that while conducting his talks, the United States and Britain would "restrain" Israel.

When Nuri had finished outlining what he thought should be the first step in a plan to meet the increasing instability in Syria, I asked him if he was thinking at all in terms of military action. He did not answer me categorically. What he said was that there were other ways than that for bringing about a "change." One thing he could say definitely: Whatever the action, he would guarantee the independence of Syria. Whatever form of government, or form of association with Iraq, the people of Syria wanted, would be acceptable to him. To determine the wishes of the people of Syria, a plebiscite might be necessary, either under the auspices of the United States and United Kingdom, or of some international agency. One thing was certain: Communism in Syria had to be "squelched and squelched now." Then, by way of added assurance, he told of an appeal that had come from Syria in 1951 when he was prime minister. Israeli planes had bombed Syrian towns near the border. The government of Syria feared that Damascus itself would be next. He was asked to dispatch some interceptor planes to help if necessary. This he did. The British Ambassador in Baghdad was very disturbed about his action, but he assured the Ambassador that when quiet had been restored the planes would be called home, and he kept his word.

We next talked about Syria in connection with a report that Syria was about to recognize Red China. I noted his comments on that occasion mainly because they revealed his deep feeling of isolation at the time from his Arab brothers. In mentioning the report to him, I asked whether through concerted Arab action recognition could be forestalled. He replied that neither Egypt nor Saudi Arabia would be interested in blocking recognition and that the existing government of Lebanon was too weak to make any "headway" with the Syrians. Then, dejectedly, he dismissed the subject with these words: "That leaves me and what I can do alone."

On October 15 I was told by the Foreign Office that it had received a report that Czech arms were beginning to arrive in Syria. When I saw Nuri two days later he expressed great concern over this latest report of growing Communist influence in Syria. "But I do not want to invade Syria or force any particular kind of association with Iraq on Syria," he said, and added, "If Iraqi military help, or some kind of association with Iraq is wanted, then that is for the Syrians to decide." The first essential, however, if he was to accomplish anything was "to freeze Saudi credits." This time he added Turkey to Israel in the guarantee he wanted of noninterference while he was "working with the Syrians."

Nuri's concern over Syria continued to the day of his death. But his ideas on what should be done, when action should be taken, and how vigorously Iraq should move varied from month to month, keeping pace with his changing moods. With a temperament as mercurial as his, the moods changed frequently and sharply.

Early 1956 found Nuri in a "wait and see" mood. He viewed Syria as pessimistically as ever, but by then he had come to feel that the situation would have to deteriorate further before any useful action could be undertaken. Populist and Nationalist leaders who had been considered pro-Iraqi, appeared still not to be overly disturbed by the trend. "Unreliable," he called them, and this in spite of the fact that they had been "subsidized" for years by Iraq. They turned out to be "two-faced" when offered bigger bribes by the Saudis. Now there was nothing to do but mark time until they saw the error of their ways. But by September, 1956, he had turned activist once again. On September 15 I found him very agitated by reports that Moscow was stepping up its plan to infiltrate officers and men into the Syrian army for training Syrians in the use and maintenance of tanks and planes. They were appearing on the scene ostensibly for these purposes, but he was convinced they were being placed there to take an active part in any hostilities that might break out. Moscow, it appeared to him, was shifting the base from which to direct possible military operations, from Egypt to Syria. It looked now as though a "solution" could only come from the "outside" and it should come soon. That was his thinking at the turn of the year and well into 1957. On February 13 he put it bluntly to me. If the green light were given him by us and the British he could "clean up" the situation quickly and effectively. "This would not be aggression for we are all brothers. We Iraqis would simply be liberating friendly and responsible elements in Syria." By September, he had come full circle again. He became cautious. Any form of precipitate action affecting Syria must be avoided. Instead, every possible effort should be made to determine whether there were not available within Syria elements through whom change for the better might be brought about. That mood of Nuri's persisted until the end of the year. With the coming of 1958 two events took place in quick succession which had the effect of neutralizing temporarily the relations between Egypt and Syria on the one hand, and Iraq on the other. In both camps there was preoccupation for a time with problems nearer home. The two events causing this were the formation of the UAR and the AU as a counterweight. Nuri's Fertile Crescent plan passed from mere abeyance into the deep freeze.

LEBANON

Lebanon never figured as prominently in my talks with Nuri as Syria. Beginning with the spring of 1958, however, he mentioned Lebanon more and more frequently.

With the formation early in 1958 of the UAR, leftists' pressures and even infiltrations from Syria into Lebanon took on serious proportions. Pressures sharpened steadily until by midsummer not only Lebanon's government, but Lebanon's independence, seemed threatened. Nuri watched the trend with growing concern. Chaos in Lebanon would create threatening repercussions not only in Iraq but also in Jordan, Iraq's partner in the AU.

On May 21 Nuri asked to see me urgently. Continuing disorders in Lebanon, he said, disturbed him greatly. The agitation appeared to him as the prelude to armed intervention. Lack of air coverage to meet such an eventuality added to his anxiety. He knew we had promised both Lebanon and Jordan some jets. He hoped we would step-up delivery. That might discourage action against Lebanon, and it certainly would bolster morale in Jordan. It looked, too, as though President Chamoun was losing out to General Chehab. He knew Chamoun well and trusted him. If Chamoun could not hold the line, he was afraid Lebanon would fall to Nasser. Were Chamoun to appeal to the Security Council, he could count on the support of the AU. Should it come to United States and British military intervention, the AU would also support that, provided the French did not participate.

The next talk I had with Nuri about Lebanon was on June 7. "Volunteers," Nuri claimed, were going into Lebanon from Syria in numbers. The sole hope now of stopping the drift was Chehab. If he failed to act firmly at once, disintegration would set in so fast that all hope of retrieving the situation would disappear.

On June 16, Nuri returned to the subject of military intervention in Lebanon. This time he said that if the government of Lebanon were to request "western military assistance," his government would not hesitate to back such a request. During my last talk with Nuri on Lebanon on July 12, he spoke frankly. He was unhappy about our failure to adopt a more positive line of action on Lebanon. Even at this late date he felt that if Chamoun were "actively" supported by friendly governments he would change his mind and stand for re-election. Any action that Iraq might take would be for the sole purpose of maintaining the independence of Lebanon. Iraqi military action on behalf of Lebanon would, he was convinced, have strong popular support. "But Iraq cannot act alone because of the lack of adequate air coverage." If only he knew what the United States contemplated doing, he could make his own plans. Would there be intervention? he asked. I had to tell him that I did not know. He looked very dejected and preoccupied as I left him.

Three days later, on the afternoon of July 15, as I was returning from my first call on Qasim, and the mob was dragging Nuri's body through the streets, our marines landed in Lebanon.

SUMMARY

Nuri was fond of saying: "My first responsibility is to Iraq." In working for Iraq, however, he never forgot the interests of the Arab nation as a whole. His vision of Arab unity was clearly set down in the Blue Book. He dreamed of the Fertile Crescent; that is, the restoration of historic Syria, to the end of his life. He had to be satisfied with a far more restricted union, the AU, but in building it he did leave the door open for other Arab states to join. He never bullied or threatened his smallest and richest neighbor, Kuwait, but instead, with respect for traditional Arab desert hospitality, proffered her what she needed most, water, and did so unconditionally, much as he wanted and needed Kuwait in the AU. He was instrumental in bringing Iraq much closer to her big neighbor, Saudi Arabia. Bitter as were the personal relations between him and Nasser, he recognized and respected Egypt's historic role in the Arab world, and when Egypt came under foreign attack he immediately reacted like every true Arab nationalist. He had a genuine fear of communism and was as deeply disturbed about its getting a foothold in Syria and Lebanon, as in his own Iraq. He stood ready to help them resist its inroads, on their terms, without thought of aggrandizement for Iraq. His record as an Arab nationalist is a consistent one and will, I am sure, stand the test of time.

VIII

NURI ON ISRAEL

Nuri's public statements on Israel differed sharply from what he had to say in private. His public statements, like those of all Arab nationalists, were bitter and uncompromising. In private, he discussed Israel calmly, reasonably, and with moderation. Public and private statements did, however, reveal his constant preoccupation with Zionism.

Zionism was mentioned in his first public statement after he resumed office in 1954. It may be remembered that he urged increased co-operation between Arab states, "To repel the Zionist menace."

Some months later during the exchanges with Prime Minister Menderes in Istanbul which led eventually to the Baghdad Pact, Zionism was uppermost in his mind. Zionism, he maintained, opposed any *rapprochement* between Turkey and the Arab states. In this it was no different from communism. It was necessary therefore equally to combat Zionist and Communist propaganda.

Although the Pact of Mutual Co-operation between Iraq and Turkey did not specifically mention Israel or Zionism, Nuri succeeded in dealing with both indirectly, and thus in keeping faith, as he thought, with his Arab brethren. The pact itself closed the door to the adherence of any state not recognized by both Iraq and Turkey. To assist Nuri further there were letters exchanged by him and Menderes at the time of the signing. Nuri, in his letter, stated that it was the understanding of the parties that the pact enabled them to co-operate in resisting aggression against either and that they would, moreover, co-operate in making the United Nations resolutions on Palestine effective. Menderes stated that his government agreed with what Nuri had to say.

A good example of how Nuri talked in public about Israel appears in his speech to the nation on December 16, 1956. This was made shortly after Jordan had requested Iraq to withdraw her troops from Jordan where they had gone, on request, during the height of the Suez crisis. Iraq complied but Nuri had this to say on the withdrawal: "We were convinced the crisis had not passed and that the danger would never be removed unless Israel herself were uprooted."

It should be said here that in private Nuri's observations on Israel usually were based on the premise that he accepted the permanency of the state of Israel. There was never any talk of "uprooting."

There is one further instance of Nuri's public pronouncements on Israel that bears mentioning. That was in connection with his venture into the field of American journalism. In a conversation on June 24, 1957, Nuri mentioned an article he had written for *Life* magazine. He had finished it some weeks before and *Life's* delay in publishing it worried him. Could it be, he asked, that it was being withheld in deference to "New York Zionists?" He had hoped to see it in print by now. If publication were put off much longer, its effectiveness would be dulled. Would I please get in touch with Mr. Dulles and see if he could expedite publication.

I called the State Department's attention to Nuri's article and his concern over its nonappearance. I do not know whether the department did anything about it, but if the article was published in Nuri's lifetime, I missed it. More than

a year after Nuri had mentioned it to me and about a month
after his death, *Life International,* in its issue of August 18,
1958, published what it termed "The Last Testament of Iraqi
Premier." The piece resembled very much the article Nuri
had mentioned to me back in June, 1957.

In the "Testament," brief as it was, Nuri touched critically
on many things; the role the United States played in the Suez
crisis, the Eisenhower Doctrine, the 1947 United Nations resolution on partition, Nasser, and the after-effects of the 1956
American intervention in the Middle East. It is recommended
reading for anyone interested in the Iraq of Nuri's day.

Two passages from the "Testament" are typical of Nuri's
public statements on Israel. For one thing, Nuri states, rather
inelegantly, that he understands Americans have had a "bellyfull" of Arab intransigence on Israel. Arab leaders have had
a "bellyfull" too, he adds, of the blindness of Americans to
the problem of Israel.

The second passage has to do with the twin "tyrannies" that
preoccupied Nuri for so long, Israel and communism. To
Arabs generally, he writes, Israel is the greater, immediate
threat.

Nuri's private comments to me give a truer picture of what
he thought about Israel than do his public statements.

Understandably, Israel came up frequently in our talks,
sometimes by itself and sometimes in connection with other
problems. Much of what he said was repetitious. What follows
now is a synthesis of the more extended and detailed observations he made to me over the years.

The United Nations resolution of 1947 on partition was
the starting point of Nuri's hopes for building a working
relationship with Israel. When Secretary Dulles visited Baghdad in 1953 he had told Dulles that he wanted a peaceful
settlement through negotiations on the basis of this resolution.
He did not ask for literal acceptance of the resolution, he
would explain, but acceptance only as a basis for negotiations,
directly between Israel and the Arab states, or through a third

party. Acceptance of the resolution as a basis for negotiations, even before any discussions could get under way, would go far to relieve tensions, he felt. There was room for compromise. He recognized Israel's right to the territory allotted her under the resolution. Claims to more, however, were not legitimate, and Israel should be prepared to bargain over the disposition of the remaining areas. Besides a compromise settlement on territory there was needed provision for the return of the refugees. He felt that if only the right of these "dispossessed" to return were formally recognized by Israel, the practical effect would be almost nil. Few, if any, refugees would actually take advantage of this and return to their homes. But with this formal recognition of the legal right of refugees to return, there should also be material compensation by Israel for the losses suffered by the refugees. This too would be subject to negotiations, again either directly or through a third party. Once an agreement had been reached in principle, and this I consider most significant, he would favor lifting the economic boycott. The existence of the State of Israel was a fact that had to be accepted. If, however, that state was to endure, Arab-Israeli tension had to be relieved. With the lifting of the economic boycott, both parties were bound to profit. But even though Jews and Arabs had lived together for thousands of years and he had no quarrel with them on religious grounds, he was afraid that the way to better relations was a long and difficult one. The root of the discord was Zionism, an alien element intruding itself into the local scene. Communism and Zionism had this in common: Just as every Communist, regardless of where he lived, owed first allegiance to Moscow, so every Zionist, regardless of where he lived, owed first allegiance to Israel. That intrusion and interference greatly complicated any search for an Arab-Israeli settlement. Even so, he would repeat, he stood ready to begin any time to seek a settlement, using the 1947 U.N. resolution as a basis for exploration and discussion.

When asked why he did not take the initiative in trying to

bring about talks on this basis, Nuri would reply that if he were to do so he would immediately be pilloried by those Arab leaders who were already accusing him of having sold his Arab birthright to the West.

The years passed with Nuri, a moderate among Arab statesmen so far as Israel was concerned, giving his real thoughts only privately on how the bitter Arab-Israeli relations might be tempered. So far as I know no effort was made to activate his moderate views. The field was left to the extremists, and the years were wasted. This is all the more tragic because Nuri's thoughts on the problem, and those expressed by Secretary Dulles in his speech of August 26, 1955, before the Council on Foreign Relations,[1] had much in common. Both started with the assumption that the Israeli state is here to stay. Neither felt the refugee and boundary problems were insoluble. Both stressed the need for co-operation in the economic field between the two groups if they were to enjoy peace and stability in the years ahead.

[1] Text in *Department of State Bulletin*, Vol. 33, September 5, 1955, pp. 378–80.

IX

THE BRITISH
IN IRAQ

Nuri's loyalty to the British was unwavering. Severely tested as it was by the British attack on Egypt in 1956, it survived even that. "How can I keep down anti-British feeling after what they have done?" were the despairing words with which he greeted me when I called on him on the morning of November 1, 1956. He was not able to stem the upsurge of anti-British feeling, but by keeping Britain out of the Baghdad Pact meetings for some months he gained time to ride out the storm. But it was a rough passage. With the aid of the police he could cope with mob and student demonstrations. It was more difficult to quiet dissension within his cabinet, where some members began sharply questioning his uncritical pro-British policy, and to deal with lower level officials who were now openly asking whether the time had not come to rid Iraq of its pro-British government. In the end, what saved Nuri was the unshaken backing of the King and the Crown Prince who, owing everything they had, position and substance, to the British, were not forgetful in this time of crisis.

172

But after Nuri had had the Suez experience with the British, he did become at times critical of them in my presence.

Nuri's loyalty to the British was not based on any material rewards. He lived simply and modestly all his life, and I do not think he possessed much more than his home in Baghdad at the time of his death. His loyalty to the British derived from their help and backing when as a young lieutenant he broke with his Turkish masters and openly espoused the cause of Arab liberation. He found congenial too, as he grew older, the pragmatic British way of doing things.

His loyalty was not founded only on what the British had done for him personally. It went beyond that to recognition of what the British had done for his country. He never lost sight of the fact that British arms and lives had opened the way for the eventual independence of Iraq. I say eventual independence because it did not come in a day but in stages, and to many Iraqis it seemed to be a long time coming. After it became a fact, there were complaints that the British, nevertheless, had tried desperately to hold on and preserve the old, privileged position of mandatory power. That put a constant strain on Nuri's loyalty.

It was not uncommon in my day in Iraq to hear Iraqis complain that the British Ambassador bore himself more like a high commissioner of the time of the mandate, than like an ambassador accredited to a sovereign state. Hard though it was for the public to substantiate, the accusation was made and widely believed that the Ambassador interfered in internal matters through pressures on the King, the Crown Prince, and Nuri, and this cost Nuri something in public esteem. It was commonly felt, too, in business circles, that the British used their entrenched position to stifle competition and to promote British trade. These complaints came from Iraqi businessmen acting as agents for foreign firms other than British, and from foreigners, other than British, conducting their own businesses in the country. Here the facts are easier to find than in the field of politics. The British presence in the country was of long standing. It was natural for them to take every possible advantage of what was left of the privileged status they had enjoyed as a mandatory power. Even after this privileged position had been watered down by treaty British control in certain fields continued. This was true in the field of transportation. During the period I am writing about, the British still had a controlling voice in the Baghdad bus system, the Iraqi State Railways, the port of Basra, and Iraqi Airways. There were also a number of British subjects scattered throughout the Iraqi government ministries in various advisory positions. Could anyone doubt that the loyal British would use the opportunities presented them by their strong position in Iraq to promote British commercial interests? Hardly. Ill-concealed zeal displayed in the economic field also, did not make Nuri's lot easier.

I personally was made to feel this British zeal to maintain the old position of supremacy in ways that helped me better to appreciate the strain such behavior put on Nuri's loyalty. Three experiences illuminated this British tendency. They were the British reaction to the presence of many American technicians in the country, the British attempts to dominate the Centurion tank ceremonies of January, 1956, and British interference in blocking later in the year the renewal of the contract of Wesley Nelson, American member of the Development Board.

The British in Iraq, both officials and those in private capacity, were none too happy, to put it mildly, about the presence in their midst of American technicians. Their attitude, unpleasant but understandable, was that here was an intrusion of amateurs into a special British preserve where only British expertise could qualify. This attitude, in contrast to how the Iraqi public looked toward the presence of American technicians, is well substantiated by the Nelson case which will be dealt with later.

It was shortly before the November, 1955, inaugural meeting of the Baghdad Pact, that we, along with the British, made a spectacular gesture in appreciation of Nuri's stand with the free world. We gave Iraq ten Mark VII Centurion tanks, while the British gave two. The ten we were giving were purchased from the British through the off-shore procurement plan.

No sooner had word reached Baghdad about the tanks than we learned that the British Embassy wished to make of this gift to Iraq "a grand show." What we did not immediately grasp was that what was meant was a "British show."

The first thing we tried to do was work out with the British and the Iraqis the wording and timing of a press release. The British suggested this wording be included in the announcement: "Ten of these tanks are supplied under the American aid program and two are a gift from the British Government." In order that the Iraqi public would understand that anything coming to Iraq under the aid program was a gift, we suggested this wording: "The twelve are without cost to the Government of Iraq." This latter wording was agreed upon by all three parties. It was also agreed by all three that the announcement would be made the week of October 30. But an unexplained "leak" occurred, and on Sunday, October 24, the Baghdad press carried the announcement, and the wording was the wording of the British: "Ten of these tanks are supplied under the American aid program and two are a gift from the British Government."

The two Embassies next arranged for cameramen to take shots of the unloading of these gifts, so that there could be adequate publicity for this joint venture to help Iraq, and through Iraq, Nuri. When the ship, loaded at a British port, arrived in Basra the cameras were in place waiting for the unloading to begin. Hatches were opened and the cranes began creaking. Up came two Centurions blazoned with huge lettering, "Gifts from Her Majesty." The cameras went to work. After that shot the cameras remained poised for the remaining ten, the gift from the United States, to be hoisted and placed on the docks. They remained poised with nothing to do for the rest of the day. For some reason or other the

American gifts had been stowed way down in the hold and did not see daylight until the next day, long after all Iraq had been alerted to Her Majesty's generosity.

But there was still more in store for us at the Embassy.

January 3, 1956, was the date fixed for the formal transfer of the tanks to the Iraqis at the Mu'askar al-Rashid Camp in Baghdad. I had agreed with the British Ambassador that we would co-ordinate our remarks for the ceremony. "Co-ordinate" it turned out meant to the British in Baghdad something quite different from what it meant to the Americans. A few days before the transfer ceremony was to take place, an official of the British Embassy called at our Embassy and left the text of the speech which it was suggested I read at the ceremony. Right then I decided to expand considerably the remarks I had intended to make, using the occasion publicly to put in perspective the nature and extent of both our economic and military aid.

After a word of praise for what Iraqis were doing themselves in the way of developing their country economically and building up its defenses, I said that we were glad to be able to play a role in these essential, interrelated programs. Through the Technical Assistance Program concluded in April, 1951, between the United States and Iraq we would have spent in Iraq by July of that year ID3,600,000, or about ten million dollars. We were providing, too, the services of over one hundred American technicians. Under the Mutual Defense Assistance Understanding between our two countries we had furnished Iraq to date with over seven hundred motor transport vehicles, artillery and rocket ammunition, eighty-five pieces of artillery and recoilless rifles, and substantial amounts of signal communications and engineering equipment. This however was not a complete list of the items we had already given Iraq, nor did it include the substantial amounts of equipment already financed by the United States but yet to be delivered. The ten Centurion tanks and thirty Ferret scout-cars then on display were only a part of the latest deliveries.

"This American aid," I concluded, "economic and military, is in recognition of the praiseworthy initiative shown by this historically old but independently young, vigorous country." Nuri, in responding, said this in part:

> The funds to which the American Ambassador has alluded and which have been spent under technical assistance call for our appreciation and gratitude. They have been spent in fields from which we expect all good for this country.
>
> It gives me pleasure too to hear the American Ambassador cite in his speech the capability and efficiency of the Iraqi army and, as I believe, my Iraqi brethren who are present here share this sentiment with me. They may be assured that we will maintain its strength and that in its training and morale building we will do our utmost to bring it to perfection. It is my firm hope that the arming program on which we have agreed with the United States will be implemented on schedule, with military equipment arriving on time—as did this first shipment of tanks we are now taking over and which ranks among the most important equipment delivered so far.

Nuri seldom missed an opportunity to advance Iraq's interests. When he was given something he was grateful, but made it clear that more was needed. He was always on the alert to use every opportunity to advance his cause, even if only a little. Generous as was his response to me there at al-Rashid Camp, he managed to insert a reminder of his repeated complaints that we were too slow in our arms deliveries. He was glad to get the tanks, as he showed, but at the same time he hoped that the rest of the program would be "implemented on schedule."

In Nuri's day, it had been the custom to have on the Development Board one English and one American engineering expert. They were not representatives of their respective governments, but specialists serving the board under individual contracts with the government of Iraq. The two Americans who served in that capacity during my time in Iraq, always scrupulously respected this relationship. They did not look to the Embassy for instructions, nor did the Embassy bring pressure to bear on them at any time to follow a particular course. They were not on the board just in an advisory capacity. They had voting powers as well, and an equal voice with their Iraqi colleagues on the board. Because of their contractual relationship with the government of Iraq, a purely personal one, and the unique voting power they enjoyed, it seemed to us at the Embassy essential that they have at all times complete freedom of action.

When I arrived in Baghdad in 1954 Wesley Nelson was the American member of the board. His contract was due to expire in 1956. Nelson's competency as an engineer was recognized at home and abroad. In Iraq he was highly respected, in and outside government circles, for the service he had rendered Iraq. Nuri was one of his greatest admirers. In view of Nelson's record and popularity in Iraq, and particularly his standing with Nuri, I had been led to believe that his contract would be renewed.

On December 21, 1955, the British Ambassador called on me at the Embassy. During our talk it soon developed that the Ambassador did not want a renewal of Nelson's contract. His replacement, by another American of course, would in his view make for smoother operations of the board. It also developed that the British member of the board had been to see him and had asked guidance. Relations between him and Nelson, it seemed, had become strained.

To all this, I replied as follows: I respected Nelson's position on the board. He was serving under a personal contract with the government of Iraq. He had always, with my encouragement, kept aloof from the Embassy so as not to give the appearance that the Embassy was in any way trying to influence him. I would not be drawn into a position now where I would have to arbitrate between him and the British member. In the last analysis their relationship was a matter for the government of Iraq to settle, and the government should have a free hand. Nelson enjoyed a fine reputation in Iraq. His reputation in the States was of the highest too. Furthermore, I did not see why the British member of the board had to go to the British Embassy with his grievances and seek guidance. He was free to express his views to the board at any time. I knew he had done this when the question of renewing the contract of an American company, which he opposed, had come up. He had been given a full hearing before the board's vote was taken, which incidentally had been in favor of the American company. Let's leave this, I urged, to Nelson, the British member of the board, and the government of Iraq. On that note we parted.

About a month later, I received a note from the Iraqi Foreign Office which surprised me for two reasons. It was written in English, the first and only communication I ever received from the Iraqi Foreign Office that was not in Arabic. Equally surprising to me was its content. In impeccable English I was informed that Nelson's contract would not be renewed. In the future foreign members of the board were not to serve more than four years. A replacement for Nelson was requested.

When word got around that Nelson's contract had not been renewed there was considerable disappointment, apprehension, and resentment. Six former prime ministers called on Nuri in a group to protest the nonrenewal of the contract on the ground that Iraq had further need of Nelson's services, and also to protest the "interference" of the British in an internal matter. A number of highly placed Iraqi government officials and Iraqis prominent in business and academic circles called on me to express disappointment of the government's decision and resentment against the British. Typical of the sentiments expressed to me were those of a former Iraqi colleague of Nelson's on the Development Board, then holding a position with a semigovernment agency. He found British "interference" in this case very disturbing, as he did British "pretensions" to play a major role in Iraq. Britain in his view lacked both the popular support for this, and the resources. It was a pity, he said, that the United States was content with the role of "silent partner" to the British. He wished we would "step out in front."

A diplomatic colleague of mine, whose country had supplied a number of technicians to help with Development Board projects, expressed uneasiness about his countrymen's future.

An American, whose firm had obtained a building contract from the board, feared the consequences of Nelson's departure. In his experience with the board he never detected any predisposition on Nelson's part to favor American firms. What he observed was a completely objective interest in the Development Program. Nelson's presence there gave the assurance, he felt, that the board would maintain high ethical and economic standards.

That was the reaction in Baghdad. In Washington the reaction was diplomatically correct. The decision against renewing Nelson's contract was not questioned.

I was sharply criticized at the time by both Americans in Iraq and Iraqi admirers of Nelson for not having protested to the government of Iraq against the way it had acted. But my hands were tied. The nature of the instructions I received from the State Department on the case made any protest impossible.

Months went by before Washington found the replacement for Nelson in the person of Clifford Wilson, previously head of our International Co-operation Administration (ICA) in India. In the interim, Nuri had become more and more impatient. On June 9, 1956, he called on me at the Embassy to discuss the problem. He needed an expert badly, he pleaded, "with the same qualifications Nelson had." I observed that in Nelson Iraq had had one of our most competent irrigation and reclamation experts and that it might have been best if his contract had simply been renewed. Clearly embarrassed, Nuri said nothing for a moment or two. Then he found an answer: "No," he said lamely, "Nelson put in four strenuous years. That's long enough for anyone on such a trying job."

The mob let loose by the July 14, 1958 coup had three objectives: The Palace, Nuri's home, and the British Embassy. The Palace was pillaged and burned, and the King and the Crown Prince killed. Nuri's home was pillaged and burned, and he was killed. The British Embassy was pillaged and partially burned, the Controller of the Household killed, and the British Ambassador and his wife were detained on the Embassy grounds for hours by an armed guard before being taken to the Baghdad Hotel for temporary residence.

On the day of these tragic events, the British Iraq *Times* of Baghdad suspended publication. It resumed publication on July 26. In that issue it had this to say editorially:

> Foreigners resident in Iraq must express to the government and people of Iraq the fullest gratitude of all those from other countries for the courteous and kindly treatment they have received in the past ten days.
>
> The care taken of foreigners has been in the best traditions of Arab hospitality, marked with that sense of responsibility for the stranger within the gate which is recognized and admired the world over.

And so, back to business as usual.

X

THE AMERICANS
IN IRAQ

The United States does not play a decisive role in Iraq, economically or politically. On January 1, 1957, the total United States capital investment in the country was only about $60,000,000, $48,000,000 of which was in petroleum operations. The rest was in plant and equipment owned by American contractors operating in the country. Iraqis from all walks of life appealed eloquently to us, particularly after Suez, to make our presence felt politically in the country. We held aloof in deference to the once mandatory power, the United Kingdom. The modest, self-effacing role we chose was nothing compared with the one we might have played, for we enjoyed a country-wide reservoir of goodwill. There were varied sources of this, three of which were especially effective. These were Baghdad College, the American University of Beirut, and the centers in the United States where Iraqis, usually graduates from one or both of these schools, went for advanced studies.

At the twenty-third annual commencement of Baghdad College held on June 15, 1958, the principal, Reverend Robert J.

Sullivan, delivered an especially appropriate address in which he noted the challenges and problems of the space age and asserted that their solutions, whatever the contribution of science, must ultimately be found in man's human and moral qualities. While pursuing survival, man must keep in mind the reasons for his desire to survive. The times, to be sure, called for good scientists, but also for better men.

Father Sullivan's words are cited because they are indicative of the positive and enlightened contribution American Jesuits have made to the educational system of Iraq and to the inspiration of sound moral and intellectual principles.

The American University in Beirut, founded and directed as its name implies by Americans, has also long contributed toward a better understanding of American ideals. Graduates of this university, like those of Baghdad College, are dispersed throughout Iraq and hold prominent positions in all fields. Many of these graduates go from the American University to do advanced work in schools in the United States. They can be, and often are, critical of us but they understand us at the same time and help immeasurably to make us better understood abroad.

Nuri's background and education were in sharp contrast to Baghdad College and the American University. Nevertheless, his understanding of us, our problems, and our way of life, was impressive. Although he had visited the United States only twice, and then briefly, he proved at all times to be a discerning and warm friend. Just before the 1956 Baghdad Pact Council meeting in Tehran Nuri said to me that he thought he understood our failure to join the pact better than other council members. He was fully aware of the domestic political considerations the President and the Secretary of State had to weigh when trying to decide whether we should join the pact. They revolved about Israel. As he saw it, we could not join the pact without at the same time yielding to pressures on the home front by giving Israel some kind of guarantee. That complicated the situation, and to raise two such issues at the same time—the Baghdad Pact and Israel—was not smart politics.

Having made this comment on the bearing that domestic political considerations have on foreign policy decisions, Nuri had a few general observations to make on our behavior in the international field. In the conduct of our foreign relations we were above all patient and reasonable. He was afraid that at times we carried these virtues too far. This line of conduct was not always understood. It blinded some countries to the depth of our determination to resist, and even fight, if pushed too far. The danger inherent in our habitually high-principled course was that some time we might delay action unduly.

In spite of the secondary role we chose for ourselves in Iraq, association with Nuri and his government was close and constant. The Baghdad Pact, our Military Assistance Understanding, and our Technical Aid Agreement contributed toward this end.

We encouraged Nuri to help create the Baghdad Pact and line Iraq up with it, and although we then shied away from joining ourselves we stayed on the scene, peripherally so to speak, as observers and members of committees. As such we became involved, day in and day out, in all the pact's discussions and planning.

When Nuri came to office in the summer of 1954 he found at hand and ready for his use the Military Assistance Understanding between our two countries. It had been effected by an exchange of notes in Baghdad on April 21, 1954, a few days before Fadhil Jamali resigned as prime minister. Nuri made full use of it in trying to build-up Iraq's military strength, and we used it to reward Nuri from time to time for his forthright stand with the free world.

There was another agreement Nuri was happy to find at hand when he assumed office in 1954. That was the agreement with us on technical co-operation. The basic agreement in this field had come into force in June, 1951. Nuri drew freely on it for the technical assistance he needed in carrying through his Development Program.

THE BAGHDAD PACT

We had two opportunities during the closing years of Nuri's life to take action that might have greatly strengthened his position and ours throughout the Middle East. The first opportunity offered us was to join the Baghdad Pact at the very start of its existence. We had found Nuri receptive to the Dulles Northern Tier concept and we encouraged him to help make it a reality through the Baghdad Pact. He fully expected, as did the other members of the pact, that we would be members from the beginning. Had we joined immediately, the reaction in Iraq, and in the other Arab states as well, would have been different. Nuri's position definitely would have been strengthened and, what is more, our intentions would have been made clear to Cairo and Moscow. As it was, we never did make our position clear. Instead, we added to the confusion by issuing statements several times a year, that while we were not prepared to join at that particular time, we did not rule out joining eventually. To compound the confusion we began joining the committees of the pact, one by one. By our day-to-day improvisations we weakened the pact and placed Nuri in a most unenviable position.

There is no simple, clear-cut answer to the question why we did not join the Baghdad Pact. I can only offer some explanations of my own on our baffling behavior. In the first place the Baghdad Pact materialized much quicker than any one in the State Department had anticipated. We gave encouragement one day to some ill-defined defense alignment, only to find the next day, before we had made up our minds on just what form the alignment should take, that a pact was in being. To catch our breath and gain time to think things through, we stalled by assuming the observer's role. What was originally only a temporary tactic, gradually became a permanent policy. I think some State Department officials honestly felt at first that eventually we would join. That, I believe, explains the department's repeated early announcements that we had constantly under review the question of joining, and why we let Menderes' statement that it could be assumed that United States adherence was only a matter of time, made at the close of the inaugural meeting of the council, stand without comment. What happened eventually to freeze us in the role of observer? I was told in the State Department when I raised that question that if we were to join, we would also have to have a pact with Israel, but the department simply did not have the stomach to face up to the debates in Congress that these issues would set off. I never understood why Israel needed a treaty with us to balance our membership in the Baghdad Pact. Our membership in the pact, in view of our consistent pro-Israeli policy, should have been sufficient guarantee to Israel that the pact would not be used to her detriment even though it had an Arab member. Moreover, if we did not join the Baghdad Pact because of Iraq's presence, why have we not joined CENTO which is free of any Arab association?

Could there still be another explanation? There might be.

I was told by a friend of mine in the State Department that Mr. Dulles, during one of his stays in the hospital not long before his death, prepared a memorandum on the Baghdad Pact. I never saw the memorandum, but according to my informant Mr. Dulles explained that what he had had in mind from the start was a purely indigenous organization for Northern Tier defense purposes, with backing, but not membership, by other interested powers. Adherence by the U.K. had fundamentally altered his original concept. Just how to align the U.S. then became the problem.

This clarification came rather late in the day. If, however, it is true, it throws some light on our fumbling and groping.

Failure to join the pact as a full member at its inception was the first opportunity we missed to strengthen a most valuable ally. We missed the second opportunity right after having successfully intervened, through the United Nations, in the Suez crisis of 1956. No sooner had our timely and determined action at the United Nations brought hostilities to a close, than a stream of callers came to the Embassy to see me. These were Iraqi business and professional men, and representatives of the academic world. There was a sprinkling of sheiks too. Some of these callers were then in public life, and some had previously been. They all had this in common: They had been following the Suez crisis closely and they hailed the prompt, determined stand we had taken, and they were grateful that, through us, aggression had been so quickly halted. They came, one by one, to express thanks to our government, and to make a plea. This, in essence, was the plea: "Having made your influence felt so decisively in the Middle East, you should keep on exerting it. A vacuum exists for the present. Fill it before it is too late. We trust you and would welcome your presence. An active, continuous role by you can assure stability and peace." Our prestige was for the moment extremely high in Iraq and beyond. It was clear that if we were to capitalize on it, we would have to act quickly.

We did react to the situation created by Suez, after a fashion. In time, the Eisenhower Doctrine was pronounced. Then, months later, the Richards mission, appointed as a result, arrived to follow through with more economic and military aid. Our responses, good enough in themselves, were however late and merely more of the same thing. They certainly failed to stir the imagination of the peoples of the area.

What more effective action could we have taken?

It was still not too late to join the Baghdad Pact. We had missed the first round, but here was the ideal, second chance. By that one single step, if taken promptly after Suez, we stood to gain much that we undertook to achieve in a drawn-out, round-about way. By joining the pact then, immediately, we

would have served notice on the world in the simplest, most
direct way open to us that we were going to continue playing
a decisive role; the plea of our friends in Iraq that we make
our presence felt more would have been answered; Nuri would
have been strengthened at home and abroad. Because of his
past close association with the British, he needed strengthening then more than ever. But still we held aloof.

Nuri, to the end of his life, worked hard and earnestly to
make the Baghdad Pact an effective instrument for the maintenance of peace and a bulwark against outside aggression in
the Middle East. To the end he maintained that only by full,
formal adherence of the United States, father of the pact,
could it be made to work fully. To the end he maintained that
only through U.S. adherence would Iraq's position within the
Arab world be above suspicion and his own position, within
and without Iraq, be made secure.

MILITARY ASSISTANCE UNDERSTANDING

The Military Assistance Understanding between the United
States and Iraq was reached through an exchange of notes.
The notes in turn were based on the Mutual Security Act
which authorizes military aid within certain limitations. When
sharp criticism of the understanding was voiced at Jamali's
trial in 1958, Jamali retorted that there was nothing sinister
about it. It was not secret and under its terms Iraq could
terminate it at any time. He added, however, that in his opinion it should have been submitted to Parliament for approval,
a formality that the prime ministers who had followed him
had overlooked.

Our military mission which administered the aid in Iraq
was a relatively small one. It consisted of about fifteen officers
and noncommissioned men. The head of the mission kept in
close touch with senior Iraqi army officers stationed in Baghdad, who worked on the army's needs. Early in the life of the

understanding the Iraqis prepared a two-phase plan, with details of the equipment they thought was needed. The ultimate objective was an all purpose force equipped to maintain internal order, to resist external aggression, and to help in regional defense efforts. During the first phase two existing divisions were to be brought up to full strength. During phase two a third division was to be fully equipped. Five years were allotted for accomplishing this. We never raised any objections to this plan. Our mission in Baghdad tried conscientiously to meet Iraq's requirements, and meet them expeditiously. But it was never entirely successful and there was continual disappointment in the Iraqi camp.

Our mission was handicapped in a number of ways. First of all, it had to work within an annual allocation of funds. In effect this ruled out any long-term planning on either side. Even after Congress had approved our annual budget, considerable time was consumed in allocating what had been appropriated among some fifty-odd countries receiving aid from us. The differences in the fiscal years between the two countries added to the uncertainty and made even more difficult any kind of systematic planning. Ours ran from July 1 to June 30. Iraq's from April 1 to March 31. This complicated every attempt to co-ordinate Iraqi needs, with what we were prepared to give.

Even so, we managed to supply Iraq with some impressive equipment for which Nuri was grateful, but which did not quiet his opponents. Opponents of his, both inside and outside Parliament, criticized him constantly for failure to obtain arms in more impressive quantities. Yet in April, 1957, during the Richards mission stay in Baghdad, Nuri told Richards that "fifty percent" of the success in keeping order had been due to the favorable impression made on the Iraqi people and army by the arms received from the United States.

The thirty-sixth anniversary of the founding of the Iraqi army fell on January 6, 1957. The evening before, Nuri broadcast to the nation. He told the public that the next day there would be on display at Rashid Camp some of the latest equipment received for Iraq's army. Among the arms to be seen were some that "none but American and some British units possess." He finished his talk on a note that was anything but bellicose. "We pray to God that we will not have to use them, and that peace and the guidance of wisdom will prevail instead of war." The next day at the display he plainly showed pride, particularly in the tanks and eight inch howitzers we had given Iraq.

Even so, Nuri too became impatient at times. This was especially so in the case of his repeated requests for better air coverage. He contended that Iraq was far from equipped to protect her northern oil fields, even temporarily, from possible air attacks from the Soviet Union. For this he estimated Iraq needed at least four squadrons of interception planes. He also maintained that should Iraq be called upon to come to the defense of her Arab neighbors, her army could not move with confidence beyond Iraq because it lacked adequate air coverage.

After years of this kind of pressure from Nuri for help in strengthening the Iraqi Air Force, I was finally able to tell him in May, 1958, that we were going to supply Iraq with some F86–F jets. First there were to be six, intended primarily for training purposes. Then more would come. This was good news that I had finally brought him, Nuri said. Then, true to his habit of never betraying too much enthusiasm when he got something, he added: "I am not familiar with that type of jet. I only hope it is a match for the MIG 17's."

But May passed and so did June and still there were no jets. On July 9, five days before the coup and six days before his death, he was still pleading for air coverage. Would we not, he begged on that day, please hurry the delivery of the jets.

The six jets intended for training purposes did arrive within the next few days, complete with training crew. For weeks after the coup, the crew waited for the sign to begin work.

When it became apparent that the nod might never be given, the crew returned home, and Qasim appropriated the jets.

July 14, 1958, marked the beginning of the end of the Military Assistance Understanding. It was only an hour after the attacks were made on the Palace and Nuri's home that Qasim's troops appeared at the Embassy, surrounded it and began checking on all who wanted to enter or leave. Next, the building across the square from the Embassy which served as an office for our military mission was searched and sealed. Work within the building was never resumed.

In the months that followed no word was forthcoming that the Qasim regime was prepared to subscribe to the terms of the understanding. With the arrival in December of Soviet military aid, and still no indication from Qasim as to his intentions, it was evident that the time had come to withdraw our military mission. This was done, but it was not until May 30, 1959, that the Republic of Iraq formally notified us that it had decided to terminate the agreement.

The history of our military aid undertaking in Iraq was, on the whole, not a happy one. I have mentioned the administrative difficulties that made operating the program difficult. There were more serious deficiencies that marred the undertaking. In the first place, in spite of the clear wording of the Mutual Security Act, there were differences in Washington as to its interpretation and application to Iraq. This was brought out during the critical days in 1956, when for a time it seemed that Iraq might move into Jordan. In the language of the act "equipment and material furnished . . . shall be made available solely to maintain the internal security and legitimate self defense of the recipient nation, or to permit it to participate in the defense of the area or in collective security arrangements and measures consistent with the Charter of the United Nations." On September 27, 1956, I received a message giving me, for my guidance, the State Department's position on the critical situation that was developing. The department,

I was told, never considered the objectives of the United States military assistance to Iraq inconsistent with Iraq's obligations, under bilateral or multilateral agreements, to assist other Arab states in the event they became victims of aggression.

That interpretation seemed sound and sensible to me. But about a month later I received a quite different interpretation, one that must have come from a group at the other end of the corridor in the department. This time I was told that it was assumed that Nuri understood that he could not take any MDAP (Military Defense Assistance Program) equipment beyond Iraq's frontiers. To make sure that he understood, I was to tell him so. I saw him on November 2 and broke the word to him as gently as possible. He was quite taken aback. "But," he countered, "if we go into Jordan it will be in defense of Jordan against aggression and I always thought that there were no restrictions on the use of this equipment against aggression." I did not pursue the matter further. As I explained to the department, Nuri looked too ill and preoccupied for me to do so.

The second great deficiency that marred the operation of our military assistance program was our failure to have thought through carefully in advance just what we were trying to achieve. The Iraqi Chief of Staff and his assistants had worked out the two-phase, five-year program. We neither approved it, nor disapproved it. Nuri, of course, was aware of it but never really concerned himself about its details. He wanted many things, and he wanted them quickly. He wanted them for various reasons, depending on the temper of the Iraqi people at a given time, or the prevailing political climate in the region generally.

To me there appeared three possible plans of action. One was to concentrate on equipping an Iraqi force capable of taking part in a general war. A second was to disregard this, but aim at building up a force intended primarily to do no more than maintain internal order during a general conflict. The third possible course might have been to disregard both these objectives and frankly concentrate on building a force for purely political ends, showy enough in types of equipment to have bolstered Nuri with his own people and to have impressed his neighbors at the same time.

I think the first course I have mentioned, aiming to equip a force intended primarily for a role in case of general war, could well have been disregarded completely. A regular Iraqi force, under any circumstances, would be relatively small and consequently no matter how well equipped and trained could play no decisive role in a general war. The burden here would have to be borne by forces of one kind or another, other than Iraqi.

For the second course of action, almost complete concentration on the formation of a force intended to maintain internal order and security during a general war, a better case could have been made out. In this instance, to be sure, the respective roles of the military force and of the police force would have had to be delimitated clearly in advance, so that there would follow the proper selection and allotment of equipment. A co-ordinate plan of action for the two, in case of war, should not have been too difficult to work out. I question though whether this type of aid, so inconspicuous, would have appealed much to the Iraqis.

The third and final course of action mentioned by me; that is, for using the program frankly for political ends, always seemed to me to make the most sense. Before dealing with this course of action in detail, I think some further word about Nuri's own feeling toward our program would be helpful.

While Nuri was grateful for what Iraq received, he was on the whole disappointed in the results of our program. We had led him to believe that the amount of aid, economic and military, that Iraq would get from us, depended on how much initiative Iraq showed and how much she was prepared to do herself to secure the Middle East from outside aggression. He showed great courage, both so far as relations with his own people were concerned and relations with the Arab world at large, in following the international course he did. He expected more from us than he got. It was not quantity he was interested in. He knew very well that there was a definite limit to how much equipment the relatively small Iraqi army could absorb, and how fast it could do so. What he was interested in was quality. He wanted the latest and the best. He wanted to impress his own people with his ability to acquire something of real value for them from abroad. He wanted, too, to gain respect, for his country and himself, among the other Arab states. And he wanted impressive equipment quickly because during those last years of his life he was continually facing crises within Iraq, as well as problems in the field of Iraq's relations with her neighbors.

We, on our part, were not ungrateful for what Nuri had done in the interests of security, nor unmindful of how helpful to him some showy pieces of the latest armament would be. We did give him some of the "big guns" he wanted so much.

There were indeed formidable barriers in the way of carrying out a program frankly aimed at bolstering Nuri politically through conspicuous, modern arms delivered in timely fashion. Even with these barriers to face we could still have provided Iraq with more modern equipment than we did, and more expeditiously too, if we had had complete freedom of action. This we did not enjoy.

The Iraqi army had from the beginning been equipped with British arms. We started our program with acceptance of that fact. Most of our money went into buying British equipment from the British through offshore procurement. This looks at first glance like a good plan. We helped two of our allies simultaneously, the British financially and the Iraqis with gifts. But the plan had two serious drawbacks. The equipment available in the United Kingdom for this program was seldom of the most modern type and, moreover, deliveries as a rule were long delayed.

My final appraisal of the program is that it did not help Nuri appreciably within or without Iraq, nor did it enhance our prestige perceptibly among Iraqis or their neighbors.

TECHNICAL AID PROGRAM

Technical aid was our third and final contact with Nuri. We tried to balance our military aid with economic aid. The economic aid we extended was largely in the nature of technical assistance. The basic agreement on technical co-operation came into force on June 2, 1951. It was amplified by a number of subsequent agreements, the last one growing out of the visit of the Richards' Mission to Iraq in April, 1957. Under the basic agreement we provided technicians and in some instances equipment for training purposes as well. The funds authorized under the Richards' agreement were intended mainly to help Iraq meet her share of costs of common Baghdad Pact projects.

As I have said, Nuri, through his close interest in the activities of the Development Board and its program, came to know well the work our technicians were doing in Iraq. He often spoke to me about their contributions with genuine gratitude.

With one exception, our technical aid program was effectively administered. The exception was that it usually took us a long time to comply with requests for additional technicians or specialists needed in some special field. It was difficult, of course, to recruit suitable specialists at a moment's notice. The really good ones were not readily available and Iraq's needs, I am afraid, did not enjoy the priority back home that we in Baghdad felt they deserved.

At the beginning of 1956 I pointed out to Washington that in Nuri we had as effective a friend as the West could expect in Iraq for some time to come and that I felt he should be strengthened, among other ways, by supporting his efforts for internal reform. We could and should implement his efforts by supplying promptly the experts he requested from time to time.

At the end of the year I urged again that we fill the post reserved for an American on the Development Board, a position that had by then been vacant for eight months.

Iraqi requests, Washington delays, Embassy promptings set the pattern to the very end.

During the weeks following the coup of July 14 there was complete confusion in all ministries of the government in Baghdad. Our technicians stood by, waiting for order to be restored and to see whether their services were wanted by the new rulers of Iraq. During August some of them resumed their work at the request of the heads of ministries. The ministries welcoming them back were Agriculture, Health, Development and Education. Public land development (*miri sirf*) and irrigation experts were particularly in demand. Others, who had established close personal relations with certain key officials, continued from day to day on a personal, friend to friend, basis. Early in September, however, I was told by one of Qasim's cabinet members that an order had gone out to each Ministry asking it to report on how many American technicians were assigned to it, what they were doing, and how extensively they could be used in the future. I never learned the nature of the replies, but from September on, less and less use was made of our technicians. On May 30, 1959, along with notification that it was terminating the Military Assistance Understanding, the Republic of Iraq gave notice that it was terminating the economic assistance agreements as well.

FAILURE

The story of our relations with Iraq from 1954 to 1958 is essentially a story of failure.

In Nuri we had a steadfast, understanding friend. He spoke well for all of us of the West, in Iraq, and in the Arab world at large. He was convinced that the way of the West was best for his people, and he had the courage to declare himself openly, amid dissenting voices from many of his own people. In the end he was killed by his own people. Did we contribute to this tragic denouement? I think we did.

If we had joined the Baghdad Pact; if we had had a clear conception of what we were trying to do with our military aid; if we had been prompt in meeting requests for technicians and specialists; would Nuri have been spared? Naturally, no one can say he would have been. But it should be clear that had we done all those things, Nuri would have been strengthened and his chances of survival, to pursue the constructive things he had embarked on in the closing years of his life, would definitely have been brighter.

Qasim took Iraq out of the Baghdad Pact. He wanted none of our military aid. He was not interested in our technicians. But all during the tense months while these activities were being liquidated, the American Jesuit fathers were permitted to carry on their work at Baghdad College and at Al-Hikma University without interference, and after the Baghdad Pact secretariat had scattered, our military aid group had left, and our technicians had gone home, the fathers were still there teaching, as they are today. Is there a lesson in this? I think there is.

Pacts, military aid, and economic assistance, when intelligently conceived and ably administered, can be used to advance our interests and to help others. But all such undertakings are at best a gamble. Through my experience in Iraq and elsewhere I have come to feel that the only area where there is any degree of certainty that efforts will be productive is in the field of education, and even there mishaps occur. There is, though, a greater hope of something lasting resulting from our support of schools, scholarships, and the exchange of students, teachers, and research workers, than from efforts in the other fields I have been discussing.

Those years of failure in Iraq coincided with the years when

John Foster Dulles was secretary of state. A discussion of them without some word about his character, personality and conception of the duties of secretary of state would be incomplete.

Secretary Dulles possessed a sharp, quick mind. With this powerful intellect came an extraordinary degree of self-confidence, and with that almost unshakable self-confidence came a certain sense of righteousness. These qualities made him a forbidding figure, and that in turn had a tendency, so it seemed to us abroad, to paralyze thought and action all through the State Department. It made little difference whether he was there in person, keeping a tight rein on everything of importance, or abroad trying himself to put out a fire. In his method of operation he reminded one of a fire chief, always on the alert to move here or there and take charge where the fire seemed most threatening. While he was concentrating on the hottest issue of the moment, whether at home or abroad, ideas and action came fast. Then, when the urgency of doing something in a particular place subsided, his attention would be shifted elsewhere and his concentration on a new set of problems would be complete. The result of these methods was that our problems in Baghdad got attention when the situation was really critical. When tension eased somewhat, they were practically ignored, and not until the next crisis developed did they again receive attention. That explains why we did not have in Iraq in the years I have covered long-term, well thought out plans and courses of action, and why, in turn, those were years of failure.

We missed and misused many opportunities. In spite of this there remains that reservoir of goodwill I mentioned at the beginning of this chapter, on which we might still someday build something worthwhile. I was reminded of this not long ago when an Iraqi friend of mine called on me at my home in Washington. He is a graduate of the American University in Beirut and has a doctorate from one of our leading universities in the United States. He was a member of Nuri's last cabinet. Like me, he deeply regretted the passing of Nuri, but his sorrow was tempered by a ray of hope. He reminded me that day that there remain in Iraq a great many understanding friends of the free world, products of the schools we have influenced abroad and of schools in our own country, whose voices would be heard again.

XI

THE 1958 COUP
AND ITS
AFTERMATH

On the morning of July 12, 1958, I made a farewell call on Nuri. On July 14 he was to leave Baghdad with King Faisal and Crown Prince Abdul-Ilah for Istanbul for talks with Prime Minister Menderes concerning the meeting in London of the council of the Baghdad Pact which was to take place late in July. As Nuri was going to be away for some months, I wanted to discuss the Lebanese situation and its effect on Iraq.

In anticipation of an appeal from Amman to move troops into Jordan, an Iraqi force had been placed on the Iraqi-Jordanian frontier. Nuri was preoccupied with Lebanon but was not so concerned that he thought he should postpone his departure. He felt that the measures that had been taken were adequate and, in any event, all that Iraq herself could do. Not knowing what the United States might do, did, however, disturb him.

I asked Nuri what the reaction in Iraq would be if Iraqi troops moved into Jordan. Nuri replied that potential trouble-makers were limited to "a few hundred students and lawyers," and these could be kept under surveillance. When I inquired about the loyalty of the army, he assured me that the army could be relied upon to support the Crown and the government.

I left Nuri at peace with his conscience. He felt that he had done all he could in preparation for his departure and absence for a time abroad.

Shortly after five o'clock on the morning of July 14, I heard gunfire. I went out into the garden where I could get a view of the streets. Traffic was normal and early risers who were passing by were untroubled. The scene in the neighborhood of the Embassy was so reassuring that I concluded that the firing was part of the ceremonial send-off for the King and his party. I had just returned indoors, when a member of my staff appeared to announce that troops were firing on the Palace and Nuri's home and that mobs were gathering in the vicinity. Most Baghdadis sleep on the roofs of their homes during the summer months as did this member of my staff. From his roof he could see both the Palace and Nuri's home.

I was fortunate to have been alerted in the early hours of the coup. Before other members of the staff could reach the Embassy, I had the second and last bit of good fortune for the day. About six o'clock an associate of Nuri appeared at the Embassy seeking asylum. The early morning gunfire had aroused his suspicions. His arrival fortunately coincided with the broadcasting of the decrees setting up the Republic of Iraq. He began immediately to translate them for us from the Arabic. By seven A.M. the new regime had established itself. A presidium consisting of Mohammad Mahdi Kubba, Khalid Naqshbandi, and Brigadier Najib Rubay'i had been appointed to replace the Royal Family. The names of the new cabinet and of other high officials had been announced, many of them unknown even to our house guest. The names of prominent military men and civilians retired to private life or arrested by the new rulers, had been broadcast. Forty military officers were retired, among them the chief of staff, Rafiq Arif and the one time assistant chief of staff, Ghazi Daghistani. Many of those whose names were broadcast were later brought to trial before a special military court.

Before the day was over it was clear that the small group which had planned the coup in utmost secrecy, had won a stunning success. In the weeks that followed there was no sign of organized opposition, either among the military or civilians. The new regime, it was clear from the start, could only be ousted by sudden and overwhelming force from outside.

On the morning of July 15 I learned that some time during the day there would be landings in Lebanon from the Sixth Fleet. I was afraid that this might set off anti-American demonstrations, and perhaps even lead to mobs breaking into the Embassy. I had these fears despite the fact that the Embassy was surrounded by tanks, and troops were encamped on the Embassy grounds for our "protection." I had misgivings because this force had not interfered with the hanging at the entrance to the Embassy of a huge anti-American banner, nor with the painting on the garden walls of anti-American slogans. Instead of preventing such incitements to mob action, our protectors busied themselves with checking and searching all who came to and left the Embassy.

Our house guest agreed that if a mob should penetrate the Embassy and find him there, it would be equally hard on us and on him. He said that if a way could be devised for him to get through the cordon of Iraqi troops and tanks into the street, he knew where he could find safety.

We made a plan and carried it out successfully. We dressed him in the uniform of an Embassy chauffeur and put him behind the wheel of an Embassy car, with one of our officers in the back seat as passenger. The car passed by the guards and beyond the tanks unchallenged, and then through the streets to the place where he felt he would be safe. There he got out and the Embassy officer brought the car back alone, the absence of his erstwhile driver escaping the notice of the guards.

Abdul Karim Qasim, the leader of the group that had executed the coup, was not widely known before July 14. At the time of the coup he was a brigade commander.

Nuri resorted to a judicious distribution of ammunition as one means to hold the army in check. When it was necessary to issue ammunition, only units trusted by him got any. Following the coup, it was learned that Nuri had at some time in the last days of his life approved the issuance of ammunition to two brigades and ordered them to move toward Jordan. One of these brigades was Qasim's. The other was under the command of Colonel Abdul Salam Arif. The two converged on Baghdad in the small hours of July 14. The trek toward Jordan ended there. Shortly, the signal to seize power was given.

Nuri escaped from his home on the morning of July 14 just ahead of the mob. At once the radio announced a reward of ten thousand *dinar* for his apprehension. Sometime during the morning of July 15 he was discovered by soldiers disguised as an Arab woman, not far from the Embassy, and shot. After his escape from his home, he found refuge for a time with the Istrabadi family, wealthy Shiahs from Kadhimain. Members of the family and their servants were later tried for aiding Nuri. Seven were found guilty and sentenced to from one to five years in prison. The eighty-year-old head of the family, whose wife was killed on the street along with Nuri, received a sentence of three years. The defense of the accused, as their sentences indicate, was feeble.

The mob, which appeared suddenly on July 14 and carried out the early morning pillaging, was made up largely of youths ranging in age from twelve to twenty. Trucks, supplied by the new regime, brought many of them into Baghdad and transported them around the city. For two days the mob, reinforced later by older hoodlums, had a free hand. Then the regime acted to put a stop to further extreme mob action. It also removed the inflammatory anti-Western signs and slogans which had bedecked the city. I think there were two reasons why the regime acted when it did. After having at first encouraged the mobs to engender at least the semblance of popular backing, it came to fear that they might get out of hand, causing deaths among foreigners and damage to their property. There was also concern over what Ba'athist and Communist leadership of the mob might lead to. Quickly on July 14, agents from both these camps took over the direction of the mob. The speed with which they moved surprised the new leaders of Iraq.

The new cabinet, which contained eleven civilians, was hastily put together. One member told me that the first word he had of his appointment was when a relative, who had heard the announcement of it over the radio, telephoned to congratulate him. Similar stories were told about some of the other appointments. These men, having been brought together on a moments notice, had no program to guide them. As a group they were not united by political philosophy or agreement on goals. Emotionally, they shared a hatred of Nuri and Hashimites. Fortunately for Qasim, four of them had had previous experience on the cabinet level.[1] This original cabinet, as might have been expected from the hasty, unplanned way in which it had been assembled, did not last long. Soon after its formation, Qasim began making changes.

On July 18 all diplomatic missions in Baghdad received notes from the new Foreign Minister telling them that the coup was a purely internal move aimed at rescuing Iraq from the evils of corrupt rule and reaction. On July 26 Qasim called his first press conference. He tried to throw light on the government's future action. After the government had effected some pressing reforms, he announced, and after it had

---

[1] Ibrahim Kubba, minister of economics; Baba Ali, minister of communications; Mohammad Hadid, minister of finance; Siddiq Shanshal, minister of news and guidance.

obtained for the people of Iraq adequate security, there would be elections. They would take place in the not too distant future "as determined by the general situation." The immediate aims were the suppression of corruption; "cleansing" of the government system; solving housing problems; and finally, "achieving prosperity."

The action of July 14 is often called a revolution, but this is misleading. "Revolution" connotes a popular uprising against those in power. What took place in Iraq on July 14, 1958, in no way resembled that. It was simply a seizure of power by a small, determined group. It is true that hordes of unruly jubilant people roamed the streets for several days. They were not representative Iraqis, but were hoodlums recruited by agitators. There was nothing spontaneous about these demonstrations. Although there was general discontent in the country and much criticism of Nuri and his government, there was no unified, determined protest, or program of reform. The July 14 coup cannot justly be called a "popular revolution." Demonstrations took place in Baghdad but across the country, among the masses, only stunned acquiescence was in evidence.

It does not follow from this that violence was new in the lives of Iraqis. Iraq had suffered much disorder and violence. Accounts of urban riots, rural tribal uprisings, and coups appear disquietingly often in her history. Prominent among these disruptive and bloody events are the Bakr Sidqi-Hikmat Sulaiman coup against the Yasin government in 1936, the Rashid Ali pro-Nazi coup of 1941, and the Portsmouth Treaty riots of 1948. The 1958 coup was no phenomenon in the history of Iraq.

The 1958 coup was planned by a small group of officers, assisted by a few liberal and leftist civilians. A member of Qasim's first cabinet told me that it had long been discussed and planned. The decision to strike on July 14, however, was taken suddenly and by only three or four members of the group.

Moscow had no hand in it but in the early stages of the

confusion that followed the attack on the Palace and the killing of the King and the Crown Prince, the closely knit band of local Communists took over the direction of public demonstrations. The Communists, as those early demonstrations revealed, were joined almost immediately by pro-Nasser agitators, mostly from the Ba'athist camp. These two elements, encouraged and assisted by some of the younger officers, one of whom was Qasim's partner, Arif, generated the frenzied street scenes of the weeks following the coup.

Almost immediately after the seizure of power Arif began his rabble rousing, first in Baghdad and then in other cities and towns from which organized groups were then brought by truck to Baghdad to return his visits. This gave him the opportunity for a second round of haranguing.

Just at this time I called on Siddiq Shanshal who was then acting foreign minister. His office was in the building of the Council of Ministers. One had to pass through a spacious courtyard to reach it, and I had difficulty getting through. The courtyard was filled with a crowd from Mosul calling for Arif. All during my talk with Shanshal the shouting of the crowd could be heard. This led Shanshal to make some comments on Arif's behavior.

He was disturbed, he said, by the stream of visitors to Baghdad from cities and towns where Arif had talked. This was taking hundreds of men away from their work. The disruptive effect on the economy was bad. What was worse was the danger that in the emotional atmosphere in which Arif met these crowds, promises would be made which could not be fulfilled. He saw trouble ahead.

By the time I left Shanshal's office and got to the courtyard, Arif had come out on the balcony overlooking the crowd and had started addressing them. He was given a tumultuous reception. Loud cheering interrupted every sentence. Each sentence was short. The language of the message was simple and its theme repeated over and over, to the accompaniment of much arm flailing. The country and government are yours,

Arif told the crowd. No longer is there a king. In fact there
is no longer any big man. We are all common people. We
are all working now for the common good.

That is what they had come to hear and they liked it.

I did not see Arif again until one evening a few weeks
later. That evening Qasim gave the first dinner of the new
regime. It was a buffet in the gardens of Amanah Hall. The
atmosphere was not an easy one. Qasim's revolver was strapped
to his side for all to see. Armed guards hovered near him.
Behind the trees and bushes surrounding the garden more
guards were stationed. One of these fired his gun during the
evening, causing additional strain until it had been determined that the shot was accidental, and not the signal for
the counterrevolution. Qasim, trim in his brigadier's uniform,
forced a strained affability. He, but not Arif, moved from
group to group to exchange pleasantries. Arif, in shirt-sleeves,
sat apart all evening, looking preoccupied. He must have
sensed what was in store for him.

Only a few days later it was announced that Arif had been
relieved of his post of deputy commander in chief of the army.
This was followed shortly by the announcement that he had
been relieved of his post of deputy prime minister as well.
To compensate him, he was appointed ambassador to the
German Federal Republic. The first intimation the German
Embassy or the Bonn government had of the appointment
was when it was announced by the Baghdad press. Nevertheless, Arif went through the motions of setting out for Bonn.
He never got there. The next news about him was an an-
nouncement made a month later that he had returned to
Baghdad and had been arrested for plotting to overthrow
Qasim and assassinate him. He was sentenced to death but
with the door left open for commutation to life imprison-
ment.

Secrecy surrounded Arif's trial, but not the trials of others
accused of crimes by the Qasim regime. A few weeks after the
coup the Iraqi press announced that 106 people charged with

"plotting against the national security and corrupting the government machinery" would be tried by a Special Supreme Military Court, presided over by Colonel Fadil Abbas al-Mahdawi, a cousin of Qasim. The trials began almost immediately. They were a shocking spectacle.

The early trials were broadcast and televised and held in the evening after working hours in order to reach as many people as possible. Radio and television sets were installed in public places. The trials were conducted in the Chamber of Parliament where the limited number of seats were reserved. Tickets for them were distributed among carefully selected supporters of the new regime whose function it was to serve as a claque, which they did with enthusiasm kept at a high pitch by Colonel al-Mahdawi. With a steady flow of unbridled and inciting words, he carried on in the dual role of judge and prosecutor. He repeatedly interrupted the defendants, standing before him in a small fenced enclosure, with accusations and tauntings, and he encouraged the spectators to do the same. Many Iraqis were sickened from the beginning by this travesty of justice. Many others tired of the nightly spectacle as the months went by. Many were shocked by the death sentences meted out to once-prominent public figures. But the show was allowed to go on into 1959. It is to Qasim's credit, however, that a number of the death sentences imposed under these conditions were later commuted to prison terms and that a number of prison terms were rescinded as well. Among those affected were some of Nuri's closest friends.

When I made my first call on Prime Minister Qasim on the afternoon of July 15, the atmosphere of the city was very tense. "Down with Western Imperialism" was the cry of the street. I was told, when I asked for the appointment, that a military escort would take me to the Ministry of Defense where the meeting was to be held, and back to the Embassy. I was pleased by the choice of my military escort. He was Colonel Damanloudgi, formerly Iraq's assistant military attaché in Washington, whose American wife was once a member of our Foreign Service. During the days that followed I made a number of trips to and from the new Iraqi officials under his protection.

The Ministry of Defense was heavily guarded. I had to pass through rows of armed soldiers to Qasim's office where I found him armed too. He was tense but friendly. His first words were: "We want to be friends with the United States." I thanked him for his greeting and then, appreciating what pressures he was under, took up the business I had come to dispatch without further preliminaries. It was disposed of quickly and satisfactorily. I asked him to give me assurance that his government would protect American lives and property. This he gave instantly. I then asked for assurance that if I were instructed to evacuate American women and dependents his government would facilitate such an operation. Here he hesitated, but only momentarily. He had, he reminded me, just assured me that American lives and property would be safeguarded. He did not think further assurances were necessary. However, as I had made the request he would go further. Should evacuation be thought necessary by Washington, his government would facilitate it.

Two days later I received instructions to start evacuation. Qasim honored his assurances. He had only one reservation to make. In order to avoid giving the impression that ours was a panic exodus, he would like us to allow some days between flights, moving our people out in gradual, orderly fashion. I agreed to this.

But this was one of those times when Washington acted promptly and with zeal. Planes were chartered from a private company in such numbers and on such closely following days that any staggered, gradual evacuation as requested by Qasim was ruled out. Qasim, however, was again obliging. In spite of the embarrassment that so rapid an evacuation might cause him, he approved the crowded schedule worked out in Washington.

On the way back from the Ministry of Defense Colonel Damanloudgi took me along the most direct route leading to the Embassy. Everything went smoothly until we were about a mile from it. There we ran into a crowd milling about, gesticulating, and yelling "Nuri." Light tanks were parked on the side of the street and at a nearby intersection, and soldiers armed with automatic rifles stood on the tanks. When they began shooting over the heads of the mob, the Colonel quickly gave directions to turn into a side street and from there we proceeded in a roundabout way to the Embassy.

Earlier that day Nuri had been apprehended and shot. The mob I encountered had learned that his body was to be taken to the morgue. The mob intercepted it, mutilated it, and dragged it through the streets. While this was taking place in Baghdad, our marines were landing on the beaches of Beirut.

During a call a European colleague of mine made on Qasim a few days after the landings, he asked Qasim whether he would have struck on July 14 if American marines had been landed in Lebanon before that date. He promptly replied "No." What follows throws light on Qasim's answer.

After our marines had landed in Lebanon I sensed fear among officials of the new regime that they might occupy Iraq as well. In fact, on my first call on the new foreign minister, Jumard, when Shanshal, minister of news and guidance, was also present, I detected from their line of questioning, uneasiness about the future movement of the marines. It was not until weeks later that Qasim and his group became less apprehensive.

Uncertainty about the future of our interests in Iraq marked the weeks following the coup. This was so even though there was no organized opposition to threaten the new regime. What would Qasim do about the Military Aid Agreement? What about our Technical Aid Agreement? Would compensation be paid to the families of the three Americans killed by the mob on July 14? How long would interference with the Embassy's normal functions by lesser military and civilian officials continue in spite of Qasim's expressed wish for friendly relations? Questions of that kind had to be weighed in deciding on a line of action and certainly before a decision could be reached on recognition.

The situation following the coup gave no reason to believe that continuation of our military and technical aid would be welcomed. Nevertheless, I did not want it to appear that we had abandoned the field voluntarily and prematurely to the Soviets. If we were to go, I wanted the new regime to take the initiative. For this reason, with the endorsement of the State Department, I informed Foreign Minister Jumard that we were prepared to continue our technical assistance if that were the wish of the government of Iraq. As to military aid I explained that this would be subject to discussion between our two governments, both as to practical details and matters of policy.

I pressed for clarification of the government's stand in my talks with Qasim and other Iraqi officials, but it was not until May, 1959, five months after my departure from Baghdad, that Qasim notified us that the agreements on military and technical aid would be terminated. For all practical purposes they had come to an end long before.

I felt that we should, if possible, get at least two assurances before we extended recognition. One was the assurance that harassment of the Embassy would be stopped so that it could carry on its normal functions. The other was assurance that the families of the three Americans killed by the mob the day of the coup would be indemnified.

Some of the obstacles which interfered with the normal functioning of the Embassy were no more than petty annoyances such as the interminable searching and questioning of visitors and staff alike, coming in and out of the Embassy. The refusal to recognize the immunity of our diplomatic couriers and the failure to clear through customs the official supplies badly needed in the day to day work were more serious. A

big problem was the interference with the freedom of movement of Embassy officials, within Baghdad itself and around
the country at large. Whenever our grievances were taken up
with a top level Iraqi official there would be relief, but only
temporarily. After a few days lower ranking military and
civilian representatives of the government would resume their
petty molestation. Once the situation got so bad that I had to
appeal to Qasim himself. The trouble, of course, was not
made by the senior members of the government, but by the
hundreds of inexperienced and zealous workers who had been
brought in at the bottom.

Among the group rounded-up by soldiers at the Baghdad
Hotel on July 14 were three American businessmen: Eugene
Burns, George Colley, and Robert Alcock. American friends
of theirs who were also staying at the hotel witnessed their
seizure and departure in trucks. A German businessman,
seized and transported with them, but who, though beaten,
managed to escape, identified the three as having been attacked and been in the truck with him. The bodies of the
three Americans were never found. The Iraqi government
claimed it could find no trace of them. We could only learn
at the hospital to which the victims of mob action were
brought, that none was brought in alive and that all bodies
were mutilated beyond hope of identification. This inability
to trace and identify the remains of the Americans complicated our efforts to get a settlement.

While we were working on these problems, but making no
headway toward a solution, the new government was becoming more impatient about our failure to recognize it. About
two weeks after the coup Foreign Minister Jumard complained to me about our "aloofness." Sixteen governments,
but all from the Communist bloc or sympathetic in their
political outlook, had by then extended recognition. "If you
are not careful," he cautioned, "you might push the new
government toward communism." Not long after this warning
Britain, Turkey, Iran, and Pakistan decided to recognize the

new regime. While uncertainties persisted, I felt that now
the point had been reached where little could be gained by
our continuing to withhold recognition. In fact, by delaying,
we might find ourselves in a dangerously isolated position.

We extended recognition early in August. At the same time
that I informed the Foreign Minister of our decision I told
him that it was our understanding that Iraq would abide by
the principles of international law with respect to the three
missing Americans, presumably dead, and that compensation
would be paid when valid claims had been established.

Claims were paid, but not until two years later.

The remaining months that I spent in Iraq were characterized by paralysis in government and stagnation of the country's economy. The ministries in Baghdad in Nuri's day were
by no means distinguished for their efficiency. The need for
training in public administration was evident. But, thanks
to a hard core of civil service employees trained in the days
of the British mandate, the essential business in the ministries
was carried out with creditable dispatch. There were, too, on
the undersecretary level, some very able, Western-trained
career officials. To work with them was generally satisfactory.
But almost immediately, with the coming of the Qasim
regime, the top level of professionals and most of the subordinate civil service employees were ousted on suspicion of
being too loyal to the old order. By the middle of October
fifty-seven percent of all government employees at the in-
spector general or director general level, in office on July 14,
excluding those in military or judicial agencies, had been
dismissed. Experienced replacements were not available and
those that remained felt too insecure to make decisions. They
just marked time.

The most important factor in keeping the economy of
the country sound had been the Development Program. Its
projects created jobs and funneled money into a variety of
business activities. The program served well as a continuous
economic primer.

One of the first things the new regime did was to call a halt to most of the big projects in order to review the contracts with the foreign firms under which they were being carried out. In addition, Western technicians and advisers were dismissed. Labor caught the revolutionary fever too. Resorting to stalling, overindulgence in sick leaves, and just plain surliness, labor succeeded in stopping almost completely the little activity that still continued on the sites of the larger projects. With the Development Program practically wrecked, the economy was paralyzed.

In charge of this wrecking program in its early stages was the young Ba'athist minister of development, Faud Rikabi. His public career lasted only a few months. It ended when Qasim suspected him of trying to extend his wrecking operations to the regime itself. Rikabi escaped to Egypt before he could be arrested.

One of the contracts Rikabi canceled shortly after becoming minister had been awarded an American engineering firm only a few days before the coup. Months later the Iraqi agent of this firm who had grown up in Baghdad with Rikabi, met him in Cairo and indulged in a little story telling. He told Rikabi that his firm had erected a monument in his honor in front of its headquarters in California because "we figured that you saved us about a million dollars by canceling our contract." Rikabi was quick with his retort. "Then you can afford to help me now. I surely could use some of those dollars." He did not get any dollars. All he got for canceling the contract was that mythical monument in California.

An Associated Press dispatch sent from Baghdad on July 15, 1961, and published in the *Washington Post* on July 16, described the celebration of the third anniversary of Qasim's coup. As part of the celebration, the dispatch read, Qasim dedicated twenty gasoline stations, fifty casinos, and ten playgrounds, all constructed under the Development Program.

Gasoline stations, playgrounds, and casinos may add to the

joy of life but they are, after all, a far cry from Wadi-Tharthar and Ramadi barrages.

The economic trend from July to December, 1958, was one of business contraction, rising prices and increasing unemployment. At the same time the political atmosphere became more charged, erupting into street fighting in November in the Karkh district of Baghdad between Communists and anti-Communist Nationalists, including Ba'athists. The clash took place near the home of the sister-in-law of the deposed Arif, where a crowd had gathered to bemoan his fate.

Far more serious than this street clash was the "imperialist plot" involving Rashid Ali al-Gailani, which Qasim uncovered early in December. Rashid Ali, who had gone into exile on the failure of his coup in 1941, was permitted by Qasim to return right after the July coup. His plotting with sheiks, mostly from the Diwanyah area, began almost immediately. With them were implicated a motley group of civilian dissidents, and some elements of the police and army. The funds to finance the uprising were said to have come from Egypt. The plot was discovered in time by a police agent in Baghdad who somehow "induced" one of the conspirators to talk, and thirty-six arrests followed. On December 9 a secret trial took place. The next day three of the accused were hanged, and six army officers and nine members of the police were shot. Rashid Ali was sentenced to five years house arrest. Various tribal chiefs received prison sentences up to twenty years.

By 1962 the Iraqi Kurds were in open rebellion, led by Mullah Mustafa al-Barzani, who like Rashid Ali had led an earlier revolt and failed, had gone into exile, and had been allowed to return by Qasim.[2]

The elections promised by Qasim in July, 1958, were never

[2] The *New York Times* editions of September 10, 11, 12 and 13, 1962, printed a series of four detailed articles on the Kurdish revolt by Dana Adams Schmidt, who spent several weeks in the Kurdish held territory of northern Iraq.

held. Iraqis with experience in government waited in vain for a call to serve their country. Because of lack of confidence, practically no capital investments were made while Qasim remained in power. On June 2, 1962, Qasim asked my successor, John Jernegan, to leave Iraq, and recalled his ambassador, Ali Haidar Suleiman, in protest against our naming an ambassador to Kuwait. At the time of the February, 1963, coup which cost Qasim his life, we were still without an ambassador in Baghdad.

By January, 1963, there were clear indications that Qasim's hold on the country was loosening rapidly and that the end for him might not be far off. During January a well-organized and widely supported strike by secondary and university students revealed how powerful nationalist sentiment against him had become. He tried to meet this threat by arresting Ba'athist civilians. He felt unsure about the army too. This led him to speed up the retirement of officers he no longer trusted. The officers plotting against him, mostly from the Air Force, saw that unless they acted quickly, retirements and transfers would ruin their chance of success. On Friday, February 8, when many senior officers had left their commands for the weekend and many soldiers were enjoying weekend passes, they struck.

While Hawker Hunters and MIG 17's from Habbaniyah kept up a steady rocket attack on Qasim's headquarters, the Defense Ministry, student groups armed with rifles and tommy guns, under Ba'athist leadership, roamed the streets. No military resistance to the coup was offered. Only the 600 men garrisoned in the Defense Ministry defended Qasim. The survivors, including Qasim and his cousin Abbas al-Mahdawi who had presided over the Special Military Court established after the 1958 coup, surrendered the following morning, February 9. Qasim and his chief aides were taken to the Radio-TV station and tried immediately by a military court, one of whose members was Qasim's former collaborator Abdul

Salam Arif. They were sentenced to death and shot on the spot. Baghdad radio announced the executions that afternoon and that evening pictures of the dead men were shown on television.

Colonel Abdel Karim Mustafa, the radio announced, was the head of the Revolutionary Council and Captain Taleb Abdel-Muttaleb et Hashemi, his aide. These were the first members of the new regime to be announced. They had been members of the Air Force who were purged by Qasim. Qasim's former associate, Arif, whom Qasim had released from prison in 1961, was named chief of state. The new rulers of Iraq pledged themselves to continue the revolution of July 14, 1958, which had been betrayed by "Qasim, the dictator." [3]

Qasim, as I remember him, usually appeared self-possessed and calm. He always answered my questions directly and promptly. He spoke calmly and softly, never excitedly, and with a ring of frankness and sincerity. This outward calm I soon detected was misleading. Inner uneasiness, tenseness, and conflict were often betrayed by a tensing and gripping of the hands. During the early calls I made on him, one or more members of his cabinet were present. This afforded some insight into the relations between him and his cabinet. While Qasim gave them opportunity to speak, they always deferred to him. While speaking, they looked to him for a nod or some other sign of agreement. He never interrupted, but he was clearly the man in charge.

Right after the 1958 coup, stories circulated that Qasim was a Communist. At no time during my association with him did he give any indication of being one. He impressed me as being at heart a well-meaning social reformer, deeply concerned with improving the living standards of the thousands of poorly fed, poorly housed, poorly clad and landless

[3] For a detailed account of the events of February 8, 1963, see the special dispatch from Beirut, Lebanon, of Dana Adams Schmidt which appeared in the *New York Times*, International Edition, February 9, 1963.

Iraqis. Unfortunately, he seized power without having had previous experience in government and without any well thought out philosophy or program of social reform to guide him.

To destroy is easy. To build is difficult.

XII

THE NURI
I KNEW

Nuri's traits and views are woven throughout the fabric of my account of the Iraqi scene from 1954–58. I have drawn on the many talks I had with him, on his public statements, and on the record of events of those days. I have not selected material in order to make an apologia. I set out to produce a clear picture of the man as I came to know him. What has emerged is neither saint nor sinner but a mixture of both, reflecting the time and environment in which he lived.

A few months after my arrival in Baghdad, I stated in a report to the State Department that of all the impressions made on me the most vivid was that of Nuri himself, who impressed me as being one of the great men of our time, not merely outstanding in the Arab world, but a world figure as well.

Nuri was above all an Arab nationalist. His first acts as he grew to maturity were on behalf of Arab independence, and throughout his life he was preoccupied with how best to safeguard and promote the interests of the Arab people. Inter-Arab rivalries and differences complicated his task. The

varying reactions of the disjointed segments of the Arab world
to international events compounded the problem he faced.
But with singleness of purpose he worked all his life to safeguard the vital interests of the Arab people. When Nasser
late in his life arrived on the scene with a totally different
outlook on Arab interests, Nuri remained true to his principles in spite of cruel, unfair and unrelenting attacks from
Nasser and his intimates. He began fighting for Arab independence in his early twenties and he was deeply preoccupied
with Arab stability and safety when he met his death.

Devoted as he was to Arab nationalism, Nuri never lost
sight of the interests of Iraq. He was a true Iraqi patriot. "My
first responsibility," he often said, both privately and publicly,
"is to Iraq."

Caractacus, the anonymous author of *Revolution in Iraq,*
says that it is unlikely Nuri thought of Iraq as his country
in any exclusive sense, or felt that Iraq had more than a
regional claim on his loyalties. My experience tells me otherwise.

Nuri was constantly preoccupied with two objectives for
Iraq. He wanted to see her secure from outside aggression
and stable within. He was convinced that Soviet communism
presented the double threat of invasion and internal upheaval. Iraq's rich oil fields, situated near the frontier of the
Soviet Union, he believed to be Moscow's prime objective.
These were his honest convictions, as anyone talking face to
face with him could feel. He wanted above all a safe and
secure Iraq, within a safe and secure Arab world, if possible. He would have preferred to realize these ends with the
co-operation of other Arab states. Without it, he would stay
the course alone, reluctantly but determinedly. That is what
he did when he aligned Iraq with the free world through the
Baghdad Pact. The underlying motivation was his concern
for the security of Iraq.

Nuri's concern for the welfare of Iraq helps one to understand the various objectives of his domestic policy. He wanted

the best weapons available for the army in order to discourage attack from outside. He wanted a well equipped police force to keep the peace within. He wanted flood control and the lesser items on the Development Program carried through as quickly as possible in order to make life richer for the masses. In spite of his professional devotion to the army, he would not let it blind him to the needs of education and public health. A fair share of the country's wealth, he insisted, must always go into these fields.

Under his direction vast sums were dispensed through the Development Program but scandal never touched him. Some of those about him enriched themselves while in office, at public expense, as was the custom of the time, but not Nuri. His honesty was proverbial.

Nuri's own people, and indeed Arabs everywhere, can be proud of the position he reached as a world figure and the respect with which his views were received beyond Arabia. He was that rare figure, a true Arab nationalist and patriot, and at the same time a recognized world figure. His knowledge and understanding of world trends and problems were impressive. He rarely dealt with the problems of Iraq and her neighbors in isolation, but usually against the background of world events. Tensions between the free world and the Soviet bloc were bound to affect, in one way or another, the political life of the Arab states and even the daily lives of individual Arabs. An open break between these two major groups would cause suffering among people everywhere. He saw this clearly and consequently was always on the alert, watching closely and studying the trouble spots around the globe. His day started by listening to the first available broadcasts from world centers. No matter how early in the morning I might call on him, I would find him abreast of the latest international developments and ready with some analysis of his own. His knowledge of world problems was often revealed during discussions at the Ministerial Council meetings of the Baghdad Pact and his diagnoses of them were always listened to with respect. He was an impressive spokesman in that setting for the free world, the Arab world, and for Iraq.

His passing was an inestimable loss for the West. Nuri understood and was friendly to the West. In him, the West had an invaluable link with the Middle East.

Loyalties were of primary importance to Nuri. The first of these was his steadfast devotion to the Hashimite dynasty. Relations between him and Crown Prince Abdul-Ilah were always strained, but Nuri never allowed this to affect his feeling for the Hashimites as a whole. Devotion to the Hashimites began with his association with Sherif Husayn, founder of the dynasty, in the days of the Arab Revolt. It continued to the day of the death of Iraq's last king, Hashimite Faisal II, which preceded his own by only twenty-four hours. The details of this record need not be repeated here. One episode in Nuri's life will suffice to show the depth of his loyalty and readiness to serve the Hashimites. This was the formation of the Arab Union.

Nuri was not enthusiastic about the union between Iraq and Jordan. He looked upon Jordan as a burden economically and of no significant help politically to Iraq in her relations with either the Arab world or the world generally. So long as wider federation along the lines envisaged in his Fertile Crescent plan was out of the question, he would have preferred for Iraq to pursue an independent course, free to use her wealth and to act politically as she saw fit. But when the two young Hashimites, Faisal and Husayn, turned to him to become the Arab Union's first prime minister and undertake the arduous task of getting it organized and functioning, he accepted with good grace and immediately concentrated all his energies on the job to be done. He gave full time and thought to the Union. His attention was thereby diverted from things Iraqi, and his control over them loosened. That I think helps explain why the Qasim coup caught him by surprise. Ironically, it was his loyal response to the Hashimite call against his better judgment that brought him and his Hashimite King to their deaths.

Nuri was equally constant in his loyalty to the British. He never lost sight of the role the British played in the struggle to break the Turkish hold on the Arabs and to make Iraq independent. In the four years that I was close to him, I never heard him utter a harsh word of criticism of the United Kingdom. He occasionally questioned some action of the British government, but he did so mildly and with balance. He was deeply shocked and hurt when the British attacked Egypt. The fact that they co-ordinated the action with the Israelis left him stunned for days. He claimed he had been misled by the British. He thought the British were planning some action against Israel. Even so, betrayed as he felt he was, and exposed as he was at the time to bitter criticism for his lifelong pro-British leanings, he lost no time in joining with Menderes to reinstate the British.

It must be admitted that sentiment was not the only factor in Nuri's loyalty to the British. Nuri, as politician, was hardheaded and practical. He saw clearly the advantages of having Iraq allied with a big power like Britain. It had both protective and material advantages. And, after all, he had no choice. There was no other big power prepared to do for Iraq what the United Kingdom was willing and anxious to do. He would have welcomed closer relations, in some formal way, with us, but he sensed early in his public life that we would scrupulously avoid any action that might impinge on the traditional British position in the country.

He saw just as clearly the advantages of staying close to the British where his public career was concerned. The Iraqi monarchy was a British creation. The king, ostensibly, made and broke prime ministers, but behind the scenes the British were present, directing the plays. To be close only to the Palace was not enough. The approach to the Palace, to be on the safe side, had to be through the British. Nuri the politician understood this very well. It does not follow, though, that as an individual he was not sincere in his loyalty to the British. He was also grateful to them for what they had done for him personally, in launching him on a public career and backing him thereafter.

Loyalty did not enter into Nuri's relations with the United States. He respected us, but his respect was primarily for our wealth and power. He questioned at times the wisdom of our hesitancy to use that power. Attachment to principle and the niceties of international conduct could, he felt, be carried too far. He understood quite well our character and our politics although he had made only two short visits to the United States. He knew about the pressures of minority groups on domestic as well as foreign issues. He was, of course, particularly sensitive to Zionist pressures.

He was genuinely grateful for our military and technical aid even though it fell short of his expectations. While he would have liked some more formal political backing too, he showed understanding of our aloofness.

Nuri had a further loyalty, which was to the sheiks. He had close relations with them during his first public service and remained close to them throughout his life. Expediency played a part in this relationship as well as sentiment. Nuri recognized the power the sheiks exercised over the country-side, and he depended on their support to control it. His devotion to order led him all too often to become their apologist, in the face of growing pressures for land reform. His loyalty to them cost him dearly in popularity with the masses, but he maintained it to the end.

I have reviewed Nuri's relations with his own people, the Iraqis; with the Arab people as a whole; with the British; and with the Americans. There remains the important subject of Israel to consider.

Nuri was an intensely loyal Arab, but at the same time moderate. He was realistic, and he was flexible, as is shown by his treatment of the Palestine issue. In his Blue Book, written in 1942, he urged the restoration of historic Syria, with semi-autonomy for the Jews in Palestine within the state, and with Jerusalem open to all religious groups. He saw in this plan a way for Arabs and Jews to live side by side in peace. This plan was never followed, reasonable and fair as it seemed to him, and to many other Arabs and non-Arabs. Instead, relations between Arabs and Jews became more complicated and strained, with growing interference from outside the Arab world, culminating in the establishment of the state of Israel, and war between Arab and Jew. Grim as the future looked and disappointed as Nuri was with the turn of events, he faced the facts and worked out a new plan. Unlike other Arab leaders whose attitude was purely negative, he let it be known that he accepted the fact that Israel as a state was here to stay, and outlined a basis for discussions on boundaries and refugees which he hoped would lead to an agreement giving some assurance of peace and prosperity to the two groups. Throughout, he was moderate, factual, and ready to compromise. His passing was a loss for Israel too.

It is difficult, because of the complexities and contradictions of his character, to present a true picture of Nuri the man, behind Nuri the officer, politician, and statesman.

He was a man of action. He acted, as a rule, quickly and firmly. He did not hesitate to resort to repressive measures to accomplish what he had to do, when once convinced that what he was doing was in the best interests of his country. Never in his long public career did he resort to such tactics to advance his personal interests in a dictatorial fashion. He never wavered in discharging his public duties. On the contrary, his impatience led him at times to act before properly preparing the ground, as was the case in 1955 when with Menderes he made the ill-fated move to bring Jordan into the Baghdad Pact.

He habitually had a set of priorities in mind to guide him in fulfilling his programs, but he did not cling to them rigidly. He shifted the emphasis when he felt it wise to do so, as in the case of the Development Program. When his pet project, flood control, was nearing completion, he began laying less stress on long-term undertakings and more on short-term ones. When it appeared that something that he was trying to accomplish was impractical or impossible of attainment, he was quick to drop it without further waste of time and leave his lively intellect and imagination free for things that seemed realizable. He was nimble, but he had his firm convictions too. This was revealed in the course he pursued in foreign affairs. He was unshakably convinced that the Soviet Union and communism were constant threats to the Middle East, and he would not be diverted from efforts to make Iraq as secure as possible in the face of this threat.

Nuri the statesman was a man of conviction, but his political opportunism permitted him to tolerate crooks. There were always some in his entourage, although his personal honesty was unquestionable.

His working habits could cause one uneasiness. There was never any evidence that he undertook to make a record of what one said to him, or, when he was talking even on the most complicated matter, that he had any notes near at hand to help him with the details. He relied completely on his infallible memory. He retained what one told him, and what he had to say without fail turned out to be accurate. Even so his total reliance on memory sometimes made me apprehensive. He had another disconcerting habit. His mind was so alert that ideas came rapidly and in great variety and he jumped from one subject to another so quickly that he was often difficult to follow.

He was a lone worker and usually insisted on seeing me alone. On the rare occasions when he wanted someone else present, he made that clear. He understood the value of teamwork, however, and could use it skillfully. For instance, at his first meeting with the Richards' mission, he had present the Chief of Staff and the key members of his cabinet. Nuri had nothing to say on that occasion except to introduce his colleagues one by one. They then listed in detail the needs of their respective departments. He had obviously given them precise instructions, and they responded magnificently with recitations of formidable requirements, under Nuri's sharp eyes.

Nuri's personal tastes and habits were simple, but in public life he could not escape becoming involved in a certain amount of ceremonial. As prime minister, he was capable of putting on an impressive show when he thought one would serve the country's interests. The military displays he organized, for the edification of the Iraqi public and Iraq's foreign friends, were examples.

When in office Nuri was always accompanied by a bodyguard. Two cars were used, one big and enclosed in which he sat, and one somewhat smaller and open in which his bodyguard sat. This bit of ostentation Nuri accepted as a requirement of public office. He always seemed a bit embarrassed by the reception this little cavalcade got at the gate of our Embassy when he came to call on me. At the entrance there was on duty a guard of half a dozen Iraqi soldiers. Word having been passed along by telephone by traffic policemen that Nuri was on his way reached the gate minutes before his arrival, so that when Nuri and his two cars got there, the guard was at its best. Orders rang out clearly and loudly, and guns were slammed about for all the neighborhood to hear. Nuri accepted it all with a tolerant air.

Nuri's usual determined bearing hid from many his delightful sense of humor and the warmer side of his nature which emerged when he was away from the ministries and among small groups of friends and intimates. His humor was mischievous but kind. He was never cruel in the jibes he took at political rivals. There was a whimsical quality about his sense of humor too. He was at the Embassy one day to check on arms deliveries when a message we had been expecting for some days arrived, with good news for him. It was brought in to me and as we sat talking I read him the contents. He was pleased, and curious too as always. He wanted to know why the message had been typed on yellow paper. I explained that it was our custom to use yellow paper for the original copy of messages and it was from the very original that I had passed the good word on to him. He liked that, and for days whenever we met, no matter where, he would loudly greet me with the query "Have you any yellow paper from Mr. Dulles for me today?"

The warmth of his nature was frequently revealed in the little thoughtful things he did for my family and me. Often when I was leaving his house after an early morning call, he went with me beyond the door into the garden and there, before I got into my car, he stopped and picked the most colorful assortment of flowers he could find, to be given with his best wishes to my wife. And when my sons arrived in Baghdad from their boarding school in the States for their annual holiday, he always found time to entertain them. The first time, he was particularly anxious that they experience something typical of Baghdad, and he arranged an evening musquf party for them on the lawn of his home along the shore of the Tigris. The preparation of this typical Baghdad fish is a delightful ritual, and Nuri did not want my sons to miss any of it. Shortly before the preparation got under way he telephoned the Embassy for them to come. He stood by explaining the intricacies of the preparation and then saw to it that they had all they could eat of the choicest bits.[1]

Nuri loved animals. There were always dogs about his house and garden, and in the river he kept flocks of ducks, geese and swans. He knew that I was fond of birds and so usually after we had finished our talk in his study, he would propose that we go down to the river and feed his flock. He

[1] Musquf is the name given locally to a fish which resembles a salmon. It is rarely found elsewhere than in the Tigris in the vicinity of Baghdad. To bring out its full flavor it should be prepared over a fire of branches from a type of thorn bush common to the banks of the Tigris. The smoke from the branches of this particular bush give it a distinct and delicate taste.

would have had prepared in advance two pans filled with bread, one for me to use and one for him. As we emerged from the house onto the lawn and approached the bank, Nuri would give a special call and before our arrival at the river's edge his ducks and geese and swans would have assembled, waiting for their treat.

One day, our talk in his study finished, Nuri told me he had something special to show me. We went down to the river and then along the bank to some bushes in an adjacent lot. There with boyish enthusiasm he pointed out a nest where one of his geese was setting. He promised me that when the young were hatched I would have one. Not long after that he presented me with a gosling, but not until I had convinced him that my big boxer would do his gosling no harm. Every now and then after the presentation when he was at the Embassy he checked on her welfare. He was relieved to find that my Duke and his Duchess got along well together.

The image of Nuri popularized by his detractors was of a man with a medieval outlook on life, an anachronism in this modern day. He was absorbed in the pursuit and enjoyment of power for its own sake. This preoccupation and singleness of purpose left no room in his character for any of the warmer human qualities. Even late in his life, when I knew him, his enemies believed this image was true.

Nuri was born and educated in a medieval atmosphere. This gave him a poor preparation for our modern world. It is remarkable that he was able to adjust to contemporary conditions. His keen, perceptive intelligence compensated for the deficiencies of his early training, and his steady lifelong growth of mind and spirit transformed his philosophy and concepts of life.

If Nuri had ever been as harsh and hard as some charged, by the time I knew him he had mellowed greatly. The Nuri I knew viewed the problems of the day calmly. He discussed them unexcitedly. His outlook on life was detached and philosophical. Warm, human relationships played a big part in his latter years. His family and friends meant much to him. Toward those with whom he had exchanged blows in the political arena, he showed no bitterness. He carried no grudges. No traces of meanness or pettiness marred his mature personality.

I began this chapter on Nuri with a quotation of my first appraisal of him, made a few months after my arrival in Baghdad. I want to finish it with what I had to say about him on the eve of my departure from Iraq, five months after the coup and five months after his death. This is what I told the State Department:

> From my personal experience and observation covering these past four years in Iraq, I would say that with the death of Nuri, illiberal as he was at times in dealing with domestic issues, Iraq lost her best leader toward an eventual life of dignity and decency, and her strongest bulwark against recurrent chaos, if not savagery.

EPILOGUE

Two weeks after the 1958 coup I asked an Iraqi friend of mine, who moved constantly among the small shopkeepers and the crowds on the streets, what the people were saying about the events of that historic day. "They say," he replied, "that they are very sorry the young King was killed, but after all neither he nor the Crown Prince had ever done anything for them."

Three months after the coup I asked him what the people were saying then. This time he said "They are frightened by the disorders, and fear the uncertainties of the future, and they say that Iraq needs another Nuri."

Five months after the coup, a few days before my departure for Washington, I put the same question to him for the third and last time. This was his answer: "The people are now saying that within ten years a monument will be erected in Baghdad to the memory of Nuri."

I hope, in fact I firmly believe, that will come to pass.

SUGGESTED
BACKGROUND READING

BIRDWOOD, LORD, *Nuri as-Said. A Study in Arab Leadership,* London; Cassell and Company, Ltd., 1959.

CAMPBELL, JOHN D., *Defense of the Middle East. Problems of American Policy,* New York; Harper and Brothers, 1958.

CARACTACUS, *Revolution in Iraq,* London; Victor Gollancz, 1959.

HUREWITZ, J. C., *Diplomacy in the Near and Middle East. Volume II. A Documentary Record 1914–1956,* Princeton; D. Van Nostrand Company, Inc., 1956.

IONIDES, MICHAEL, *Divide and Lose. The Arab Revolt of 1955–1958,* London; Geoffrey Bles, 1960.

IRELAND, PHILIP WILLARD, *Iraq. A Study in Political Development,* London; Jonathan Cope Ltd., 1937.

KHADDURI, MAJID, *Independent Iraq. A Study in Iraqi Politics from 1932 to 1958,* Second Edition, London; Oxford University Press, 1960.

LONGRIGG, STEPHEN HEMSLEY, *Iraq, 1900 to 1950. A Political, Social, and Economic History,* London; Oxford University Press, 1953.

NURI AL-SAID, *Arab Independence and Unity,* Baghdad; Government Press, 1943.

SETON-WATSON, HUGH, *Neither War nor Peace. The Struggle for Power in the Postwar World,* New York; Frederick A. Praeger, Inc., 1960.

SHWADRAN, BENJAMIN, *The Power Struggle in Iraq,* New York; Council for Middle Eastern Affairs Press, 1960.

WARRINER, DOREEN, *Land Reform and Development in the Middle East. A Study of Egypt, Syria, and Iraq,* London; Oxford University Press, 1957.

INDEX

Abdul-Ilah, Crown Prince: seeks Nuri as prime minister, 5; proclaimed Regent, 5n; and Sarsank talks, 23; requests assistance, 40; and United States adherence, 78; relationship to government, 89–91; and King Saud, 152–54; killed in Qasim coup, 206

Agreement for Technical Co-operation: text available, 8

Agreement of June 18: between Saudi Arabia and the United States, 29

Ali, Chauri Mahamad: and Pakistani delegation to Permanent Council, 66

Ali Hasain: and Iranian delegation to Permanent Council, 66

Ali, Omar: and Kurds, 120–21

Al-Hikma University, 125

American businessmen: killed in Qasim coup, 147; and indemnity, 211; victims of mob action, 212; claims paid, 213

American Jesuit priests: and Baghdad College, 124–25; contribution to Iraq, 183

American University of Beirut, 182–83

Anglo-Egyptian Agreement. See British-Egyptian Agreement

Anglo-Iraqi Treaty: termination of, 13, 28; negotiations for new treaty, 51; terminated, 59–60; mentioned, 22, 24

Arab Collective Security Pact: basis for defense pact, 24; Nasser rejects expansion of, 24; responsibilities beyond Iraq, 28; Iraqi participation in, 35

Arab independence proclaimed, 12

Arab League: Iraqi participation in, 35; emergency meeting of, 39. See also Cairo conference

Arab nationalism: promoted by Nuri, 14. See also Nuri

Arab Security Pact, 55

Arab Union: formed, 84; economic and military aid for Jordan, 137–43 passim, 145–46; federation announced, 142; Nuri first prime minister, 143; portfolios, 143–44; first Union Parliament meeting, 144; constitution of, 145; Faisal I head of, 145n; Iraq withdrawn from, 147; financial needs of, 150

Arif, Abdul Salam: and Qasim coup, 203; rabble rousing, 206–7; relieved of post, 207; arrested, 207; named chief of state, 217

Arif, Rafiq: retired, 202

Army: needs of, 30; chief officers support Crown, 92; shared opinions of civilian population, 91–92. See also Military Aid; Military Understanding Agreement; Nuri

Assali-Azm: and Syria, 160

Atasi: Jamali visits, 40; and events in Syria, 160

Atomic Energy Library: presented, 112

Ba'athist propaganda: sparks riots, 78

Ba'athists: and mob leadership, 204

Baban, Ahmad Mukktar: succeeds Nuri, 121
Baghdad College: founded by American Jesuit priests, 124–25; positive contribution, 182–83
Baghdad-Kut-Basra railroad: and Richards' mission, 81
Baghdad Pact: justification for treaty, 35–36; aid offered Jordan, 70; deputies' work "observed," 71; Security Organization, 71; on deputies' level, 71–73; firmly established, 72; Nuri defensive about, 72; pressure on United States to join, 73–74, 77–78; economic aid and Richards' mission, 80–81; headquarters sealed by Qasim troups, 85; Iraq's withdrawal, 85–87; mentioned, 14, 22. *See also* Turkish-Iraqi Pact; CENTO
Baghdad Pact Council. *See* Permanent Council
Baghdad press: comments on proposed Turkish-Iraqi agreement, 37–38
al-Barzani, Mustafa: rebellion led by, 215
Bashayan, Burhanuddin: and press communiqué, 34; at first deputies' meeting, 71
Bayar, Celal, 56
Beirut: and marines landing, 210
Ben-Gurion: Eisenhower's approach to, 76–77
Bilateral pacts: with non-Arab states, 29–30
Blue Book: 134–35. *See also* Fertile Crescent Plan
British: Nuri's loyalty to, 172–73; anti-British feeling, 172–73; and independence of Iraq, 173; economic control, 174; and Centurion tanks, 175–77; and Nelson contract, 178–79; Embassy pillaged and burned, 181; Iraq *Times* suspended, 181; position in Iraq, 223–24

British air bases, 28
British Ambassador, 173
British-Egyptian Agreement on Suez: initialed, 23; and British reoccupancy, 25; and Menderes-Nuri talks, 27; welcomed by Iraq, 36
British Mandate: termination of, 13. *See also* Anglo-Iraqi Treaty

Cairo: radio campaign against Nuri, 38–40, 57; counterattack by Baghdad radio, 40
Cairo conference: Iraqi report on, 46; response of delegates, 46–48; delegates visit Baghdad, 46–49
Campaign: preceding June 9, 1954, elections, 4
Capital Development Works Scheme, 13
Caraway, Forrest: and Permanent Council, 66–67
Casey, Richard: and Blue Book, 134
Cassady, John A.: and Permanent Council, 66–67
CENTO: Baghdad Pact renamed, 87; United States as observers, 87; mentioned, 58
Chadirchi, Kamil: leader of National Democratic party, 127; forced political retirement, 127; a liberal, 127; conditions in Iraq, 127–28; criticizes Nuri, 128
Chamber of Deputies: supports proposed Turkish-Iraqi Pact, 43–44
Chamoun: letter to Nasser, 41–43; and King Saud, 154; losing out, 165; mentioned, 40
Communist activity: repression of, 6, 121
Communist agents, 95
Communist propaganda: measures to check, 27; reached threatening proportions, 48, 67, 68; sparks riots, 78
Communists: and mob leadership, 204

Constitutional Union Party: Nuri's followers, 2; dissolution of, 5; and Nuri's Parliament, 6–7

Cornwallis, Kinahan: as ambassador to Iraq, 128

Council of Ministers, empowered to control activities, 6

Coup: February 8, 1963, 216. See also Coups; Qasim coup

Coups: prominent in Iraq, 205

Criticism of Nuri: petition for Nuri's removal, 128–29; petition signers and Qasim cabinet, 129; memorandum to King, 129; masses need enlightenment, 131

Crown Prince Abdul-Ilah. See Abdul-Ilah, Crown Prince

Da ghara: anthropologists' description of, 118–19

Defense of Middle East: against aggression, 21; preoccupied Washington, 21

Democratic Youth activities: outlawed, 6

Development Program: and flood control, 1, 105–6, 108; and Iraqi army, 30; established, 105; Nuri chairman, 105; and projects, 105–8; Salter evaluates program, 106–7; publicity by USOM, 111–12; Nelson contract cancellation, 178–79; and Qasim celebration, 214–15. See also Technical Aid Program

Development Works Scheme: forerunner of Development Program, 13

Dhahran airfield: use of by United States, 30

Domestic Policy: and the Palace, 89–91; and land, 113–19; criticism of, 126–31; evaluation of, 131–32

Dulles, John Foster: visit to Middle East, 21; and MEDO, 21; report on Middle East tour, 22; congratulates Menderes and Nuri,

37; press conference and Turkish-Iraqi Pact, 46; attends Ankara meeting, 83; and Israeli problem. 169, 171; and failure in Iraq, 198

Eden, Prime Minister: and Baghdad Pact, 73

Education, 123–25

Egypt: attacks Turkish-Iraqi agreement, 37–40; emergency meeting of Arab League, 39; Mutual Defense Agreement, 57; Nasser-Nuri and Egyptian-Iraqi relations, 156; and Baghdad Pact, 156; leadership in Arab world, 156–58; and Soviet military equipment, 158–59. See also Cairo; Turkish-Iraqi Pact; United Arab Republic

Eisenhower Doctrine, the, 79–81

Eisenhower, President: and Baghdad Pact, 73

Elections: of September 12, 1954, 6; few candidates opposed, 6

Faisal I: first King of Iraq, 5n; highly revered, 90; mentioned, 13

Faisal II: crowned, 5n; death of, 5n; summer home at Sarsank, 23; relationship to government, 89–91; criticized, 90

Fattah, Sami: and press liberties, 99

Fertile Crescent Plan: outline for Arab unity, 134–35; caused debates, 159

Flood control: priority in Development Program, 1, 105–6, 108; effective, 108; plan for, 111; and irrigation, 111. See also Ramadi dam; Wadi-Tharthar

Floods: spring of 1954, 1; estimated damage, 1; relief for sufferers, 1; and course of government, 1

al-Gailani, Rashid Ali: and "imperialist plot," 215

Ghazi: succeeded Faisal I, 5n
al-Ghita, Kashif: and Atomic Energy Library, 112
Ghods-Nakhai: Iranian ambassador: relieved, 63; at deputies' meeting, 71
Goksenin: represents Turkey at deputies' meeting, 71

Habbaniya: British air bases at, 28; ceremonies marking transfer of control, 61–62. See also Anglo-Iraqi Treaty
Hai, Kut: Communist demonstrations at, 118
Hashim, Ibrahim: killed, 147
Hashimite dynasty, 89
Health: and Technical Aid Agreement, 123
Husayan, King: not informed, 41; message to, 70

Iran: staff talks with, 31; and adherence, 63–65
Iraq: small-town life, 119
Iraqi Legation in Moscow: closed, 31
Iraq Petroleum Company: oil revenues, 108–9; stations blown up, 109–10; loan agreement, 110
Iraq under Qasim: and harassment of Embassy, 211–12; recognition extended, 212–13; economy paralyzed, 213–14; and Development Program, 214
Israel: Zionist propaganda, 167; and rapprochement between Turkey and Arab states, 167; Nuri's statements on, 167, 168; permanency of, 168; and Dulles policy, 169, 171; synthesis of Nuri's observations, 169–71
Istanbul talks: summary of minutes, 25–26
Istiqlal party: anti-western, 3; and Nuri's Parliament, 7

Jabr, Salih: chief rival of Nuri, 2; and meetings at Palace, 35; refuses to revive political party, 101; memorandum to King, 129
Ja'far, Dhia: and Development Board publicity, 111–12; and tax reform, 122; mentioned, 104
Jamali, Fadhil: as prime minister, 1; flood relief program criticized, 1; and Abdul-Ilah, 2; resigns, 2; declines Nuri's offer, 2; heads delegation to Bandung, 3; Nuri's attitude toward, 3; and meetings at Palace, 35; seeks Syrian support for pact, 40–41; represents Nuri, 47
Jawdat, Ali: succeeds Nuri, 83
Jernegan, John: asked to leave Iraq, 216
Jordan: offered aid to join Baghdad Pact, 70; reacts violently to aid offer, 70; artificial political entity, 137; aid for, 137–43 passim, 145–46; and Qasim coup, 147. See also Arab Union
Jumard: and Qasim view of Baghdad Pact, 85–86

Kadhim, A. H.: minister of education, 123; and summer camps, 124
Kanna, Khalil: and press relations, 104; and tax reform, 122; minister of education, 123–24
Karachi: Permanent Council meeting at, 81–82
Khalidi, Awni: and the Baghdad Pact, 71
Khan, Ayub: and Karachi meeting, 82
al-Khayyal, Abdullah: Saudi Arabian minister, 34
al-Khouri, Faris: government falls, 160
Kurds: resist assimilation, 119, 121; and Communist activity, 120; aghas, 120; Omar Ali, mutasarrif, 120–21; and Arab Union, 121; in

rebellion, 215; articles by Dana Adams Schmidt, 215n; mentioned, 2

Kuwait: and the Arab Union, 147–51; and water, 148–49; port of Umm-Qasr, 149; and the Arab League, 151; claimed as Iraqi territory, 151

Land: law of inheritance, 113; provisional ownership, 117n; unsatisfactory conditions, 118, 119

Land Ordinance: issued, 116–17; increase in *miri sirf* land, 117

Land registry: by sheiks, 115

Latifiya: and land reform project, 116

Lazma, 117n

League of Nations: Iraq becomes a member of, 13, 28

Lebanon: leftist pressures, 164; and promised jets, 165; military intervention, 165; lack of air coverage, 165; marines landed, 166; Nuri preoccupied with, 200; landings from sixth fleet, 202

Life International: The Last Testament of Iraqi Premier, 169

Lowlow: and Nuri's ancestry, 9

Macmillan, Harold: and the Permanent Council, 66–68

Madfai, Jamal: and meetings at Palace, 35

Mahir, Muzahim: at Shu ayba ceremonies, 63

Mahmud, Nuraddin: and meetings at Palace, 35

Menderes: and Istanbul talks, 26; in Baghdad, 29, 32, 51; addresses Iraqi Parliament, 35; description of, 51–52; death of, 52; contribution to Permanent Council, 69; at the Rose Palace, 76–77; and Britain's return to participation in Baghdad Pact, 77, 78; and United States adherence, 78; mentioned, 223

Menderes-Nuri talks, 25–37

Middle East security, 25–37. *See also* Defense of Middle East

Military aid: Nuri urges speed up of, 15–16; needed urgently, 18, 19; Nuri presents needs, 19–20. *See also* Military Assistance Understanding

Military Assistance Advisory Group: urges speed up of deliveries, 16

Military Assistance Understanding: text available, 8; Advisory Group urges speed up deliveries, 16; based on Mutual Security Act, 188; military mission small, 188; two-phase, five-year plan, 189; handicapped by fiscal year, 189; and display at Rashid Camp, 190; and air coverage, 190; building searched and sealed, 191; interpretation of, 191–92; evaluation of, 192–93; results of program, 193–95; and British arms, 194; agreement terminated, 211

Miri sirf: and landless peasants, 116

Mirza: and meeting of Moslem Pact members, 75

Moslem sects, 2

Murjan, Abd-al-Wahhab: Jawdat succeeded by, 84; and Chamber of Deputies, 104

Mutual Defense Agreement: entered into by Egypt and Syria, 57

Nasser: and Arab Collective Security Pact, 24; and Nuri, 156. *See also* Egypt, Turkish-Iraqi Pact

National Democratic party: suspended, 127

National Front: and June, 1954 elections, 4; influence of, 4; caused uneasiness, 5

National party. *See* Istiqlal party

Nelson, Wesley: and Development Board contract, 178–79; 180–81

Neutrality: unrealistic, 55

Northern Tier concept: replaced MEDO dream, 22; mentioned, 14

Nuri: returned to office in 1954, 1; and conditions for becoming prime minister, 5; dissolved political parties, 5; reputation as strongman, 6; and flood control, 7, 108; birthplace, 9; origin of family, 9; enters primary military school, 10; attends Military College, 10; commissioned, 10; begins military service, 11; takes Staff College course, 11; joins "Young Turks," 11; flees homeland, 11–12; married into al-Askari family, 11; prisoner of war, 12; staff positions, 12; summoned by King Husayn, 12; joins desert revolt, 12; becomes prime minister, 13; helps organize police and army, 13; in office during stress, 13; summary of achievements, 13–14; as independent worker, 17; description of, 17–18; sees Nasser, 24; to Istanbul to see Menderes, 25; and Soviet threat, 27, 48, 226; sensitive to Arab criticism, 37–38, 70; and objections to Anglo-Egyptian agreement, 44–45; addresses Parliament on Turkish-Iraqi Pact, 44–45; bolstered by Dulles, 46; rejects martial law, 49; resigns, 82–83; prime minister of Arab Union, 84; and United States adherence to Baghdad Pact, 85; and public order, 92; and public relations, 103; relied on key individuals, 103–4; and political associates, 104; ignored clamor, 108; interest in health and education, 123; prime minister fourteenth time, 142; and Zionism, 167; farewell call on, 200; shot, 203; body mutilated, 210; as Arab nationalist,

219–20; as Iraqi patriot, 220–21; passing a loss for the West, 222; and the Hashimites, 222–23; loyal to British, 223–24; respected United States, 224; and the Sheiks, 224; and Israel, 225; personal habits and tastes, 221, 225, 226, 227, 228; an appraisal of, 230. See also Baghdad Pact; Criticism of Nuri; Menderes-Nuri talks; Turkish-Iraqi Pact

Nuri's Parliament: analysis of composition, 7

Offshore purchases: for Iraqi army, 30; mentioned, 19

Oil: government percentage of revenue, 109; and development, 109

Omer, van, Colonel. See Van Omer, Colonel

Pact of Mutual Co-operation between Turkey and Iraq. See Turkish-Iraqi Pact

Palace, the: turns to Nuri, 5; and Baghdad Pact, 35; called to, 41–43; and policy, 89–91; troops firing on, 201. See also Abdul-Ilah, Crown Prince

Pasha, Jafar: minister of defense, 12

Peace Partisan activities: outlawed, 6

Penal Code: authority extended, 6

Permanent Council: establishment of, 65; participants at inaugural meeting, 66; Washington established liaison with, 66, 67; United States contribution to, 70–71; United States joins Military Committee, 81–82

Permanent Council meetings: Baghdad, 66–71; Tehran, 73–74; Karachi, 81–83; Dulles at Ankara meeting, 83; Ankara meeting, 83–85

Police: Nuri's use of, 92–93; and student demonstrations, 93–94; and Communists, 93–95; Nuri solicitous of, 95. *See also* Qazzaz, Said

Political parties: dissolution of, 99; Organic Law, 100; two party system proposed, 101–2. *See also* Nuri

Portsmouth Treaty: rejected by Iran, 29n; and riots, 38

Presidium: to replace royal family, 201

Press: Nuri revokes licenses, 6, 97–99; Press Ordinance, 97; Press Ordinance criticized, 98; and Khalil Kanna, 104

Purge Bill: Law for Regularization of Government Machinery, 126

Qasim, Abdul Karim: leader of coup, 203; first press conference, 204; first call on, 208; hold loosening, 216; sentenced to death, 216–17; as a leader, 217

Qasim coup: Baghdad Pact headquarters sealed, 85; and Jordanian ministers, 147; and Technical Aid Program, 196; takes place, 201–7; evacuation of American dependents, 209; and aid agreements, 210–11

Qasim trials: shocking, 208

Qazzaz, Said: and public security, tried by Qasim, 96–97

Qureishi: and Pakistan's adherence, 63; and deputies' meeting, 71

Radio equipment: Nuri requests, 49–50

Radio Free Iraq, 56–57

Ramadi dam: flood control project, 111

Rashid Ali revolt, 61–62

al-Rawi, Falil: visits Damascus and Beirut, 40; interview with Atasi, 41

Refugees, Arab: and Israel, 170

Richards' mission, 79–81

Rikabi, Faud: and Development Program, 214

Riots: during Suez crisis, 78, 79

Sa'dabad Pact: and Iraq, 36

Salim-al-Sabah, Fahad bin: and Kuwait negotiations, 149–50

Salim, Salah: and Sarsank talks, 23–24

Salter, Lord: evaluates program of Development Board, 97, 106–7

Salter Report, the: stresses balanced program, 107

Samara dam: dedication of, 111

Sarsank talks, 22–25

Saud, King: and Abdul-Ilah, 152–54

Saudi Arabia: relations with Iraq strained, 151–52; King Saud and Crown Prince meet in Washington, 152–53; King Saud visits Baghdad, 153, 154; co-operation with Iraq, 155–56

Senate: appointment and tenure, 7n

Shabandar, Musa: foreign minister, 15; in Washington, 16; at Habbaniya ceremonies, 61–62

Shah, the: talks with Nuri, 64

Shanshal, Siddig: attack on Nuri, 39; opposes Baghdad Pact, 86; and Arif, 206

Sheiks: supported Nuri, 113; title to tribal lands, 114–16; in Parliament, 116

Shias: Moslem sect, 2; representation on cabinet, 2

Shu ayba: British air base at, 28; transfer to Iraq, 62–63

al-Shubailat, Farhan: minister to Iraq, 69

Special Agreement of April 4, 1955: treaty between Britain and Iraq, 13, 60

Speech from the Throne: outlines Nuri's objectives, 104–5
Staff College: founded by Nuri, 13
Stassen, Harold: accompanies Dulles, 21
Strikes, 94
Students: suspended, 79; and summer camps, 124
Suez Canal base: preliminary agreement, 22
Suez crisis: and attacks on Nuri, 74–79; Mirza calls meeting of Moslem Pact members, 75; Britain excluded from deliberations of pact, 75–76; embarrasses Baghdad Pact members, 75–78; Rose Palace emergency meetings, 76–78; and pressure on United States to join pact, 77–79
Suhrawardy: and Rose Palace meetings, 77; and Permanent Council, 82
Sullivan, Robert J.: president, Baghdad College, 182–83
Sunnis: Moslem sect, 2; representation on cabinet, 2
Suweidi, Tawfig: and meeting at Palace, 35
Syria: politically unstable, 30, 160–64; opposed to Turkish-Iraqi Pact, 40–41; and petroleum pipeline, 41; French and Saudi intrigue, 43, 160; fears coup, 53; aid requested, 53; and Mutual Defense Agreement, 57; and Fertile Crescent Plan, 159; leftist trend, 160, 162; arms from Soviet bloc, 161, 162; Nuri and independence of, 162; Iraqi military help, 163; Nuri's concern vascillates, 163–64

Taha, Said: Nuri's father, 10
Talib, Sayyid: and Iraqi revolutionaries, 12
Tapu: provisional ownership, 117n
Taxation: and tax reform, 121–22;

and USOM, 122; new law passed, 122
Technical Aid Program: and public health, 123; provided technicians, 195; Washington delays, 196; and Qasim coup, 196; terminating economic agreements, 196; agreement terminated, 211
Technical Co-operation Agreement with Iraq: and United States Operation Mission, 111
Treaty of Alliance: bilateral pact with non-Arab state, 29
Treaty of Preferential Alliance. See Anglo-Iraqi Treaty
Turkish-Iraqi Pact (Pact of Mutual Co-operation between Turkey and Iraq): preliminary talks, 25–37; and al-Rawi interview, 41; and Chamoun letter, 41–42; signing of, 50–56; Washington's attitude toward, 51; Britain's attitude toward, 51; and Palestine letters, 52–53; and United Nations Charter, 53; adherence by other states, 53–54; replaced agreement of Friendly Co-operation, 54; ratified by Iraqi Parliament, 54; and Permanent Council, 54; debated in Chamber, 55–56; early adherence urged, 57–59; and British adherence, 59–61; Pakistan joins, 63; Iran joins, 63–65; to be called Baghdad Pact, 67. See also Baghdad Pact; CENTO; Permanent Council; Permanent Council meetings
Turkish-Pakistani Agreement: and Northern Tier concept, 22; opposed by Egyptians, 23; and Menderes-Nuri talks, 27; too broad, 54; mentioned, 25

al-Umari, Arshad: as prime minister, 3; called for elections, 3; resigns, 4; and meetings at Palace, 35

Umma party: Populist or People's party, 2; moderate and pro-western groups, 3–4; and Nuri's Parliament, 7

United Arab Republic, 84, 141

United Nations Charter: and Defense Pact based on Articles 51 and 52, 28, 30, 31, 33; and Pact of Mutual Co-operation, 53

United Popular Front: and Nuri's Parliament, 7

United States: and intrigue in Syria, 48; enjoyed goodwill, 182; role not decisive, 182; American University of Beirut, 182–83; and Baghdad College, 182–83; and Baghdad Pact, 184; Nuri aware of domestic political considerations, 183–84; Nuri on United States foreign relations, 184; association with Nuri, 184; Iraqi's request decisive influence, 187. *See also* Military Assistance Understanding; Technical Aid Agreement; United States Operating Mission

United States Operating Mission: and Development Program publicity, 111–12; operating agency for technical aid to Iraq, 112–13

al-Uzri: and Arab Union finances, 150

Van Omer, Colonel: head of MAAG mission visits Nuri, 19–20

Wadi-Tharthar: flood control project, 111

Washington: view on Turkish-Iraqi intention, 45–46; position explained to Embassies, 46

Wilson, Clifford: replaced Nelson on Development Board, 180

Wright, J.: represents British at Shuʿayba ceremonies, 62

Wright, Michael: British ambassador, 52; at Habbaniya ceremonies, 61–62; at deputies' meeting, 71

Yezidis: and devil worship, 3

"Young Turk": Nuri joins Al-Ahad group, 11

Zayd, Amir: Iraqi ambassador in London contacts Nuri, 5

Zionist propaganda: measures to check, 27

Zionists: and allegiance, 170

Zorlu: and American adherence to pact, 51; description of, 51–52; death of, 52

IRAQ UNDER GENERAL NURI:
MY RECOLLECTIONS OF NURI AL-SAID, 1954–1958

BY WALDEMAR J. GALLMAN

designer:	EDWARD D. KING
typesetter:	VAIL-BALLOU PRESS, INC.
typefaces:	BASKERVILLE, PERPETUA
printer:	VAIL-BALLOU PRESS, INC.
paper:	WARREN'S 1854
binder:	VAIL-BALLOU PRESS, INC.
cover material:	BANCROFT ARRESTOX C

General Nuri al-Said was one of the Middle East's most able statesmen in this century, one of Nasser's chief rivals for Arab leadership and power. Unfortunately for history, however, he kept few records of his activities, even while in office.

These recollections, written by the former United States Ambassador to Iraq, come from the author's almost daily associations with Nuri from 1954 to 1958, crucial years for Iraq and the Middle East generally. Several issues discussed by the author have never been made public until now—particularly the plight of Anglo-American relations in Iraq from 1954 to 1958.

Dictatorial and generally unpopular, Nuri was anti-Communist and pro-West, with deep understanding of the United States. His contributions to Iraq's welfare went far beyond political achievements.

The author is critical of former Secretary of State Dulles and of American policy on the Middle East in regard to the Baghdad Pact. He relates how Dulles instructed him to